MILITARY VETERAN REINTEGRATION

AF765331

MILITARY VETERAN REINTEGRATION

Approach, Management, and Assessment of Military Veterans Transitioning to Civilian Life

Edited by

CARL ANDREW CASTRO
Suzanne Dworak-Peck School of Social Work
University of Southern California
Los Angeles, CA, USA

SANELA DURSUN
National Defence Canada
Ottawa, ON, Canada

ELSEVIER

ACADEMIC PRESS
An imprint of Elsevier

Academic Press is an imprint of Elsevier
125 London Wall, London EC2Y 5AS, United Kingdom
525 B Street, Suite 1650, San Diego, CA 92101, United States
50 Hampshire Street, 5th Floor, Cambridge, MA 02139, United States
The Boulevard, Langford Lane, Kidlington, Oxford OX5 1GB, United Kingdom

Copyright © 2019 Elsevier Inc. All rights reserved.

No part of this publication may be reproduced or transmitted in any form or by any means, electronic or mechanical, including photocopying, recording, or any information storage and retrieval system, without permission in writing from the publisher. Details on how to seek permission, further information about the Publisher's permissions policies and our arrangements with organizations such as the Copyright Clearance Center and the Copyright Licensing Agency, can be found at our website: www.elsevier.com/permissions.

This book and the individual contributions contained in it are protected under copyright by the Publisher (other than as may be noted herein).

Notices

Knowledge and best practice in this field are constantly changing. As new research and experience broaden our understanding, changes in research methods, professional practices, or medical treatment may become necessary.

Practitioners and researchers must always rely on their own experience and knowledge in evaluating and using any information, methods, compounds, or experiments described herein. In using such information or methods they should be mindful of their own safety and the safety of others, including parties for whom they have a professional responsibility.

To the fullest extent of the law, neither the Publisher nor the authors, contributors, or editors, assume any liability for any injury and/or damage to persons or property as a matter of products liability, negligence or otherwise, or from any use or operation of any methods, products, instructions, or ideas contained in the material herein.

Library of Congress Cataloging-in-Publication Data
A catalog record for this book is available from the Library of Congress

British Library Cataloguing-in-Publication Data
A catalogue record for this book is available from the British Library

ISBN: 978-0-12-815312-3

For information on all Academic Press publications visit our website at https://www.elsevier.com/books-and-journals

Publisher: Nikki Levy
Acquisition Editor: Nikki Levy
Editorial Project Manager: Barbara Makinster
Production Project Manager: Sujatha Thirugnana Sambandam
Cover Designer: Matthew Limbert

Typeset by TNQ Technologies

Working together to grow libraries in developing countries
www.elsevier.com • www.bookaid.org

Contents

5. Self-assessment of need for assistance with military-to-civilian transition

James M. Thompson, Sanela Dursun, Jennifer E.C. Lee, Alla Skomorovsky, Wendy Lockhart, and Mary Beth MacLean

6. Challenging missions: vulnerable veterans leaving the armed forces and promising avenues to support them

Jacco Duel, Lauren Godier-McBard, Mary Beth MacLean, and Matt Fossey

7. Development of a Medical Release Transition Framework

Jennifer E.C. Lee, Kimberley Watkins, and Sanela Dursun

8. Disability and compensation principles in military-to-civilian transition support

Mary Beth MacLean, Ryan Murray, and Raun Lazier

Contributors

Nick Caddick Veterans and Families Institute for Military Social Research, Anglia Ruskin University, Chelmsford, United Kingdom

Carl Andrew Castro Suzanne Dworak-Peck School of Social Work, University of Southern California, Los Angeles, CA, USA

Linda Cooper Veterans and Families Institute for Military Social Research, Anglia Ruskin University, Chelmsford, United Kingdom

Jacco Duel Netherlands Veterans Institute, Doorn, the Netherlands

Sanela Dursun National Defence Canada, Ottawa, ON, Canada

Martin Elands Netherlands Veterans Institute, Doorn, the Netherlands

Matt Fossey Veterans and Families Institute for Military Social Research, Anglia Ruskin University, Chelmsford, United Kingdom

Lauren Godier-McBard Veterans and Families Institute for Military Social Research, Anglia Ruskin University, Chelmsford, United Kingdom

Raun Lazier United States Department of Veterans Affairs, Washington, DC, USA

Jennifer E.C. Lee National Defence Canada, Ottawa, ON, Canada

Maj Neil Lewis Ministry of Defence, Whitehall, London, United Kingdom

Wendy Lockhart Veterans Affairs Canada, Charlottetown, PE, Canada

Mary Beth MacLean Veterans Affairs Canada, Charlottetown, PE, Canada

Ryan Murray Veterans Affairs Canada, Charlottetown, PEI, Canada

David Pedlar Canadian Institute of Military and Veteran Health Research and Professor, School of Rehabilitation Queens University, Kingston, ON, Canada; Center for Innovation and Research for Military and Veteran Families, University of Southern California, Los Angeles, CA, United States

Kadri Raid Faculty of Social Sciences and Education, University of Tartu, Estonia

Alla Skomorovsky National Defence Canada, Ottawa, ON, Canada

James M. Thompson Department of Public Health Sciences, Queens University, Kingston, ON, Canada

Tiia-Triin Truusa Ühiskonnateaduste Instituut, Institute of Social Studies Tartu Ülikool, University of Tartu, Estonia

Kimberley Watkins National Defence Canada, Ottawa, ON, Canada

Nathan Williamson United States Department of Veterans Affairs, Washington, DC, USA

Foreword

The vast majority of military personnel transition successfully back to civilian life, going on to become productive members of society. Likewise, most are neither dangerous, drug addicted, depressed, nor otherwise damaged, even if that is the clear impression given by the media, and sadly reflected in surveys of public opinion. But that is not to say that many do not face challenges in adjusting to new circumstances. Transition is always a time of risk and uncertainty—whether we are talking about children leaving home to start college, those with mental disorders discharged from hospital, or service personnel leaving the Armed Forces. For the latter group, a particular challenge can be finding civilian employment that gives them the same sense of pride and accomplishment that their military service may have afforded them.

It will come as no surprise to learn that these issues are not randomly distributed, and in particular those with significant mental health and/or physical injuries have the most difficulties. Policies and programs that assist veterans and their families' are therefore needed for those in need.

This volume, edited by Castro, Dursun, and Harrison, ably assisted by a wealth of talented contributors, provides a balanced approach to the issues releasing service members face and what nations need to consider when designing and implementing programs to assist service members and their families during the transition. The authors accomplish this by presenting the major issues in straightforward, easy-to-understand language (even if a Brit like me wishes they had stuck with our way of spelling), along with practical considerations for successfully implementing programs. As one would expect given the pedigree of the authors, evidence-based approaches and best practices are emphasized throughout the volume. The contributors explain, for example, that evaluating and refining existing programs is a more reliable approach than creating new and untested ones. It seems like we all suffer from the disease of "pilotis"—a condition affecting funders and service providers across the world in which the desire to "innovate" and "think outside the box" and where "standing still is not an option" prevails, leading to vast numbers of eye catching pilot programs that briefly flash across the screen but then fade leaving very little behind other than an incomplete evaluation report, soon to join a myriad of other dust-covered slender reports replete with glossy photos of happy families but little else. Real improvements in service use less catching techniques such as gradual and continuous quality improvement, and instead of overhyped pilots, properly funded trials with decent follow-up. Call me old fashioned if you wish, and I will happily plead guilty.

But on the same theme, affordable, replicable programs that may do less are better than unaffordable ones, which can only be delivered in circumstances and by staff that are not going to exist beyond a handful of centers, and may in the end leave veterans and their families without the services they have come to rely on.

Furthermore, the contributors avoid the common mistake of assuming that one size fits all. Instead, the authors provide the key general principles relevant to all nations and then suggest how different countries' cultures, institutions, and other contextual factors come to bear on the programs they create and the challenges their veteran members face. Leveraging, building on, or modifying civilian programs, for example, may make more sense in some countries than creating military programs for transitioning service members. None of this is a surprise, and indeed frankly should be something to celebrate—how dull life would be if indeed one size really did fit all.

This volume is unique in being the first to take a multinational approach to understanding the military-to-civilian transition. Every nation with a military will be interested in what the authors of these chapters have to say because each chapter contains a treasure trove of empirical research and thoughtful advice for governmental and military policy makers and program developers. Nongovernmental military veteran organizations will also find the material in this volume valuable, especially as the number of veterans' charities increases.

Of course, even if all the principles of military-to-civilian transition laid out in this volume were followed, which will never happen, some of the challenges releasing many service members and their families face will remain. But the situation would definitely be improved.

That is more than enough from me. Now read on.

Professor Sir Simon Wessely
Regius Chair of Psychiatry, King's College London
Director, King's Centre for Military Health Research

CHAPTER

1

Introduction to military-to-civilian life transition

Carl Andrew Castro[1], *Sanela Dursun*[2]

[1] **Suzanne Dworak-Peck School of Social Work, University of Southern California, Los Angeles, CA, USA;** [2] **National Defence Canada, Ottawa, ON, Canada**

Military service is generally seen as a duty in nations that have conscription and as an honorable act where military service is voluntary, and many nations see military service as both a duty and an honorable act. Regardless of the reasons for serving, military personnel must eventually transition back to civilian life. Most service members will transition successfully and, as with any other major life transition, some will experience bumps in the road. For a significant number of separating service members, however, substantial challenges will arise—one of the most prominent being obtaining a good paying job that provides a sense of accomplishment, among others.

In this volume, we have tried to identify the major challenges that separating service members encounter when they leave the military and transition back to civilian life and how governments should support service members leaving the military. The authors of these chapters were members of a NATO Human Factors and Medicine Research and Technology Group, which examined this topic over a 3-year period. Many of the observations reported in this volume were enhanced by a survey of NATO nations, which was conducted to assess the support provided by various nations to service members and their families leaving the military.

We begin by observing that the military culture is a unique one, with a unique set of characteristics that must be understood to help separating service members navigate the transition to civilian life (Chapter 2). Alongside understanding its military culture, each nation must also decide who is a military veteran. How a veteran

Military Veteran Reintegration
https://doi.org/10.1016/B978-0-12-815312-3.00001-2

© 2019 Elsevier Inc. All rights reserved.

and their family are defined, after all, will determine which former service members are eligible for which benefits. Thus, the exact definition of military veteran adopted by each nation will have a profound impact on the support that separating service members receive during their transitions to civilian life (Chapter 2).

We also provide a conceptual framework for understanding the military-to-civilian life transition (Chapter 3), which is useful for identifying key predictors of both a successful transition and a transition in which the veteran is likely to struggle. This framework also pinpoints the important outcomes that determine whether a veteran has had a successful transition. Finally, the framework identifies areas where interventions might be used to ensure a successful transition. As will be seen, the conceptual framework is comprehensive, assessing multiple outcomes for determining whether a veteran's transition has been successful.

We next provide an understanding of how policies and procedures aimed at helping transitioning service members—including both governmental and nongovernmental activities—can be developed and implemented to ensure success (Chapter 4). The sheer complexity of the array of available support programs and services for separating service members can be a barrier to service access as they navigate the transition process, particularly if they are not aware that such services exist, or if they think they do not need additional supports. People undergoing major life transitions might not reflect sufficiently on their preparedness for aspects of the transition process. There is a need for tools that enable separating service members to seek and use services (Chapter 5).

Much has been written about vulnerable military populations and the additional support these populations need as they transition to civilian life. These populations are discussed in detail (Chapter 6), along with the service members who have been physically or psychological wounded during military service (Chapter 7). Service members who have been wounded in combat rightly receive considerable support throughout the transition process. Yet service members who fail to complete their initial term of service generally receive the least support from their governments, even though they are one of the most vulnerable groups who struggle during the transition back to civilian life. While most nations have sought to help those service members with the greatest need in their transition back to civilian life, more support should be considered.

Following the chapters on vulnerable populations, we turn to how veterans are recognized for their service (Chapter 8). Recognition of military service varies by nation, yet it typically includes a variety of compensation schemes. Best practices are presented on how service members might be compensated for both injuries suffered during military service and lost earnings as a result of military service. While national differences may necessitate different policies in different places, the best practices outlined in this volume are likely to improve transitions for all veterans and their families.

Families are often forgotten when service members leave the military, so the reasons for including support for families in the military-to-civilian life transition are explained in Chapter 9. In particular, the importance of developing an adequate definition of a family is highlighted here because few nations actually define what a military family is. Thus, we identify the unique needs of families in the transition process and recommend ways of addressing these needs.

Another important but overlooked issue is the role of media in the military-to-civilian life transition (Chapter 10). How the military describes the service member and the veteran is particularly important for how society will see the military veteran. A media portrayal of the military veteran as mentally ill and physically broken, for instance, will negatively affect potential employers' perceptions of military veterans. Conversely, if real issues are minimized in the media, then veterans may not receive adequate support.

We conclude this volume by identifying the essential components in the military-to-civilian life transition. While it is tempting to prescribe in detail exactly what each nation must and must not do to assist service members transitioning to civilian life, there is no single optimal approach for all nations. Each must consider its own unique national culture and historical experiences of the military in deciding how and what support to provide transitioning service members. Still, it is hoped that the essential components, conceptual framework, and best practices provided in this volume will help each nation better formulate how it approaches the military-to-civilian transition.

CHAPTER

2

Definition of a veteran: the military viewed as a culture

Tiia-Triin Truusa[1], *Carl Andrew Castro*[2]

[1] Ühiskonnateaduste Instituut, Institute of Social Studies Tartu Ülikool, University of Tartu, Estonia; [2] Suzanne Dworak-Peck School of Social Work, University of Southern California, Los Angeles, CA, USA

OUTLINE

Military Veteran Reintegration
https://doi.org/10.1016/B978-0-12-815312-3.00002-4

© 2019 Elsevier Inc. All rights reserved.

The definition of veteran, why does it matter in the transition process?

In 2014, at the NATO summit in Wales, the heads of state and government acknowledged the demanding nature of military service and reaffirmed their nation's support to the men and women of the armed forces and their families, while still serving, but also after service (NATO, 2014). While this document does not include the word "veteran," it certainly includes veterans in its scope. The reason is simple. In an international context, using the term "veteran" would cause undue confusion, as nations have defined who is a veteran quite differently, let alone the differences in who the public in any given country considers to be a veteran. Because this book is about military veterans transitioning to civilian life, we are going to take a closer look at who do we mean when discussing issues connected to military–civilian transition. Who exactly are veterans?

Generally speaking, the definition of a veteran is based on either the length or the nature of the service, ranging from broadly inclusive to quite narrowly exclusive (Dandeker, Wessely, Iversen, & Ross, 2006). The most inclusive and broad definition of a veteran encompasses all those who have served in the armed forces for any period of time. For example, in the United Kingdom, the length of service to qualify as a veteran is a single day. In this case, the underlying factors are the intent and initiative of the person to serve and the subsequent acceptance of service by the armed forces. In essence, a life-long binding contract exists after a single day of service. For other nations, like the United States, the length of service is 2 years, yet that service must have occurred on active duty, along with having served "honorably" during the entire time of service.

The most exclusive or strict definition of a veteran only includes those who have served in combat. Many nations even make the further distinction between being a "combat veteran" or simply a "veteran," with the former obviously being seen in a more favorably light than the latter. In practice, however, most nations include as veterans those who have served on any type of operational mission (i.e., deployed outside of their home nation). For example, the Dutch and Australians, as well as many other nations, define a veteran either as a former or current military service member who has served on a peacekeeping or peace enforcement mission in another nation. Indeed, this definition of a veteran appears to be the most widely accepted.

Both extremes of the definition spectrum have drawbacks, as well as advantages. More inclusive definitions are clearer and can potentially allow even the newest members of the armed forces to position themselves as a part of a larger veteran community. Yet, at the same time, calling someone a veteran who had not even successfully completed basic combat training may diminish the contributions of other service members who did. Likewise, referring to service members who may have been dishonorably discharged from the military may also diminish the status of being a veteran.

Paradoxically, a strict or narrower definition of a veteran can also create unintended drawbacks. For instance, in the United States, someone who has served honorably in the National Guard or reserves, yet never served on active duty for the required 2 years, would not be considered a veteran, even if they served for 30 years. Such a situation would also be true for those nations that require serving on an operational deployment to be considered a veteran. Determining who is and is not a veteran is important, as being a veteran often determines the level and eligibility of support that a service member leaving the military will receive.

There are a range of aspects that determine whom a nation acknowledges as a veteran, including the nation's history, civil–military relations, force structure (Dandeker et al., 2006), and social factors such as economic wealth and the social welfare system that exists within the nation (Danilova, 2010). The historical background of a nation can include many factors. For example, veteran status may be linked to participating in a specific war or conflict, with specific service required during a specific time period. If the service member served during that period, then they are acknowledged as a veteran of that conflict. The Croatian definition is one that can be given as an example in this context, as veterans are those who participated in the Croatian Homeland War 1991–95, members of National Liberation Movement (i.e., partisans) in WWII, members of Home Guard in WWII, and former active duty personnel who served after 1996 (Survey). The Croatian example also includes people who technically were not members of the official armed forces but nevertheless participated as combatants in an armed conflict. Therefore, some nations may include individuals who never wore the uniform.

Estonia can be given as an example when considering the force structure of the definition of veteran. Estonian Defence Forces are structured according to the principle of a reserve force, employing conscription and voluntary service for its Defence League and reserve units. Thus, the Estonian definition includes those who have participated in the military defense of the country as part of the Defence Forces (which in the Estonian case is a part of the definition looking into the future), a person who has participated as part of the Defence Forces on either international or collective defense operations and those who have sustained permanent incapacity for work while discharging duties in the Defence Forces or as an active member of the Defence League. Thus, the definition supports the logic of the national defense model and also takes into account the contribution to national defense made by conscripts, Defence League members, and reservists (Veterans Policy, 2012). Countries with historically controversial civil-military relations are trying to find a different way of how to frame and understand the new emerging group of veterans. This process adds a specific set of challenges (Michael, Nicola, & Naser-Lather, 2018).

The official definitions of veteran may be viewed as political statements. How one defines a veteran can be used to promote veteran issues to help those who need help, but they can always be used to further other political goals. There are some groups of former military service members who have not been recognized by their nation as "veterans." Typically, these former service members denied veteran status participated in unpopular or controversial conflicts and wars. For example, during the Soviet–Afghan War, because it was considered to be unsuccessful one already while it was still going on, those service members killed in action were sent home in closed zinc coffins and families had to bury them in the dead of night (Aleksievich, 1992). These veterans were only later recognized by the current Russian government, with some arguing purely for political gains (Porter, 2017).

Definition of veteran frames not only how we as individuals but also as societies understand and relate to the men and women who come under this definition. It determines who is eligible to receive financial support and services, public recognition, and private gratitude. In other words, definitions influence governmental policies and distribution of and access to resources—that is the sociological framework and more widely the social inclusion or exclusion within any given society (Burdett et al., 2013). In short, how a nation defines a veteran will determine how that nation recognizes and supports that service member after their military service is completed.

Because of the fact that some countries have a strict as opposed to a broad (Dandeker et al., 2006) definition of veteran, not all military service members are entitled to the same services and support. Indeed, even veterans from different wars may be entitled to different services and support, depending on the laws of that nation. In the United States, for example, the highly popular and successful education program that supports veterans obtaining an advanced college degree, known as the GI Bill, varies from one conflict to another, with the veterans of WWII receiving more generous support to attend the college or university of their choice compared with the veterans of the Vietnam War of those who served in Iraq or Afghanistan.

Despite the importance of how veteran status is defined, our aim here is to show that regardless of how each nation defines a veteran, all service members leaving the military will require some level of support as they are transitioning back into civilian life. Transitions can be stressful, and military transitions in particular entail moving from the military culture to the civilian culture, producing changes in relationships, assumptions, work context, and personal and social identity (Castro & Kintzle, 2014). An unsuccessful transition will be a burden on the social networks of the veteran and a burden for the community and for the state. So when discussing different aspects of the transition process, it is important to bear in mind that in terms of transition, the most inclusive idea of who is a veteran should be applied.[1]

It should be kept in mind that research shows most military service members do not experience major difficulties in their transition process (see Elnitsky, Fisher, & Blevins, 2017, for a comprehensive review). In addition to the more obvious reasons as to why some transitioning military service members need support, such as mental and physical health issues that they acquired during their military service, it has been proposed that transitioning from the military culture back to the civilian culture plays a significant role. Bergman, Burdett, and Greenberg (2014) propose that there is a "reverse" culture shock that separating service members experience. The "first" cultural shock being the one experienced when joining the military. Cultural shock denotes the feelings of unease and stress that people experience when the cultural practices that they are used to no longer serve them well in a new environment, causing them to rethink and adjust the competences they used to thrive in one cultural context to another cultural context (Raud, 2013). In the case of military service personnel, we can frame their experience as a reverse culture shock as they are in fact returning to a civilian culture where they used to have cultural competences, much like someone who has spent a significant amount of time abroad will have to readjust to their country of origin once they return. Although it can be argued that for those who have joined the military at a young age, culture shock may be more salient than reverse culture

[1] Another point to be made is that this book does not look into the transitional needs of conscripts or the continuous transition of the members of the reserve forces but concentrates on the professional soldier. Finnish studies with conscripts have shown that also during conscript service socialization into the military organization will trigger adaptation to military culture and values (Salo, 2008). With regard to reservists Lomsky-Feder, Gazit, and Ben-Ari (2008) have proposed the concept of transmigration, i.e., reservists are equally proficient in military and civilian cultures and can move between the two with ease.

shock because they are in fact transferring into a culture where they have never gained competence or capital as grown-ups.

Arguably, the militaries of nations employ different force and organizational structures between the different services of the armed forces, let alone the armed forces of different countries. Nonetheless, various military organizations share certain traits that stem from the unique purpose of militaries, namely that the primary goal is to produce operationally ready units (Siebold, 2001) and thus the occupational culture of militaries is subjugated to that ultimate goal.

Military-to-civilian transition seen through the lens of cultural transition

To begin our short discussion on how military culture influences transitioning military service members, we need to determine what is culture or rather how we see culture within the context of this chapter. Culture has been much used and at times overused and has not always been clearly or well defined (Minkov, 2012). There are also those who have denied the utility of using the concept of culture (Barber, 2008). However, we propose to use Raud's (2013) fairly straightforward definition of culture: it is a loosely tied set of representations, texts, and practices that give meaning to a person's environment. Cultural practices are the things that people do and actively participate in, creating meaning and maintaining meaning. Culture is always learned and essentially a group phenomenon. Another useful definition that will help understanding the role of culture in transitioning between cultures is that proposed by Hofstede, Hofstede, and Minkov (2010), with culture being "the software of the mind," the sources of this software lie within the environments not only where people grew up but also where they collected their life experiences. This software allows us to make sense of the loosely connected sets of texts, representations, and practices within our cultural environments, but for those with different software or cultural background our environment might seem different or even not make sense at all (Raud, 2013). Military culture as any culture can be discussed on micro- and macrolevels, but, in this chapter, we are going to discuss culture more on the macrolevel, yet acknowledging that culture is practiced and performed by individuals in different and sometimes even contradicting ways even within the same cultural environment and among people with the same essential software.

So what makes the military culture distinct and separate from other occupational cultures? As the military is a large and constant organization in most countries, it has been the focal point of a lot of research and there have been various attempts in trying to establish what military culture is. Grimell (2015) points out that the commonalities of military cultures across militaries include traits such as valuing the collective, having an anti-individualistic perspective, as the group is placed above the individual and camaraderie is reenforced as much as possible. These bonds are more often than not mainly within the military culture, forming a strong in-group identity (Tajfel, 1974). The people in the in-group form close psychological attachments to each other. This often leads to forming a psychological distance between the military and civilian worlds (Coll, Weiss, & Yarvis, 2011). Military culture generally promotes qualities such as unity, discipline, physical fitness, duty, and self-sacrifice, where the latter two are prominent among military personnel (Grimell, 2015; Rahbek-Clemmensen et al., 2012). At the same time, military culture also has values that conventionally are not often associated with the military mind-set, values that seemingly clash with common idea of what the military is. Coll et al. (2011) bring out that armed forces also value restraint, obedience, and peacefulness. They explain that peacefulness is valued through preserving harmony that in some cases also means waging war to re-establish balance, restraint in using lethal power only as a last resort. Obedience to orders has to be seen as more complicated than simple compliance, as only orders that are just and morally justified should be carried out, though as Coll et al. (2011) concede it is unlikely that a direct order by a superior will be challenged.

One way of discussing military culture is through considering cultural dimensions that Hofstede produced in his large-scale research on culture in different organizations and countries. Hofstede et al. (2010) present the idea that cultures, especially national cultures, have four dimensions, i.e., aspects of culture, which can be measured relative to other cultures. These dimensions are power distance, collectivism versus individualism, femininity versus masculinity, and uncertainty avoidance. Later, on Minkov's research, two more dimensions were added, which are the long-term versus short-term orientation and indulgence versus restraint (Hofstede et al., 2010).

Hofstede is careful to point out that national culture dimensions are not fully applicable when explaining organizational cultures, if only because people usually do not grow up in organizations. However, Soeters, Winslow, and Weibull (2006) have demonstrated in their research that national cultures have a strong influence on their militaries. At the same time, as pointed out earlier, it is the purpose of the military organization to produce operationally ready units, an aim that underlies all the activities taking place within the military organization. This singular purpose gives the militaries of different nations a starting point that reaches beyond the national borders and forms a military culture that shares commonalities across nations. That is to say that not all military cultures are the same, but as discussed above, there are universal traits that all militaries share.

The first dimension that Hofstede et al. (2010) discuss is the way cultures handle that people are in fact unequal. This is measured by the power distance index; in countries where the power distance is low, there is a smaller emotional distance between superiors and subordinates and thus subordinates have fewer trepidations in approaching or contradicting their superiors. The collectivism (Hofstede et al. 2010) refers to the power of the group, how willing are people to put the collective, common good above the needs of the individual. Hofstede et al. (2010) see masculinity in cultural dimensions as referring to traits such as assertiveness and competiveness that are highly valued within the cultural environment. Avoidance of uncertainty according to Hofstede et al. (21010) refers to how tolerant cultures are to ambiguous and uncertain situations. They continue that long-term goal orientation stands for the fostering of virtues oriented toward future rewards—in particular, perseverance and thrift, but also include such traits as willingness to subordinate oneself for a purpose, respect for circumstance, and concern with personal adaptiveness. The last and final dimension that Hofstede et al. (2010) bring forth deals with restraint, which reflects a conviction that instant gratification needs are to be curbed and regulated by strict social norms. Indulgence here refers to the disposition in cultures to have fun and enjoy life, not indiscriminately gratifying human desires.

Military culture tends to be more masculine, collective, with greater power distance, less tolerance for ambiguity, and geared toward restraint. These were also findings in Soeters et al.'s (2006) research, which also showed that cultural dimensions within the military culture are at least to an extent explained by the differences in cultural dimensions of national cultures. It is quite plausible that transitioning from a more collective military culture into a strongly individualistic national culture will present certain readjustment issues. The same difficulties can be found when considering all the cultural dimensions that we have discussed. Relatively high ambiguity avoidance within the military culture is not an easy match for the fast paced and changing societal life of contemporary western societies.

We have so far concentrated on the military culture, but as pointed out by Atuel and Castro (2018), military identity can be considered as a role identity that develops within the military cultural environment. Research has shown that military identity can supersede that of race and ethnicity, but at the same time there is little research to establish a direct causal link. Without question, the rigorous training and the socialization into military values and culture leaves a lasting mark. Whether individuals who self-select into the military already possess military values and integrate these values into their lives also remains a possibility. It is clear that the military aims to create through a rigorous socialization process a strong collective identity. One of the purposes of collective identity is to create strong emotional attachment to the group; this emotional attachment makes them loyal to the group (Ellemers, Kortekaas, & Ouwerkerk, 1999), which in the case of militaries all over the world is a desirable goal. Still this very same loyalty to the group and one's own identity connected to the military group and culture is one of the more difficult transitions that a former service member will experience after leaving the armed forces.

In the often-discussed transition from a civilian to a soldier, the new recruit's perceptions, goals, motives, and behaviors will come under the influence of military culture and military leaders (Halonen, 2007), but when the transition into a civilian happens, then there is no such rigorous training program to undergo, although some militaries do use some forms of re-acculturation programs. At the same time, it is clear that some form of cultural readjustment will take place, regardless of the period of time spent serving in the military, and the rate and success of such an adjustment also depends on the willingness to unlearn some of the cultural competences and in the case of a military service member transitioning back into his or her original cultural environment, to relearn forgotten or changed cultural competences that are important within the civilian culture that they are returning to. There is some research on the obstacles to a successful transition, usually involving people who have physical or mental-health hampering transition into their civilian live. There is less research on an average transition and we have tried to show that looking at the military as culture can add to the understanding that all members of the military experience some form of transitional difficulties when they move from one cultural environment to another.

There is no one typical veteran or former military service member, just as there is no one typical veteran, but veterans carry some values and traits of military culture just as a member of a nation carries some values of his or her national culture, but not all. Some of these values and traits can be of great use in a transition process, whereas others might be a hindrance.

Transitioning back to civilian society

As noted earlier, research shows that most veterans ultimately transition back to their civilian communities successfully (cf. Elnitsky et al., 2017). It has been argued that skills obtained during military service aid the veteran in this transition process (see Castro & Kintzle, 2016), as many of these skills have direct application to civilian jobs. Other skills that aid veterans in transition include adaptability, enhanced decision-making, and tolerance for ambiguity, among others.

This is not suggested even for these veterans transitioning successfully that there will not be bumps in the road to transition. The transition from military service back to civilian life has been described as a reverse "culture shock" (see Beverly, Bergman, Howard, Burdett & Greenberg, 2014), with the initial cultural shock occurring with the veteran first joining the military. The reversed cultural shock is dramatic for a number of reasons, including loss of status on leaving the armed forces. However, often not appreciated is that veterans feel like strangers in their own country, with many veterans reporting that they "just don't fit in" (Castro & Kintzle, 2014).

The veteran as an immigrant

In this section, we use "the immigrant" as a metaphor for elucidating the many challenges that all veterans will be confronted with as they leave the military and rejoin their civilian communities, recognizing, of course, that military veterans are not immigrants, yet having to deal with many of the challenges that all immigrants must deal with. Therefore, if one were to immigrate to another country, what are the things that they would have to sort out to have a successful transition? First, they would need a job and place to live. Next, they would have to figure out where to shop, where to bank, and where they would receive their health care. If they had a spouse and children, they would have to figure out where they would go to school and where their spouse might work. There are literally thousands of details, both big and small, that someone immigrating to another country would need to figure out. For a service member transitioning back to civilian life, they too have to figure out all of these details. Therefore, in a very real sense, service members transitioning back to civilian life are like new-comers in their own country.

As noted earlier, the military has its own distinct culture, differing in many ways from its civilian counterpart. However, often not appreciated is that the military also consists of a different economic structure as well. Namely, the military is basically a socialist system, existing in most cases within a civilian culture that is capitalistic. Like the nuclear family in nearly every society in the world, the military strives to meet every need of the service member (and to a lesser extent their families). Albeit, some armed forces, especially those of smaller countries', would be more closely connected with their parent society and a larger integration is promoted.

First and foremost, every service member in the military has a job. While this might seem obvious as serving in the military is a job, the military culture differs from the civilian culture in many important respects. The military goes beyond just providing employment to all its service members. The military is structured so that every entry position in the military can lead to a career lasting 20 to 30 years until retirement. In the civilian world, this is not the case. While a civilian may have a job for life, many of these civilian positions are not ones that would be considered a career. In addition to every job in the military leading to a career, most career pathways in the military come with required education and training that is provided by the military, while most civilians have to figure out for themselves what career they want and the educational requirements for obtaining it.

Service members' careers are also actively managed by trained professionals so that they are provided increasingly challenging assignments that prepare them for promotion. Once again, civilians are expected to figure this out for themselves unless they are in a trainee position, while service members have someone to do this for them. Furthermore, when a service member desires a career change, there is typically a structure to help the service member change their career, all the while remaining in the military. For example, many militaries have processes whereby an infantryman may become an intelligence officer. If a civilian wants to make a career change, they have to figure out how do it by themselves and typically have to leave the organization in which they are working to do so.

In addition to the military providing a highly structured career and promotion processes, the military also provides other services that are indicative of a social system. Key among these include food, housing, and health care, which are typically provided free to all service members. Even in nations where there is a national health care system, there is typically a parallel military health care system that provides priority support to service members.

Once a service member leaves the military, they must figure out where they will live and how to access the civilian health care system. In the United States, former service members must pay for their health care, including their dental care, which was provided free when they were in the military. Oftentimes, service members have very little concept of the costs of food, housing, and health care, because these are provided either for free or at greatly reduced costs to them. Other services may be provided by some militaries such as commissaries, military shopping centers, schools for their children, and day cares, which are also heavily subsidized, which masks the true costs of these services. For civilians, managing all of these expenses is just part of life. Many service members leaving the military lack the practical experience to appreciate these costs.

Furthermore, employment in the civilian culture is very individualistic. Unlike in the military culture where a premium is placed on working as a team, the civilian culture is more interested in individual achievements and skills. This can lead many veterans to view "civilian" employment as self-promoting, with a "dog-eat-dog" mentality. Many military skills have no direct civilian equivalent, which makes it difficult for former military personnel to obtain a job and leaving them with the feeling that their military skills are not appreciated by civilians.

Finally, military pay and benefits are standardized. No matter how "good" a service member thinks they are, they will receive exactly the same pay and benefits as every other service member of the same rank and time they have been in the military. For example, there are over 40,000 sergeants (E-5) in the U.S. Army, and the best sergeant receives exactly the same pay and benefits as the worst sergeant, as would be expected in a socialist system. In civilian society, this would not be the case. There would be significant pay and benefit differences based on performance. Yet, while the best sergeant is likely to be promoted to the next rank earlier than the worst sergeants, there is still a degree of frustration that can set in that can demoralize a service member that causes them not to give 100% effort, a situation that is frequently seen among workers in socialist systems.

Transitioning back to the civilian community: avoiding the bumps

Despite the challenges in transitioning from a military culture back to a civilian culture, most former service members do eventually transition successfully, albeit with a few bumps along the way. To have the smoothest transition possible, service members must remember that the military culture differs significantly from most civilian cultures. Therefore, they must plan every aspect of their transition as if they were moving to another country. Second, service members must maintain their aggressive, competitive spirit. Separating service members should not expect anything to be handed to them. They must expect to compete for everything they want, including their civilian job. In short, they must maintain their hustle. Third, they must learn to adapt their military identity to their new civilian culture. Civilians are not their enemies. Approaches and behaviors that were successful in a military culture may not be successful in a civilian culture, and in fact some aspects of a military culture might interfere or impede a successful transition.

Identity shift that will inevitably occur when transitioning from the military to civilian culture is likely to be just as difficult as it is for immigrants who struggle to embrace the new culture that they find themselves in. Part of the difficulty is the difference of the military ethos, the particular combination of a number of core values, which differ from the ethos of the society as Bar-Tal (2000) has termed it. Ehala (2017) points out that when core values are questioned or come under attack, it instigates moral outrage and this makes identity shifts particularly difficult to navigate.

The military must support service members in the transition process. The most important thing that militaries can do is to provide adequate time for service members to prepare for their transition. This might include the time to retrain or obtain critical certifications or education that will allow the former service member to compete for job and career opportunities as a civilian. Regardless, if the service member is leaving the military after 1 week or 30 years, every service member needs time and support to have a successful transition. Indeed, the shorter the length of service, the more support a service member typically needs.

Governments and local communities also have an important role in assisting former service members in their transition. At the governmental level, essential programs and services must be provided to separating service members, particularly housing and employment programs. Local communities must anticipate veterans returning to their communities and welcome them back. Civilians who have not served must understand that while some veterans might have mental and/or behavioral health issues, most do not. Veterans overall make an important contribution to every community that they are a member of.

Conclusion

The military represents a unique culture. Service members leaving the military are in essence moving from one culture, the military culture, to another, the civilian culture. There are aspects of the military culture that can result in challenges that a former service member has not encountered before. Yet, through individual preparation and support by the military, government, and local community, every former service member can have a successful transition, with minimal bumps along the way.

References

Aleksievich, S. (1992). *Zinky boys: Soviet voices from a forgotten war.* Chatto & Windus.

Atuel, H. R., & Castro, C. A. (2018). Military cultural competence. *Clinical Social Work Journal*, 1–9. https://doi.org/10.1007/s10615-018-0651-z.

Bar-Tal, D. (2000). *Shared beliefs in a society: Social psychological analysis*. Thousand Oaks, London, New Delhi: Sage Publications Inc.

Barber, N. (2008). *The myth of culture : Why we need a genuine natural science of societies/.* Newcastle, UK : Cambridge Scholars Publishers.

Bergman, B. P., Burdett, H. J., & Greenberg, N. (2014). Service life and beyond – institution or culture? *The RUSI Journal, 159*(5), 60–68. https://doi.org/10.1080/03071847.2014.969946.

Burdett, H., Woodhead, C., Iversen, A. C., Wessely, S., Dandeker, C., & Fear, N. T. (2013). Are you a veteran?" Understanding of the term "veteran" among UK Ex-service personnel a research note. *Armed Forces and Society, 39*(4), 751–759. https://doi.org/10.1177/0095327X12452033.

Castro, C. A., & Kintzle, S. (2014). Suicides in the military: The post-modern combat veteran and the hemingway effect. *Current Psychiatry Reports, 16*(8). https://doi.org/10.1007/s11920-014-0460-1.

Coll, J. E., Weiss, E. L., & Yarvis, J. S. (2011). No one leaves unchanged: Insights for civilian mental health care professionals into the military experience and culture. *Social Work in Health Care, 50*(7), 487–500. https://doi.org/10.1080/00981389.2010.528727.

Dandeker, C., Wessely, S., Iversen, A., & Ross, J. (2006). What's in a name? Defining and caring for "veterans" the United Kingdom in international perspective. *Armed Forces & Society, 32*(2), 161–177. https://doi.org/10.1177/0095327X05279177.

Danilova, N. (2010). The development of an exclusive veterans' policy: The case of Russia. *Armed Forces & Society, 36*(5), 890–916. https://doi.org/10.1177/0095327X09351224.

Ehala, M. (2017). *Signs of identity.* Routledge: The anatomy of belonging.

Ellemers, N., Kortekaas, P., & Ouwerkerk, J. W. (1999). Self-categorisation, commitment to the group and group self-esteem as related but distinct aspects of social identity. *European Journal of Social Psychology, 29*(2–3), 371–389. https://doi.org/10.1002/(SICI)1099-0992(199903/05)29:2/3<371::AID-EJSP932>3.0.CO;2-U.

Elnitsky, C. A., Fisher, M. P., & Blevins, C. L. (2017). Military service member and veteran reintegration: A conceptual analysis, unified definition, and key domains. *Frontiers in Psychology, 8*, 369. https://doi.org/10.3389/fpsyg.2017.00369.

Grimell, J. (2015). A transitional narrative of military identity: Eris's story. *International Journal for Dialogical Science, 9*(1), 135–157.

Halonen, P. (2007). *Puolustusvoimien koulutuskulttuurin rakentuminen.* Tampere University Press. Retrieved from http://tampub.uta.fi/handle/10024/67698.

Hofstede, G., Hofstede, G. J., & Minkov, M. (2010). *Cultures and organizations: Software of the mind* (3rd ed.). McGraw Hill Professional.

Lomsky-Feder, E., Gazit, N., & Ben-Ari, E. (2008). Reserve soldiers as transmigrants: Moving between the civilian and military worlds. *Armed Forces & Society, 34*(4), 593–614. https://doi.org/10.1177/0095327X07312090.

Michael, D., Nicola, S., & Naser-Lather, M. (Eds.). (2018). *Conflict veterans: Discourses and living contexts of an emerging social group.* Cambridge Scholars Publishing.

Minkov, M. (2012). *Cross-cultural analysis: The science and art of comparing the world's modern societies and their cultures* SAGE.

NATO. (2014). *Armed forces declaration by the NATO heads of state and government.* Retrieved April 22, 2018, from http://www.nato.int/cps/en/natohq/official_texts_112745.htm.

Porter, J. (2017). The restoration of the Soviet military veteran—Soviet veterans of the war in Afghanistan and their place (and purpose) under president Vladimir putin. In *Presented at the Inter-university seminar on armed forces and society:2017 IUS Biennial Conference, Reston, Virginia, USA.*

Rahbek-Clemmensen, J., Archer, E. M., Barr, J., Belkin, A., Guerrero, M., Hall, C., et al. (2012). Conceptualizing the civil–military gap a research note. *Armed Forces & Society, 38*(4), 669–678. https://doi.org/10.1177/0095327X12456509.

Raud, R. (2013). *Mis on kultuur? Sissejuhatus kultuuriteooriasse.* Tallinn, Estonia: Tallinna Ülikooli Kirjastus.

Salo, M. (2008). *Deteminants of military adjustment and attrition during Finnish conscript service* (PhD Thesis). Helsinki: University of Tampere. Retrieved from http://tampub.uta.fi/bitstream/handle/10024/67908/978-951-44-7470-5.pdf;sequence=1.

Siebold, G. (2001). Core issues and theory in military sociology. *Journal of Political & Military Sociology, 29*(Summer), 140–159.

Soeters, J., Winslow, D., & Weibull, A. (2006). Military culture. In G. Caforio (Ed.), *Handbook of the sociology of the military* (pp. 237–254). Springer Science & Business Media.

Tajfel, H. (1974). Social identity and intergroup behaviour. *Social Sciece Inforamtion, 13*(2), 65–93. https://doi.org/10.1177/053901847401300204.

Veterans Policy. (2012). Retrieved April 22, 2018, from http://www.kaitseministeerium.ee/en/objectives-activities/veterans-policy.

CHAPTER

3

Military-to-civilian transition theories and frameworks

David Pedlar[1,2], *James M. Thompson*[3], *Carl Andrew Castro*[4]

[1] Canadian Institute of Military and Veteran Health Research and Professor, School of Rehabilitation Queens University, Kingston, ON, Canada; [2] Center for Innovation and Research for Military and Veteran Families, University of Southern California, Los Angeles, CA, United States; [3] Department of Public Health Sciences, Queens University, Kingston, ON, Canada; [4] Suzanne Dworak-Peck School of Social Work, University of Southern California, Los Angeles, CA, USA

OUTLINE

https://doi.org/10.1016/B978-0-12-815312-3.00003-6

© 2019 Crown Copyright and Elsevier Inc.
All rights reserved.

The challenges faced by troops returning to civilian life after military service have been of interest to societies throughout recorded human history. During the First World War, Canada, like other countries, established a range of benefits and services for veterans including a network of hospitals, clothing allowances, a land settlement scheme, a life insurance plan, and disability benefits (Neary, 2004). During the Second World War, in response to a sense in several countries that not enough had been done for First World War veterans, governments were determined that returning veterans would have more support. Resettlement benefits and services were expanded across key areas of life, including health care, rehabilitation, employment, housing, education, and finances (Allport, 2010; Neary, 2004; Rogers, 1944; Hollingshead, 1946; Woods, 1953). In 1944, Rogers reported that 65%–85% of releasing personnel in US Separation Centers wished counseling of some sort to assist them with adaptation to civilian life. Since then, longitudinal studies of Second World War veterans have demonstrated the positive and negative impacts of military service across the life courses of Second World War veterans in Canada (Tate, Cuddy, & Mathewson, 2015) and the United States (Spiro, Settersten, & Aldwin, 2016).

Today, while there is evidence that many releasing military personnel manage to negotiate military-to-civilian transition (MCT) challenges to integrate successfully into civilian life, a sizable proportion continue to face substantial adjustment issues in Canada (Thompson et al., 2014), the United Kingdom (Ashcroft, 2016; Cooper, Caddick, Godier, Cooper, & Fossey, 2016; Cooper et al., 2017), and the United States (Castro, Kintzle, & Hassan, 2014; Coll & Weiss, 2013; Kintzle, Rasheed, & Castro, 2016). It is well accepted that MCT is a key turning point in the lives of military personnel that variously brings both challenges and opportunities and has implications for well-being in many areas of life after service (Ahern et al., 2015; Ashcroft, 2016; Blackburn, 2017; Castro et al., 2014; Curry, Wood, Passmore, & Atkins, 2017; Faulkner & McGaw, 1977; Jolly, 1996; Kintzle et al., 2016; Pinch, 1980; Spiro et al., 2016; Veterans Affairs Canada Ombudsman, 2016).

The challenges provide opportunities for growth as well as adverse outcomes. The challenges can be profound, including shifting from a deeply rooted military identify to a new post-service identity, shifting from the structured military culture to unstructured civilian culture; lack of sense of purpose; unemployment or underemployment; insufficient income, relationship and family problems; inadequate accommodation including precarious housing and homelessness; role disability related to physical or mental health problems; problems accessing health care and rehabilitation services; addiction; social isolation; difficulty accessing complex supports from various levels of government; and suicide (Ahern et al., 2015; Ashcroft, 2016; Bergman, Burdett, & Greenberg, 2014; Blackburn, 2016, 2017; Coll & Weiss, 2013; Cooper et al., 2016, 2017; Demers, 2011; Faulkner & McGaw, 1977; Hatch et al., 2013; Jolly, 1996; Keeling, 2019; Kintzle et al., 2016; Rogers, 1944; Sayer, Carlson, & Frazier, 2014; Sayer et al., 2011; Thompson et al., 2015, 2017; Thompson, Pedlar, Jetly, & Sudom, 2016). Transitioning families variably experience similar challenges and opportunities, including living with a transitioning veteran (Jolly, 1996; Rogers, 1944; Veterans Affairs Canada Ombudsman, 2016).

This chapter reviews emerging MCT theories and frameworks. While MCT is generally understood to be a period of preparation, reintegration, and adaptation that all military personnel enter as they approach release from service (Ashcroft, 2016; Blackburn, 2017; Castro, Kintzle, & Hassan, 2015; Cooper et al., 2016, 2017; Keeling, 2019; Robinson, Littlefield, & Schleuning, 2017), there is no widely accepted comprehensive theory or framework for the phenomenon, which hampers systematic MCT policy and program development (Blackburn, 2017; Robinson et al., 2017; Shields et al., 2016). The objectives of this chapter are to (1) summarize the life-course approach to understanding well-being in life after service and (2) describe the current status and utility of MCT theories and frameworks that are being devised to inform the complex work of supporting transitioning military personnel and their families in their adaptation to life after service.

Definitions, theories, and frameworks

Definitions, theories, and frameworks are necessary for policy, programming, service delivery, and research, particularly when dealing with complex phenomena like MCT. A *definition* is a statement of the exact meaning of a word or phrase. Simple definitions cannot portray the nature of complex concepts like life course, MCT, well-being, or health; for that we need theories and frameworks. Theories and frameworks provide an integrated way of looking at a complex problem. They are constructed from building blocks called *concepts,* ideas that combine the particulars about an entity. A *theory* is a system of ideas that provides explanations and enables predictions (hypothesis formation) for complex phenomena (Imenda, 2014). A *validated theory* is a conceptual system based on and consistent with real-world observations. A *framework* is derived from a set of concepts drawn either directly from a theory (*theoretical framework*) or constructed from real-world observations in the absence of a theory (*conceptual framework*).

The life courses of military veterans

The life-course view states that biological, physical, psychological, and socioeconomic influences earlier in life independently, interactively, and cumulatively affect well-being later in life (Hertzman & Power, 2003; Kuh, Ben-Shlomo, Lynch, Hallqvist, & Power, 2003). The life-course view breaks down siloed thinking by integrating risk and growth factors into causal chains and temporally ordering exposures and outcomes, thereby encouraging interdisciplinary, interagency solutions (Kuh et al., 2003). Longitudinal studies of Second World War veterans laid the foundation for the life-course view of veterans' experiences (Settersten & Patterson, 2006; Spiro et al., 2016). Hollingshead (1946) described three main phases and several subphases of military members' lives: pre-military (cultural preconditioning for military service), military (induction, basic training, specialized training, combat, post-combat, and demobilization), and post-military (indeterminate length and character, acquisition of veteran status).

The concept of "linked lives" is a key principle, meaning the interconnectedness of life courses and importance of relationships between people (Bengston, Elder, & Putney, 2005). Military personnel have shared experiences in service that lead to the formation of strong bonds and a shared identity that persists and influences life after service. The life-course view emphasizes the importance of time, place, and cultural context, and the role of critical or sensitive periods of human development in which people are most likely to be susceptible to certain influences. The importance of the life-course view of MCT (Fig. 3.1) is that events, experiences, and decisions earlier in life contribute to predicting and mitigating outcomes for veterans during MCT and in life after service (Settersten & Patterson, 2006; Spiro et al., 2016). Another key principle of the life-course view is the importance of transitions and their timing in people's lives (Bengston et al., 2005).

Culture, relationships, and identity in life-course transitions

Transitions are times of both opportunity and vulnerability characterized by adjustments to cultural shifts that require management of relationships and social identity (Praharso, Tear, & Cruwys, 2017; Robinson et al., 2017; Sayer et al., 2014). All people experience major life-course transitions like entering adulthood, graduating at school, obtaining or losing a job, marriage, acquiring health problems, bereavement, and retirement. Transitions normally challenge everybody to some degree in many areas of life and can be extremely stressful for some. Military personnel experience a variety of transitions during service, including rank promotion, unit transfers, and operational deployments that impact themselves and their families. Two major transitions in particular are unique to the military life course: the cultural shift from civilian to military service and the cultural shift from military to post-service life (Atuel & Castro, 2019; Castro & Kintzle, 2014; Robinson et al., 2017). Both are major transitions characterized by identity challenges and cultural adjustment (Adler, Zamorski, & Britt, 2011; Keeling, 2019; Pinch, 1980; Sayer et al., 2011, 2014).

It is important to understand the effects of culture on life-course transitions in military personnel (Castro & Kintzle, 2014; Demers, 2011; Keeling, 2019; Lancaster, Kintzle, & Castro, 2018). Demers (2011) found high levels of distress among US veterans of Iraq and Afghanistan who were experiencing identity crises, caught between military and civilian cultures. Hofstede described culture as *"the collective mental programming which separates members of one group from the other"* (Bergman et al., 2014, p. 62). The US Marine Corps defined culture as the set of norms and behaviors that one can activate within a social group, while the US Air Force defined culture as *"the creation, maintenance and transformation across generations of semi-shared patterns of meaning, sense making, affiliation, action, and organization by groups"* (Watson, 2010, p. 95). Military culture is both

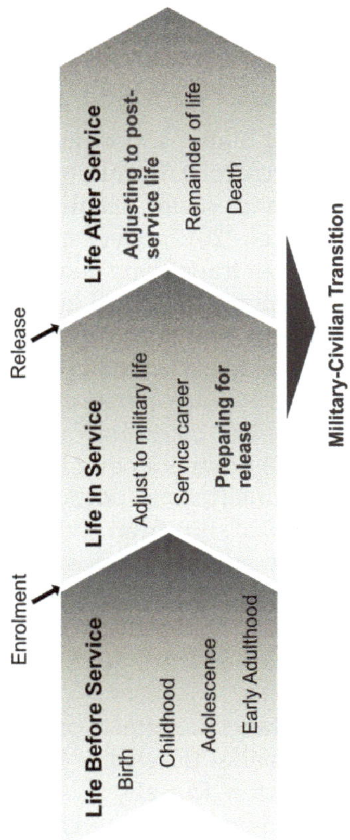

FIGURE 3.1 Military–civilian transition in the life courses of military personnel.

similar to and differs in important ways from the civilian culture that it serves (Capstick, Farley, Wild, & Parkes, 2005; Johansen, Laberg, & Martinussen, 2013; Pinch, 1980). There are several military cultures within a single nation, for example, "professional" versus "idealistic" (Johansen et al., 2013) or "exclusionary" versus "inclusive egalitarianism" (Dunivin, 1997). Military cultures evolve in the context of civilian cultural evolution (Pinch, 1980).

Fundamentally, humans are intensely social creatures: they need effective social relationships to survive and thrive. During life-course transitions, people need to reorient themselves in many areas of life at once, in particular redefining the way they relate to others in social settings (Amiot, Terry, Wirawan, & Grice, 2010; Atuel & Castro, 2019; Castro & Kintzle, 2014; Jetten, Haslam, & Haslam 2012; Lancaster et al., 2018; Praharso et al., 2017; Sayer et al., 2014; Sayer et al., 2011). The ability to reconcile losses of former relationships and to form new relationships in transitions from one culture to another is a key to transition success.

Social identity theory is a useful way of understanding what happens to people across major life transitions like MCT (Atuel & Castro, 2019; Lancaster et al., 2018; Thompson et al., 2017). Social identity is that part of a person's self-concept that derives from their memberships in valued social groups (Tajfel & Turner, 1986; Amiot et al., 2010). Social identities allow people to see their "*interests, attitudes, and behaviors as aligned with those of other members of the groups to which we belong (in-groups) but as different from those of groups to which we do not belong (out-groups)*" (Cruwys et al., 2014, p. 128). People become aware of themselves (the "self") at a young age, and then begin early in life to develop personal identities that distinguish them as unique (Cruwys et al., 2014; Kroger, 2007). As people develop through adolescence into early adulthood, they develop social identities in which they obtain memberships and roles in social groups and then adopt the norms and values from the cultures of valued groups to which they belong (Kroger, 2007; Sneed, Schwartz, & Cross, 2006; Stets & Burke, 2000). Social identities grow out of and enable meaningful relationships in people's families, schools, workplaces, and communities. Social identities constantly evolve, particularly during and after major life transitions from one culture to another and can have protective functions, for example, protecting against depression (Cruwys et al., 2013, 2014; Haslam, Cruwys, Haslam, Dingle, & Chang, 2016) and enabling employment (Griffin & Stein, 2015) when adapting to new life circumstances.

Life in civilian cultures before service

There is no stereotypical military member or veteran life-course trajectory: heterogeneity is the norm (Cooper et al., 2016, 2017; Curry et al., 2017; Hollingshead, 1946; Robinson et al., 2017; Spiro et al., 2016; Thompson et al., 2014). The uniqueness of life-course trajectories and post-service transition experiences has roots in life before service, well before enrolling in the military. Recruits differ widely in terms of pre-service life-course trajectories and well-being determinant exposures, including families of origin, ethnicity, adverse childhood experiences, socioeconomics, prior education, and civilian work experience. During the 2000–12 Afghanistan mission, the CAF recruited members in their 30s, 40s, and 50s who had special skills and knowledge. Many of these mature recruits had established civilian occupations and professions before entering service.

Although selected for good health, recruits nevertheless vary in terms of physical fitness and prior mental health experiences (Kessler et al., 2014; Pethrus et al., 2017). Public policies that influence the well-being of children and adolescents, particularly physical and mental health and fitness, can increase the proportion of the population who could provide military service, as well as prepare recruits for the rigors of military duty with long-term well-being benefits later in life.

Many recruits are young, often just out of high school, never established in the civilian workforce and with incomplete adult identity formation. Furthermore, there is evidence that people today often delay development of adult social identities until their 20s (Bergman et al., 2014; Kroger, 2007), which means that young recruits are likely to form adult identities while in the military. The culture shock consequences and impact on relationships can be profound at release from service, both for young adults who release early with incomplete military identities and for older adults with longer service and deeply established military identities (Bergman et al., 2014).

Enrollment and military acculturation

The transition from civilian to military life usually starts with a period of intense cultural adaptation that begins in basic training and can be described as culture shock or identity conflict (Bergman et al. 2014; Blackburn, 2016; Butler, Eren, & Budgell, 2014; Hollingshead, 1946; Smith & True, 2014). *"Transition is formidable because the military is a 'total institution' with high levels of social integration, regimentation, and social control"* (Smith & True, 2014, p. 152). Unlike preparation for transition out of the military, recruit acculturation is population-wide, efficient, and thorough (Bergman et al., 2014;

Blackburn, 2017; Smith & True, 2014). Entry to military life is a challenging period of profound adjustment that can be stressful and difficult owing to separation from the civilian world, adaptation to living in a highly structured communal lifestyle, deference to authority, downward flow of directives through a chain of command, extreme mental and physical challenges in rigorous training, and adaptation to new and often tightly woven social networks as recruits begin to form a military identity (Bergman et al., 2014; Blackburn, 2017; Butler et al., 2014). Early in their careers, military personnel are encouraged to view themselves as special, particularly compared with civilians, which can have implications in post-service adjustment to civilian life (Dentry-Travis, 2013; Hollingshead, 1946). Successful recruits begin to identify with the military, an identity that tends to deepen with rank promotion and new, shared experiences during service, especially combat (Smith & True, 2014).

Recruits join the military for many reasons, including family tradition, patriotism, economic security, educational and career opportunities, adventure, challenge, or mandatory service (Smith & True, 2014). Recruits come from all walks of life and differ in terms of age and gender, though most are young men. Recruits in noncommissioned ranks more often have less education and adverse childhood experiences than members in commissioned officer entry ranks (Hollingshead, 1946; Iversen et al., 2007; Thompson et al., 2014). Women are a minority in military populations, but there are more women in military service than in the past and women have now entered combat roles (Di Leone, Wang, Kressin, & Vogt, 2016).

Military service is a unique vocation. Unlike civilians, military personnel can be ordered into harm's way by their employer at any time, on short notice. Families often are separated for long periods of time by training and operational deployments (Veterans Affairs Canada Ombudsman, 2016). Military life is defined by rules and regulations, rank hierarchy, rapid decisions, adherence to orders, and unique military values including the subordination of self to group, obedience, sacrifice, self-discipline, and the total commitment to purpose essential for being effective in dangerous military operations (Ashcroft, 2016; Bergman et al., 2014; Blackburn, 2016, 2017; Curry et al., 2017; Keeling, 2019; Smith & True, 2014). The military provides basic needs for most aspects of life including salaries, housing, education, clothing, food, insurance, hygiene, recreation, and health care (Ashcroft, 2016; Hollingshead, 1946; Robinson et al., 2017; Smith & True, 2014). Even the language is different: military acronyms, slang, and humor often are not understood by civilians (Curry et al., 2017; Keeling, 2019).

Military work life is built on successful integration into military units where members live, train, and work together in preparation for military operations. These units, designed to achieve success in high intensity military operations, have high levels of social cohesion, closeness, intensity of relationships, and a sense of purpose rarely found in civilian life. Military service is demanding on physical, mental, social, and spiritual health, involving exposure to occupational hazards uncommon in civilian occupations such as intense military training, exposure to weapons and other occupational hazards in extreme environments, combat operations in war zones, and participation in complex humanitarian situations including natural disasters, failing states, and civil wars. These challenges can confer advantages and lead to personal growth in later life (Spiro et al., 2016). Physical and mental illnesses and injuries during service can have chronic health sequelae in post-service life, sometimes arising years after release from service (Settersten & Patterson, 2006).

Military personnel continue to experience common life transitions during military service including marriage, pregnancy, building families, sometimes of two serving military personnel, loss of relationships and family members, family moves with new postings, reunion after prolonged absences and deployments, and loss of friends and comrades through death or separation. Military personnel also have family, recreational, and employment roles in civilian life outside the military, particularly reservists and professionals like physicians. All members continue to identify to varying degrees with civilians, both pre-service social groups with whom they maintain contact and new ones that they engage with after entering service.

Acculturation during release and life after service

Release from the military occurs in several ways. Some are released voluntarily on request or owing to planned retirement, while others are released involuntarily owing to acquiring medical employment limitations, end of a service contract, force downsizing, or unsatisfactory service or misconduct (Blackburn, 2016). Researchers from the First World War onward have pointed out that most modern era military personnel release into the civilian workforce rather than retire from the workforce, contrary to the prevailing stereotype (Curry et al., 2017; Iversen et al., 2005; MacLean, Keough, Poirier, McKinnon, & Sweet, 2016; Robinson et al., 2017; Stanford, 1971; Thompson et al., 2014).

Varying degrees of culture shock appear to be universal among releasing military members (Bergman et al., 2014; Robinson et al., 2017). Particularly for those in the full-time regular force, released members move abruptly from the military collectivist community where life is quite structured to the unstructured and more individualist experience of civilian life (Adler et al. 2011; Ahern et al., 2015; Blackburn, 2016, 2017; Coll & Weiss, 2013; Cooper et al., 2016, 2017; Robinson et al., 2017; Rogers, 1944; Smith & True, 2014). Post-release (and post-deployment) stress and stress reactions are universal to varying degrees and can be regarded as normal. Rogers (1944) described the extent of disturbed self-esteem, loss of sense of purpose, difficulties with roles in marriages and families, hostility, and need for support services to appreciate MCT difficulties in many areas of life among returning Second World War veterans. Since then, multiple authors have described the identity disruption and culture shock that often occurs on release from service, including loss of sense of communal purpose, sense of alienation from their familiar military world sometimes described as the "military family," relationship challenges, weak sense of community belonging, alienation from other civilians, lack of civilian structure compared with the military, disorienting sense of autonomy and anger toward the system that released them in midcareer, especially in those released involuntarily (Adler et al., 2011; Ahern et al., 2015; Ashcroft, 2016; Bergman et al., 2014; Coll & Weiss, 2013; Keeling, 2019; Sayer et al., 2011, 2014; Stanford, 1971). It is commonly understood that career interruption owing to unanticipated release on medical grounds often is associated with adverse MCT experiences (Van Staden et al., 2007). However, a Canadian study of former Regular Force CAF members found that of the 27% released since 1998 who reported having difficult adjustments, a majority (60%) had not been medically released (Thompson, Sweet et al., 2016). The majority of that subgroup had been voluntarily released and had disproportionate prevalences of health and socioeconomic well-being problems.

Identity challenges in MCT

Transitions normally challenge the transitioner's sense of self. A substantial literature from civilian research over recent decades have found that major life transitions like MCT are periods not only of opportunity but also of risk owing to elevated stress and increased vulnerability to harm and poor outcomes including suicide (Kroger, 2007; Jetten, 2012). In recent years, identity researchers have turned their attention to MCT (Adler et al., 2011; Atuel & Castro, 2019; Blackburn, 2017; Lancaster et al., 2018; Orazem et al., 2016; Smith & True, 2014). Release from military service tends to be associated with normal but often unanticipated identity crises of varying degrees as released members adjust to living in civilian society (Atuel & Castro, 2019; Butler et al., 2014; Coll & Weiss, 2013; Keeling, 2019; Orazem et al., 2016; Robinson et al., 2017; Smith & True, 2014; Thompson et al., 2017), described by Bergman et al. (2014), as "reverse culture shock." Butler et al. (2014) described military identity as reflecting a combination of national and military cultures in which members live, including values, principles, and imperatives. The military culture becomes "home" to many military personnel, including the formation of relationships in the military so close and meaningful that they often describe as the military as "family."

Orazem et al. (2016) found that reintegrating Afghanistan and Iraq veterans reported feeling that they did not belong in civilian society, held negative views of civilian society, and had difficulty finding meaning. Achieving integrated post-military social identities, including roles that confer a sense of purpose, is thought to be an important determinant of success in adapting to post-service life. Veterans identify with new post-service social groups when they attain group memberships and value their roles so that the "we" becomes "me," answering "Who am I in this civilian world?" and "What is my purpose?" (Atuel & Castro, 2019; Keeling, 2019; Smith & True, 2014; Thompson et al., 2017). Not uncommonly, released members can withdraw socially, which serves to heighten their isolation and delay achievement of civilian acculturation and post-military identities (Bergman et al., 2014; Keeling, 2019; Smith & True, 2014). Settersten and Patterson (2006) found variations in how veterans viewed their military service at release and how they made meaning of their military service throughout later life. Lancaster et al. (2018) found that in US military personnel, military identity strength (viewing military as family and having desire to return to the military) was associated with years of service and number of deployments. Following release, those with strong military identities more often had poorer post-military functioning, whereas high levels of personal and public regard for the military and feeling connected (lack of feeling like an outsider) were associated with less distress and higher life satisfaction.

Lifelong effects of military service

In their review of military veteran life-course research, Spiro et al. (2015) concluded that the positive and adverse effects of military service on military veterans are lifelong, often reverberating throughout life; affect multiple domains of life; lead to both gains and losses; are experienced within social relationships; and are affected by era-specific sociocultural contexts. They developed a life-course conceptual framework for modeling positive as well as negative trajectories for military veterans. Their framework identifies several core concepts that influence veteran life courses, including individuals' characteristics before and at entry to service, followed by military factors that act as determinants of positive or negative outcomes later in life, and then by post-military pathways including midlife experiences, government benefits, and midlife outcomes. In Canada, the ongoing longitudinal study of Second World War airmen that began in 1946 continues to shed light on successful biological and psychosocial aging, which the narrative evidence suggests should be viewed as a lifelong dynamic process of transition (Tate et al., 2015).

Well-being across the life course

There is no internationally accepted construct for defining "success" in life-course transitions. "Well-being" is a widely used concept for describing various states of human existence and often is cited as a key public policy objective (White, 2015). Etymologically, the compound word "well-being" is a noun originating in the 1610s when it arose from the adverb "well" and the noun function of the verb "be" (Online Etymology Dictionary, n.d.). The term therefore describes the state of "being" in the sense of existing and "well" in the sense of satisfactory, successful, sufficient, comfortable, or healthy. Good well-being is generally understood to be desirable, while poor well-being is not. A simple definition is not, however, readily operationalizable in programming and research, so a variety of well-being *constructs* (mental constructions derived from real-world observations) have evolved in psychology, sociology, and economics. Some are subjective, for example, when people are asked to describe their quality of life (psychological well-being), while others are objective, based on observing how people are doing, for example, measurements of income or the state of a community's economy.

In recent years, a number of superordinate, composite well-being constructs have been developed to assess well-being subjectively and objectively across multiple areas of life. Internationally, the Organisation for Economic Co-operation and Development (OECD) well-being framework recognizes 11 domains of individual well-being in two sectors: (1) quality of life (health status, work-life balance, education and skills, social connections, civic engagement and governance, environmental quality, personal security, subjective well-being) and material conditions (income and wealth, jobs and earnings, housing) and (2) well-being sustainability over time based on natural, economic, human, and social capital (Organisation for Economic Co-operation and Development, 2013). In Canada, the Canadian Well-being Index accounts for the full range of social, health, environmental, and economic concerns of citizens in addition to national economic indicators and including the living standards of households, health, community vitality, democratic engagement, leisure and culture, time allocation, education, and the environment (Langlois, 2014). The First Nations Community Well-Being Index aggregated multiple indices across four dimensions of well-being: education, labor force participation and employment, income, and housing (Cooke, 2005). The UK national well-being framework, which was designed to inform development of statistical measures for the general population, took the view that individual subjective well-being was a key domain affected directly by the domains of social connections, health, work and leisure activities, residence, personal finance, and education/skills, and indirectly by the domains of societal governance, regional economy, and the natural environment (Beaumont, 2011).

In the United States, Robinson et al. (2017) proposed that successful MCT encompasses multiple dimensions of "wellness." "Well-being" is used by Veterans Affairs Canada (Thompson, Sweet et al., 2016). There are no widely accepted definitions for these terms and, confusingly, they are often used interchangeably. However, a resolution for this confusion is emerging.

The superordinate, composite well-being construct developed by Veterans Affairs Canada and used as way to assess transition outcomes gathers all other well-being constructs, such as subjective psychological well-being, quality of life, and objective economic well-being into a superordinate construct (Thompson, MacLean et al., 2016). In this construct, well-being refers to how a person is doing subjectively and objectively in seven domains or key areas of life: employment or other purposeful activity, finances, health, life skills/preparation, social integration, housing/physical environment, and cultural/social environment (Fig. 3.2). Well-being is measured at each stage of life in each well-being domain on continua from poor to good (or worse to better) using subjective and objective descriptors (indicators) and fluctuates across the life course in response to determinants from all the other domains. The construct includes the classic determinants of health but accommodates bidirectional causal relationships between domains, as well-being in any one domain is influenced by determinants from it and all the other domains.

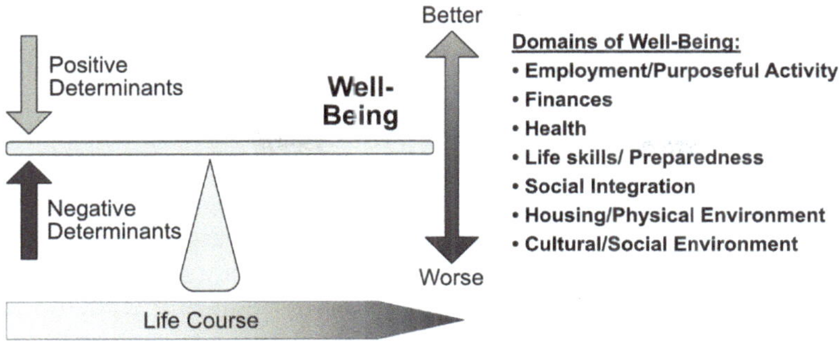

FIGURE 3.2 Well-being theory.

The "wellness" concept used in the US report included similar dimensions to the VAC well-being construct, including mental and physical health, family, housing, transportation, occupation/ employment, education/training, finances, legal interactions, social capital/connectedness, self-actualization, and transition literacy (Robinson et al., 2017). They provided a comprehensive list of measures in each dimension. They did not explicitly define the term "wellness," but their use of the term would be consistent with the VAC well-being construct if it is understood that "wellness" means ways of living to achieve good well-being and "health" is viewed as a well-being domain reserved for the physical, mental, social, and spiritual functioning of the individual (Thompson, MacLean et al. 2016). This approach resolves confusion between the three terms (well-being, health, and wellness) that results when they are used interchangeably. It also allows for all three to be operationalized commonly in policy, service programming, and research between nations.

Military–civilian transition theories and frameworks

This section describes comprehensive MCT frameworks and theories designed to aid policy, services, and research in developing supports for transitioning military personnel when they leave service. That portion of the life course in which MCT occurs (Fig. 3.1) is of particular interest because there is considerable evidence that transition is a vulnerable time and transition experiences impact not only well-being during MCT but throughout the later life course (Adler et al., 2011; Ahern et al., 2015; Castro & Kintzle, 2014; Robinson et al., 2017; Smith & True, 2014).

MCT definitions

There is no widely accepted definition for MCT (Blackburn, 2017; Pinch, 1980; Robinson et al., 2017; Shields et al., 2016). Citing Claude Tapia, Blackburn (2017, p. 2) noted that the term "transition" evokes *"the idea of a passage, from one state to another, from one position to another, a passage that takes place gradually, progressively, with something happening in the middle"*. Authors have variously described MCT as a process that occurs over a period of time beginning sometime prior to release from the military to sometime after entering civilian life, characterized as a time of stress and uncertainty; and comprised of preparation, psychological adaptation, administrative functions, identity shift, and socioeconomic adjustments (Ashcroft, 2016; Blackburn, 2017; Curry et al., 2017; Kintzle et al., 2016).

However, a simple MCT definition cannot be operationalized owing to the complexity of the phenomenon. Simple definitions, because they cannot account for the variety of MCT influences and experiences across varying individual life courses, lead to stereotyping and oversimplification in policy and programming. One size does not fit all releasing members. For example, before the 1990–91 Gulf War, many observers described released members as "retired"; however, considerable research has shown clearly that in the post-Second World War period, a majority release from the military into the civilian workforce (Kintzle et al., 2016; MacLean et al., 2016; Pinch, 1980; Thompson et al., 2014). Initial government approaches to post-release employment have tended to take a blanket approach, such as accepting merely that released members found any, rather than suitable, employment (Ashcroft, 2016; Cooper et al., 2016, 2017; Rutherford et al., 2013), or adopting an oversimplified definition of MCT (Robinson et al., 2017).

MCT frameworks and theories

Unlike simple MCT definitions, theories and particularly frameworks can be operationalized to effectively guide policy, programming, and research. There is a long history of attempts to describe MCT comprehensively, but none have been widely accepted (Blackburn, 2017; Cooper et al., 2017; Pinch, 1980; Shields et al., 2016).

Working with Second World War Veterans, Hollingshead (1946) described a conceptual framework with three phases of life: *pre-military* (civilian life before service with preconceived notions of war and the military), *military* (indoctrination, training for war, development of a warrior identity that sets apart from civilian peers), and *post-military* (loss of communal military supports except veteran benefits and fending for oneself independently in civilian settings). Working with Vietnam War Veterans, Faulkner and McGaw (1977) developed a conceptual framework with three major phases: *moving from war* (disengaging from intense friendships in military life), *moving back to civilian life* (handling shifts in homecoming expectations), *and moving toward consolidating social involvement* (taking responsibility for fitting in). In the Canadian Forces, Pinch (1980) developed a framework for analyzing midcareer MCT that included psychosocial and economic determinants of successful transition from the perspectives of the individual, society, and the military. In the United Kingdom, Jolly (1996) described a conceptual framework based on three stages in the process of change: *confrontation*, where the person acknowledges and confronts the change that might have been thrust on them rather than by choice; *disengagement*, which typically is "muddled" and can be aided by reflection until ready to move in a productive new direction; and then *resocialization*, the process of assuming a new identity. In the United States, Burkhart and Hogan (2015) developed a theoretical framework based on work with female veterans in which they conceptualized coping with military life transition process in seven categories: choosing the military, adapting to the military, being in the military, being a female in the military, departing the military, experiencing stressors of being a civilian, and making meaning of being a veteran civilian. These frameworks were life-course oriented and converged in several ways but did not capture the full complexity of MCT.

More recent proposals include the life-course conceptual framework in the Forces in Mind Trust study (Curry et al., 2017), a well-being/life-course conceptual framework developed in Canada (Thompson, MacLean et al., 2016; Thompson, Pedlar et al., 2016), a four-phase life-course conceptual framework proposed in Canada (Blackburn, 2016), a Bourdieusian MCT theoretical framework in the United Kingdom (Cooper et al., 2016, 2017), and the MCT theory in the United States (Castro & Kintzle, 2014).

In the United Kingdom, the Forces in Mind Trust study (Curry et al., 2017) organized findings into factors determining MCT outcomes by using a basic conceptual framework with four life-course stages: prior to joining, in service, in service during formal resettlement activity, and after leaving. For example, they used the framework to demonstrate that those who begin to prepare early in military service tend to do better after leaving than those who only engage with preparation just before leaving or not at all.

Also in the United Kingdom, Cooper et al. (2017) proposed a theoretical framework based on concepts elaborated in theories by

French sociologist Pierre Bourdieu. Bourdieu *"conceived the possibility of transformation and social mobility through the application of social, cultural, economic and symbolic capital and movement between social spaces"*. His concepts *"shape the understanding of the variations in how [military] personnel approach their transition process based on their own backgrounds, experiences and contextual understandings, and [the] conceptual framework can be applied across national and geographical settings"* (Cooper et al., 2017, p. 158). They viewed MCT as a period of navigating a complex cultural transition, where the challenge for releasing members is to acquire cultural competence in the civilian world (field). Their framework can be used to visually model individual trajectories across the life course from pre-service through service to post-service using the concepts of habitus (subconscious dispositions acquired in developing an identity), capital (rank, military experiences, ability to manage in military social groups, and other social, cultural, economic, and symbolic resources), and space (or field, e.g., military or civilian life). Military habitus and capital are suited to the military space but not necessarily the civilian space.

In Canada, Thompson, Pedlar et al. (2016) suggested a conceptual framework based on the life-course view and well-being composite construct (Thompson, MacLean et al., 2016). In their well-being framework (Fig. 3.3), a person's status at any point in the life course including MCT is operationalized as poor to good well-being using the superordinate, composite well-being construct described above. The system can be used to identify service opportunities by considering well-being determinants in all the well-being domains in each life-course stage, and to evaluate policy and program effectiveness by measuring related well-being indicators. The framework emphasizes a whole-of-community approach by distinguishing the roles of the veteran and his or her family, the Canadian Armed Forces and Department of Defence before release, Veterans Affairs Canada after release, both agencies throughout MCT, and other public and private sector actors.

Also in Canada, Blackburn (2016) described a similar conceptual framework that he called the MCT process model. He felt that the MCT theory described by Castro and Kintzle (2014) was US-centric and felt that a different approach was needed for the Canadian context. He identified four life-course phases: *"pre-release"* starting when the member faces release; *"release"* starting when the release process begins administratively and is divided into two parts, the first where the Canadian Armed Forces plays a major role and the next where Veterans Affairs Canada plays a major role; and finally the *"post-release"* phase where the released member begins to subjectively feel adapted to civilian life. For each phase, Blackburn

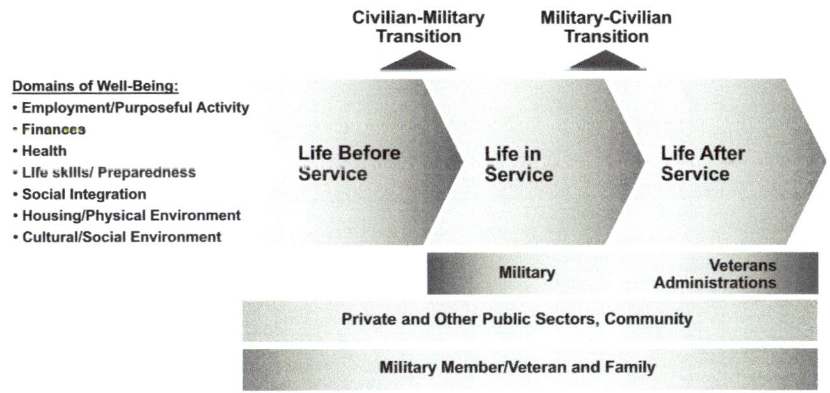

FIGURE 3.3 A life-course/well-being conceptual framework emphasizing the domains of well-being and roles of various agencies in promoting the well-being of military members and veterans across their life courses.

identified the start, end, duration, things to consider, measures to take, use of the transitioner's time to prepare or adapt (particularly important during military service where time is not the transitioner's own), and the role of the key support agency (CAF or VAC).

In the United States, Castro and Kintzle (2014) proposed an MCT theory which states that the transition of entering the military, transitions during military service, and the transition of leaving the military create opportunities for growth and susceptibilities to negative outcomes. They described three interacting and overlapping components. The first component, *"approaching the military transition,"* outlines the personal, cultural, and transitional factors that create the base of the MCT life-course trajectory. These include military cultural factors such as type of military discharge and combat history, personal characteristics such as health, expectations, and personal preparedness, and factors describing the nature of the transition (expected/unexpected, positive/negative). The second component, *"managing the transition,"* refers to factors impacting the individual's progression from service member to post-service life. Members' progressions are affected by individual adjustment factors (life skills and knowledge, coping styles, attitudes, and beliefs) and social support from family, friends, community, and society. Military transition management includes navigating the resources provided by the military, such as Veterans Affairs benefits, education benefits, and career planning. Community and civilian transition support includes factors that the nonmilitary population can utilize to support transitioning service members. The final segment, *"assessing the transition,"* describes outcomes associated with transition, measured through the categories of work, family, health, well-being, and community. Examples include adequate employment, re-acclimation to family life, and adjustment to new family roles, physical and psychological health, adaption to new social networks, and engagement in the community. Outcomes impact one another. For example, challenges to physical health may create challenges in finding employment. However, success or failure in one outcome does not indicate success or failure in overall transition.

All of these conceptualizations share common features (Table 3.1). They all view MCT as a highly individual process that takes place over a period of time, from some point in service to some point after release from service. They all account for the variety of interacting determinants that variously affect well-being across the life course in all major areas of life, various ways of measuring well-being across domains, and the broad heterogeneity of life-course trajectories known to occur in the transitioning population. All capture

TABLE 3.1 Common features of MCT (military-to-civilian transition) frameworks and theories.

- MCT is a process that takes place over a variable period of time from before release to after release.
- MCT is multidimensional, involving changes in multiple domains of well-being or areas of life.
- MCT is characterized by opportunity, challenge, and vulnerability.
- Life-course view: influences earlier in life impact well-being later in life.
- Like adaptation to military life at enrollment, MCT is a major event in the life courses of military veterans.
- Heterogeneity of life courses: each member's journey through MCT is unique, requiring an individualized approach.
- MCT, like all major life transitions, commonly is associated with identity disruption requiring psychological adaptation to an unfamiliar culture in addition to employment, health care, relationship, and housing challenges.
- The diminished well-being that is commonly experienced by releasing members can be mitigated with policies, programs, and services throughout the life course, meaning before release, during service, and during MCT.
- Important for serving military members to begin preparing for their MCT well before release.
- There are roles for the whole community in promoting good well-being during MCT, including the transitioning member, their family, the military, veterans' administrations, other government agencies, nongovernmental agencies, the private sector, and their communities.
- Transition requires coordination among policy and service actors.

factors are thought to be important in determining and defining successful MCT outcomes including life skills preparedness, managing identity disruption, finding a new sense of purpose, civilian employment, financial support, social and family support, adequate housing, and access to effective support services including health care (Ashcroft, 2016; Atuel & Castro, 2019; Curry et al., 2017; Kintzle et al., 2016; Thompson et al., 2017).

The MCT theory proposed by Castro and Kintzle (2014) and the Bourdieusian theoretical framework described by Cooper et al. (2017) are useful for constructing hypotheses to guide research. The conceptual frameworks described by Forces in Mind Trust (Curry et al., 2017), Thompson, Pedlar, et al. (2016), and Blackburn (2016), seem to be generally consistent with the theoretical approaches but could be more readily operationalizable by policy and program designers in their countries. Together, all five provide valuable examples for consideration by nations in their unique cultural and legislative contexts.

Implications

Life course-based MCT theories and frameworks capture the broad range of factors that need to be considered in understanding, predicting, influencing, and measuring the well-being of military veterans across their life courses, particularly as they transition from military service to post-service life. They capture MCT principles that can be used to systematically guide policy and services and inform further research (Table 3.1). Understanding the importance of the cultural environments of military personnel during their major life transitions into and out of the military is key. Transitioners' ability to form effective relationships and establish new social identities unlocks access to resources promoting good well-being in all domains of their lives after military service.

For policy, programming, and services

MCT frameworks and theories encourage policy and program designers and service providers to broadly consider both prior and current factors across multiple areas of life in supporting the present and future well-being of transitioning military personnel. It is widely accepted that while individualized planning for MCT is associated with better outcomes, many leave with little preparation (Adler et al., 2011; Ashcroft, 2016; Castro et al., 2014; Curry et al., 2017; Forkin, 2015; Jolly, 1996; Rogers, 1944; Shields et al., 2016). Over the centuries, militaries have become very efficient at inducing military identities in recruits; however, less attention has been paid until recently to helping military members transition to post-military identities (Ashcroft, 2016; Atuel & Castro, 2019; Bergman et al., 2014; Blackburn, 2016; Curry et al., 2017; Hollingshead, 1946; Robinson et al., 2017): *"They spent 13 weeks turning me into a Marine, but only 3 days turning me back into a civilian"* (Robinson et al., 2017, p. 19).

Castro et al. (2015) pointed out the "veteran paradox": while transition stress is normal, many would benefit from adaptive counseling. Others have suggested training to prepare releasing members with life skills such as financial management, job seeking, house-hunting, and resolving military and post-military identities (Keeling, 2019; Rogers, 1944; Ashcroft, 2016; Thompson et al., 2017). Those with mental illness and physical health problems also require access to therapeutic treatment. Family support is widely recognized as playing important roles in assisting members undergoing MCT (Curry et al., 2017). Numerous authors have emphasized the importance of peer supports for transitioning members, including navigator support from a veteran with a shared identity (Ahern et al., 2015; Brown, 2016; Keeling, 2019; Klaw, Diaz, Avalos, & Li, 2017).

Theories and frameworks have a technical feel that suits researchers and administrators but does not resonate with those living the experience of "getting out." The lay-friendly "journey" concept is emerging in the United States and Canada as a way of understanding individualized MCT experiences at a more personal level. In the United States, Robinson et al. (2017) described the "Journeys of Veterans" map and "personas" used to identify points during MCT when transitioners could benefit from predictive outreach by service providers. A tool for encouraging transitioning military personnel to reflect on their preparedness and need for assistance has been developed that prompts self-assessment in several well-being domains (Thompson, Dursun et al., 2019).

All the MCT models described here can be used to inform policy and service delivery to aid members and their families along their journeys. The life-course/well-being framework described by Thompson, MacLean et al. (2016) can be used to identify opportunities for certain agencies to influence determinants of well-being in various domains at each stage of life before and after release (Fig. 3.3). The framework described by Blackburn (2016) emphasizes the roles of the military before release and Veterans Affairs after release in supporting members through transition, preparedness in multiple areas of life, the nature of the release, preparing for release while doing their military jobs until release, and managing development of post-military identities. The Bourdieusian framework proposed by Cooper et al. (2017) emphasizes the importance of acquiring cultural capital appropriate to the member's stage of life and across transitions. The MCT theory described by Castro and Kintzle (2014) comprehensively draws attention to the pre-MCT factors that establish MCT trajectories, the types of factors to consider during MCT, and factors to consider in assessing transition outcome across multiple areas of life (domains of well-being). Keeling's work (Keeling, 2019) emphasizes the importance of attending not just to employment, health care, and social support but also to the normal impact on identity and need to join social groups where they can find purpose and meaning.

No one agency is solely responsible for the well-being of members during their journeys: all play roles including veterans, their families, all levels of government, nongovernmental agencies, and the private sector. Each transitioning member has to take responsibility for developing a realistic MCT plan, and society is responsible for early preparation of military personnel for eventual release, structuring the release process to provide a wide range of needed supports and creating safety nets to support well-being as needed during life after service (Ashcroft, 2016; Blackburn, 2016; Robinson et al., 2017).

Future research

Much work remains to be done to unpack and understand the complex nature of MCT (Ahern et al., 2015; Cooper et al., 2017); however, the enormous upswing in worldwide research on the well-being of military personnel and their families through transition has led to proposals for MCT frameworks and theories that have great potential. While there are many programs and services that purport to support veterans and their families in transition, there is little evidence of effectiveness for many of them. There is need now to validate the theories, refine theoretical frameworks for practical applications, and use them to assess the effectiveness of MCT support policies, programs, and services for both military personnel and their families (Rutherford et al., 2013).

There is need for longitudinal studies across MCT and for studies of the long-term outcomes of MCT needs and experiences for veterans, their families, and subgroups such as female and LGBTQ identities (Blackburn, 2017; Rutherford et al., 2013). Most of existing research focusses on full-time military rather than Reserve Force members who increasingly play roles in military operations. Although there is good evidence that identity resolution is a key element of the MCT experience, further research is required to understand how best to support the development of post-military identities that support good well-being (Atuel & Castro, 2019; Keeling, 2019; Lancaster et al., 2018; Thompson et al., 2017).

Conclusions

MCT is a major transition in the life courses of military veterans. It is a period of opportunity and vulnerability that has to be managed as efficiently as the orchestrated transition to military life. The well-being of military personnel in life after service can be conceptualized as having multiple domains, for example, employment or other purposeful activity, finances, health, life skills, and preparedness for managing transition, social integration, housing and physical environment, and culture and social environment. Well-being in life after service is influenced by well-being influences earlier in life, including during MCT. Successful MCT requires successful negotiation of challenges with employment, finances, housing, health care, and veterans' benefits. It also requires reconciliation of military and post-military identities and the formation of effective relationships in post-military cultures that are unlike military cultures. Simple definitions are not sufficient to describe a complex issue like MCT. Progress is being made toward a unifying MCT theory and theory-based frameworks for shaping policy, programs, services, and research. Comprehensive unifying MCT frameworks and theories are emerging that consider the complex factors operating on veterans across their life courses. These conceptual systems go beyond stereotypes to account for the diverse heterogeneity of MCT journeys. They emphasize whole-of-community roles in good MCT outcomes for veterans, their families, their communities, the military, veterans' administrations, and all other public and private sector agencies.

Acknowledgments

We are grateful to Fulbright Canada; the Center for Innovation and Research on Veterans & Military Families (CIR) at the USC Suzanne Dworak-Peck School of Social Work; and The Canadian Institute for Military and Veteran Health Research (CIMVHR) for their generous support of this research project.

References

Adler, A. M., Zamorski, M., & Britt, T. W. (2011). Psychology of transition: Adapting to home after deployment. In A. M. Adler, P. D. Bliese, & C. A. Castro (Eds.), *Deployment psychology: Evidence-based strategies to promote mental health in the military.* ashington, DC: American Psychological Association. https://doi.org/10.1037/12300-000.

Ahern, J., Worthen, M., Masters, J., Lippman, S. A., Ozer, E. J., & Moos, R. (2015). The challenges of Afghanistan and Iraq veterans' transition from military to civilian life and approaches to reconnection. *PLoS One, 10*(7), e012599. https://doi.org/10.1371/journal.pone.0128599.

Allport, A. (2010). *Demobbed: Coming home after the world war two*. New Haven, CT: Yale University Press.

Amiot, C. E., Terry, D. J., Wirawan, D., & Grice, T. A. (2010). Changes in social identities over time: The role of coping and adaptation processes. *British Journal of Social Psychology, 49*(4), 803–826.

Ashcroft, M. (2016). *The veterans' transition review – second follow-up report*. London, UK: Veterans Transition Review. Retrieved from http://www.veteranstransition.co.uk/.

Atuel, H. R., & Castro, C. A. (2019). Military transition process and identity. In E. L. Weiss, & C. A. Castro (Eds.), *American military life in the 21st century: Social, cultural, economic issues, and trends*. Santa Barbara, CA: Praeger/ABC-CLIO.

Beaumont, J. (2011). *Measuring national well-being*. Discussion paper on domains and measures. London, UK: Office for National Statistics. Retrieved from http://apps.bps.org.uk/_publicationfiles/consultation-responses/Measuring%20National%20Well-Being%202%20-%20cons%20paper.pdf.

Bengston, V. L., Elder, G. H., & Putney, N. M. (2005). The life course perspective on ageing: Linked lives, timing and history. In M. L. Johnson (Ed.), *Cambridge handbook of age and ageing* (pp. 493–509). Cambridge, UK: Cambridge University Press.

Bergman, B. P., Burdett, H. J., & Greenberg, N. (2014). Service life and beyond – institution or culture? *Armed Forces & Society, 159*(5), 60–68. https://doi.org/10.1080/03071847.2014.969946.

Blackburn, D. (2016). Transitioning from military to civilian life: Examining the final step in a military career. *Canadian Military Journal, 16*(4), 53–61.

Blackburn, D. (2017). Out of uniform: Psychosocial issues experienced and coping mechanisms used by veterans during the military–civilian transition. *Journal of Military, Veteran and Family Health, 3*(1), 62–69. https://doi.org/10.3138/jmvfh.4160.

Brown, N. A. (2016). Combat veterans: Adaptation to transition. *Psychiatric Times, 33*(6), 1–3. Retrieved from http://www.psychiatrictimes.com/special-reports/combat-veterans-adaptation-transition/page/0/3 viewed 08 February 2017.

Burkhart, L., & Hogan, N. (2015). Being a female veteran: A grounded theory of coping with transitions. *Social Work in Mental Health, 13*(2), 108–127.

Butler, A., Eren, E., & Budgell, G. (2014). *Literature review: Theories, concepts and measures of professional, organizational, and military identity. (Human resources systems group ltd, a report for director general military personnel research and analysis)*. Ottawa, ON: Defence Research and Development Canada.

Capstick, M., Farley, K., Wild, B., & Parkes, M. (2005). *Canada's soldiers – military ethos and Canadian values in the 21st century: The major findings of the army climate and culture survey and the army socio-cultural survey.* Ottawa, ON: Director General Land Capability Development, Department of National Defense.

Castro, C. A., & Kintzle, S. (2014). Suicides in the military: The post-modern combat veteran and the Hemingway effect. *Current Psychiatry Reports, 16*(8), 1–9.

Castro, C. A., Kintzle, S., & Hassan, A. M. (2014). *The state of the American veteran: The Los angeles county veterans study.* Los Angeles, CA: Center for Innovation and Research on Veterans and Military Families, University of California School of Social Work.

Castro, C. A., Kintzle, S., & Hassan, A. M. (2015). The combat veteran paradox: Paradoxes and dilemmas encountered with reintegrating combat veterans and the agencies that support them. *Traumatology, 21*(4), 299–310. https://doi.org/10.1037/trm0000049.

Coll, J. E., & Weiss, E. L. (2013). Transitioning veterans into civilian life. In A. Rubin, E. L. Weiss, & J. E. Coll (Eds.), *Handbook of military social work* (pp. 281–300). Hoboken, NJ: John Wiley and Sons.

Cooke, M. (2005). *The first nations community well-being Index (CWB): A conceptual review.* Ottawa, ON: Strategic Research and Analysis Directorate, Indian and Northern Affairs. Retrieved from http://www.publications.gc.ca/collections/Collection/R2-400-2005E.pdf.

Cooper, L., Caddick, N., Godier, L., Cooper, A., & Fossey, M. (2016). Transition from the military into civilian life: An exploration of cultural competence. *Armed Forces & Society, 44*(1), 156–177. https://doi.org/10.1177/0095327X16675965.

Cooper, L., Caddick, N., Godier, L., Cooper, A., Fossey, M., & Engward, H. (2017). A model of military-to-civilian transition: Bourdieu in action. *Journal of Military, Veteran and Family Health, 3*(2), 53–60. https://doi.org/10.3138/jmvfh.4301.

Cruwys, T., Dingle, G. A., Haslam, C., Haslam, S. A., Jetten, J., & Morton, T. A. (2013). Social group memberships protect against future depression, alleviate depression symptoms and prevent depression relapse. *Social Science & Medicine, 98*, 179–186. https://doi.org/10.1016/j.socscimed.2013.09.013.

Cruwys, T., Haslam, S. A., Dingle, G. A., Dingle, G. A., Haslam, C., & Jetten, J. (2014). Depression and social identity: An integrative review. *Personality and Social Psychology Review, 18*(3), 1–24. https://doi.org/10.1177/1088868314523839.

Curry, A., Wood, B., Passmore, C., & Atkins, N. (2017). *The Transition Mapping Study UK: Understanding the transition process for service personnel returning to civilian life*. London, UK: Forces in Mind Trust. Retrieved from http://www.fim-trust.org/wp-content/uploads/2017/07/FIMT_TMS_Report_2017_FINAL_PDF.pdf.

Demers, A. L. (2011). When veterans return: The role of community in reintegration. *Journal of Loss & Trauma, 16*(2), 160–179.

Dentry-Travis, S. J. (2013). Canadian soldiers' constructions of their role-sets. *Personal Construct Theory and Practice, 10*, 28–39.

Di Leone, B. A., Wang, J. M., Kressin, N., & Vogt, D. (2016). Women's veteran identity and utilization of VA health services. *Psychological Services, 13*(1), 60–68.

Dunivin, K. O. (1997). *Military culture – a paradigm shift? (Maxwell Paper No. 10). Maxwell Air force base.* AL: Air War College.

Faulkner, R. R., & McGaw, D. B. (1977). Uneasy homecoming: Stages in the reentry transition of Vietnam veterans. *Urban Life, 6*, 303–328.

Forkin, K. A. (2015). Transition assistance – being proactive in the 21st century. *Marine Corps Gazette, 99*(9), 27–34.

Griffin, C. L., & Stein, M. A. (2015). Self-perception of disability and prospects for employment among U.S. veterans. *Work, 50*(1), 49–58.

Haslam, C., Cruwys, T., Haslam, S. A., Dingle, G., & Chang, M. X. (2016). Groups 4 health: Evidence that a social-identity intervention that builds and strengthens social group membership improves mental health. *Journal of Affective Disorders, 194*, 188–195.

Hatch, S. L., Harvey, S. B., Dandeker, C., Burdett, H., Greenberg, N., Fear, N. T., et al. (2013). Life in and after the armed forces: Social networks and mental health in the UK military. *Sociology of Health & Illness, 35*(7), 1045–1064.

Hertzman, C., & Power, C. (2003). Health and human development: Understandings from life-course research. *Developmental Neuropsychology, 24*(2–3), 719–744.

Hollingshead, A. B. (1946). Adjustment to military life. *American Journal of Sociology, 51*(5), 439–447.

Imenda, S. (2014). Is there a conceptual difference between theoretical and conceptual frameworks? *Journal of Social Sciences, 38*(2), 185–195.

Iversen, A. C., Fear, N. T., Simonoff, E., Hull, L., Horn, O., Greenberg, N., et al. (2007). Influence of childhood adversity on health among male UK military personnel. *British Journal of Psychiatry, 191*(6), 506–511. https://doi.org/10.1192/bjp.bp.107.039818.

Iversen, A., Nikolaou, V., Greenberg, N., Unwin, C., Hull, L., Hotopf, M., et al. (2005). What happens to British veterans when they leave the armed forces? *The European Journal of Public Health, 15*, 175–184.

Jetten, J., Haslam, C., & Haslam, S. A. (Eds.). (2012). *The social cure: Identity, health and well-being*. London, UK: Psychology Press.

Johansen, R. B., Laberg, J. C., & Martinussen, M. (2013). Measuring military identity: Scale development and psychometric evaluations. *Social Behavior and Personality, 41*(5), 861–880.

Jolly, R. (1996). *Changing step*. London, U.K.: Brassey's Ltd., 178.

Keeling, M. (2019). Stories of transition: US veteran's narratives of transition to civilian life. *Journal of Military, Veteran and Family Health* (in press).

Kessler, R. C., Heeringa, S. G., Stein, M. B., Colpe, L. J., Fullerton, C. S., Hwang, et al. (2014). Thirty-day prevalence of DSM-IV mental disorders among nondeployed soldiers in the US army: Results from the army study to assess risk and resilience in service members (army STARRS). *JAMA Psychiatry, 71*(5), 504–513. https://doi.org/10.1001/jamapsychiatry.2014.28.

Kintzle, S., Rasheed, J. M., & Castro, C. A. (2016). *The state of the American veteran: The Chicagoland veterans Study.* Los Angeles, CA: Center for Innovation and Research on veterans and Military Families, University of California School of Social Work.

Klaw, E., Diaz, J., Avalos, R., & Li, K. (2017). VET (Veterans Embracing Transition) connect: An emerging peer leadership program for veterans on campus. *Journal of Military, Veteran and Family Health, 3*(1), 70–76. https://doi.org/10.3138/jmvfh.4116.

Kroger, J. (2007). *Identity development: Adolescence through adulthood.* London, UK: Sage.

Kuh, D., Ben-Shlomo, Y., Lynch, J., Hallqvist, J., & Power, C. (2003). Life course epidemiology. *Journal of Epidemiology & Community Health, 57*(10), 778–783 (Erratum in Journal of Epidemiology and Community Health, *57*(11), 914.).

Lancaster, S., Kintzle, S., & Castro, C. S. (2018). Validation of the warrior identity scale in the Chicagoland veterans study. *Identity, 18*(1), 34–43.

Langlois, S. (2014). Wellbeing in Canada. In W. Glatzer, L. Camfield, V. Moller, & M. Rojas (Eds.), *Global handbook in quality of life.* New York, NY: Springer.

MacLean, M. B., Keough, J., Poirier, A., McKinnon, K., & Sweet, J. (2016). *Labour-market outcomes of veterans (research Directorate technical report No. V32-261/2016E).* Charlottetown, PE: Veterans Affairs Canada.

Neary, P. (2004). *Honoring Canada's commitment: "Opportunity with security" for Canadian forces veterans and their families in the 21st century.* Charlottetown, PE: Canadian Forces Advisory Council, Veterans Affairs Canada.

Orazem, R. J., Frazier, P. A., Schnurr, P. P., Oleson, H. E., Carlson, K. F., Litz, B. T., et al. (2016). Identity adjustment among Afghanistan and Iraq war veterans with reintegration difficulty. *Psychological Trauma, 9*(Suppl. 1), 4–11. https://doi.org/10.1037/tra0000225.

Organisation for Economic Co-operation and Development. (2013). *How's life? 2013: Measuring well-being.* Washington, DC: OECD. https://doi.org/10.1787/9789264201392-en.

Pethrus, C. M., Johansson, K., Neovius, K., Reutfors, J., Sundstrom, J., & Neovius, M. (2017). Suicide and all-cause mortality in Swedish deployed military veterans: A population-based matched cohort study. *British Medical Journal Open, 7*, e014034. https://doi.org/10.1136/bmjopen-2016-014034.

Pinch, F. C. (1980). *Mid-career transition in the military institution: A review of the issues and framework for analysis (Canadian forces personnel applied research Unit).* Ottawa, ON: Department of National Defence.

Praharso, N. F., Tear, M. J., & Cruwys, T. (2017). Stressful life transitions and wellbeing: A comparison of the stress buffering hypothesis and the social identity model of identity change. *Psychiatry Research, 247*, 265–275.

Robinson, J., Littlefield, P., & Schleuning, A. (2017). *Transforming veterans' experiences during military-to-civilian transition: Gaps and opportunities.* Washington, DC: Center for Innovation, U.S. Veterans Administration.

Rogers, C. R. (1944). Psychological adjustments of discharged service personnel. *Psychological Bulletin, 41*(10), 690–693.

Rutherford, G. W., Alegia, M., Bazarian, J. J., Blazer, D. G., Cernak, I., Corrigan, J., et al. (2013). *Returning home from Iraq and Afghanistan: Assessment of readjustment needs of veterans, service members, and their families (committee on the assessment of readjustment needs of military personnel, veterans, and their families).* Washington, DC: Board on the Health of Select Populations Institute of Medicine, National Academy of Sciences, National Academies Press.

Sayer, N. A., Carlson, K. F., & Frazier, P. A. (2014). Reintegration challenges in U.S. service members and veterans following combat deployment. *Social Issues and Policy Review, 8*, 33–73.

Sayer, N. A., Frazier, P., Orazem, R. J., Murdoch, M., Gravely, A., Carlson, K. F., et al. (2011). Military to civilian questionnaire: A measure of postdeployment community reintegration difficulty among veterans using department of veterans Affairs medical care. *Journal of Traumatic Stress, 24*(6), 660–670.

Settersten, R. A., & Patterson, R. S. (2006). Military service, the life course and aging, an introduction. *Research on Aging, 28*(1), 5–11.

Shields, D. M., Kuh, D., Lutz, K., Frender, J., Baumann, N., & Lopresti, P. (2016). *Mental health and well-being of military veterans during military to civilian transition: Review and analysis of the recent literature (Report prepared for Veterans Affairs Canada Road to Civilian Life Program of Research).* Vancouver, BC: Veterans Affairs Canada.

Smith, R. T., & True, G. (2014). Warring identities, identity conflict and the mental distress of American veterans of the wars in Iraq and Afghanistan. *Society and Mental Health, 4*(2), 147–161.

Sneed, J. R., Schwartz, S. J., & Cross, W. E. (2006). A multicultural critique of identity status theory and research: A call for integration. *Identity, 6*(1), 61–84.

Spiro, 3rd A., Settersten, R. A., & Aldwin, C. M. (2015). Long-term outcomes of military service in aging and the life course: A positive re-envisioning. *The Gerontologist, 56*(1), 5–13. https://doi.org/10.1093/geront/gnv093.

Stanford, E. P. (1971). Retirement anticipation in the military. *The Gerontologist, 11*(1), 37–42.

Stets, J. E., & Burke, P. J. (2000). Identity theory and social identity theory. *Social Psychology Quarterly, 63*(3), 224–237.

Tajfel, H., & Turner, J. C. (1986). The social identity theory of intergroup behaviour. In S. Worchel, & W. G. Austin (Eds.), *Psychology of intergroup relations* (2nd ed., pp. 7–24). Chicago, IL: Nelson-Hall.

Tate, R. B., Cuddy, T. E., & Mathewson, A. L. (2015). Cohort profile: The manitoba follow-up study (MFUS). *International Journal of Epidemiology, 44*(5), 1528–1536. https://doi.org/10.1093/ije/dyu141.

Thompson, J. M., Dursun, S., Lee, J., Skomorovsky, A., Lockhart, W., & MacLean, M. B. (2019). Self-assessment of need for assistance with military to civilian transition. Ch. 5. In Castro, et al. (Eds.). *Military veteran reintegration.* Elsevier.

Thompson, J. M., Lockhart, W., Roach, M. B., Atuel, H., Bélanger, S., Black, T., et al. (2017). *Veterans' identities and well-being in transition to civilian life – a resource for policy analysts, program designers, service providers and researchers (report of the veterans' identities research theme working group, Canadian Institute for military and veteran health research Forum 2016, cat. No. V32-279/2017E).* Charlottetown PE: Research Directorate, Veterans Affairs Canada. Retrieved from https://cimvhr.ca/documents/Thompson%202017%20veterans%20Identities%20Technical%20Report.pdf.

Thompson, J. M., MacLean, M. B., Roach, M. B., Banman, M., Mabior, J., & Pedlar, D. (2016). *A well-being construct for veterans' policy, programming and research (Research Directorate Technical Report).* Charlottetown PE: Research Directorate, Veterans Affairs Canada.

Thompson, J. M., Pedlar, D., Jetly, R., & Sudom, K. (2016). Toward a theoretical framework for military to civilian transition. In *Presentation to the military to civilian expert Panel.* Los Angeles: University of Southern California.

Thompson, J. M., Sweet, J., Van Til, L., Poirier, A., & MacKinnon, K. (2016). *Correlates of mental health problems in Canadian armed forces veterans – 2013 life after service survey*. Charlottetown, PE: Research Directorate, Veterans Affairs Canada. Retrieved from http://www.veterans.gc.ca/eng/about-us/research-directorate/publications/reports/correlates-mental-health-lass-2013.

Thompson, J. M., Van Til, L., Poirier, A., Sweet, J., McKinnon, K., & Pedlar, D. (2014). *Health and well-being of Canadian armed forces veterans: Findings from the 2013 life after service study (research Directorate technical report, cat. No. V32-252/2014E-PDF)*. Charlottetown, PE: Veterans Affairs Canada. Retrieved from http://publications.gc.ca/collections/collection_2016/acc-vac/V32-252-2014-eng.pdf.

Thompson, J. M., Van Til, L., Zamorski, M. A., Garber, B., Dursun, S., Fikretoglu, D., et al. (2015). Mental health of Canadian Armed Forces veterans – review of population studies. *Journal of Military Veteran Family Health, 2*(1), 70–86.

Van Staden, M. A., Fear, N. T., Iversen, A. C., French, C. E., Dandeker, C., & Wessely, S. (2007). Transition back into civilian life: A study of personnel leaving the UK armed forces via "military prison. *Military Medicine, 172*(9), 925–930.

Veterans Affairs Canada Ombudsman. (2016). *Support for military families in transition: A review*. Charlottetown, ON: Veterans Affairs Canada Ombudsman. Retrieved from http://www.ombudsman-veterans.gc.ca/eng/reports/reports-reviews/support-family-review.

Watson, J. R. (2010). Language and culture training: Separate paths? *Military Review*, 93–97. March–April.

Well-being. (n.d.). *In Online etymology dictionary*. Retrieved from https://www.etymonline.com/word/well-being.

White, S. C. (2015). Introduction: The many faces of wellbeing. In S. C. White, & C. Blackmore (Eds.), *Cultures of wellbeing* (pp. 1–44). London UK: Palgrave MacMillan.

Woods, W. S. (1953). *Rehabilitation (A combined operation). Being a history of the development and carrying out of a plan for the re-establishment of a million young veterans of World War II by the Department of Veterans Affairs and its predecessor the Department of Pensions and National Health*. Ottawa, ON: Queen's Printer.

CHAPTER

4

Military-to-civilian transition policies, processes, and program efforts

Matt Fossey[1], Raun Lazier[2], Maj Neil Lewis[3], Nathan Williamson[2], Nick Caddick[1]

[1] **Veterans and Families Institute for Military Social Research, Anglia Ruskin University, Chelmsford, United Kingdom;** [2] **United States Department of Veterans Affairs, Washington, DC, USA;** [3] **Ministry of Defence, Whitehall, London, United Kingdom**

OUTLINE

Military Veteran Reintegration
https://doi.org/10.1016/B978-0-12-815312-3.00004-8

© 2019 Elsevier Inc. All rights reserved.

Introduction

Countries typically provide transition support through policies, processes, and programs that offer valuable resources to veterans transitioning from military to civilian life. In contrast, the academic literature on military-to-civilian transition (MCT) within NATO countries has focused on problems that veterans sometimes encounter such as mental health issues, homelessness, prison, and a purported sense of alienation or disconnection from civilian life, as opposed to the positive outcomes that veterans also experience due to their military service (Ahern et al., 2015; Danish & Antonides, 2013; van Staden et al., 2007). Moreover, research has placed an excessive emphasis on pathology and has considered veterans primarily as a "social problem" to be solved (Bulmer & Jackson, 2016). Indeed, comparatively little research has considered what might be termed "pathways to success" among service leavers transitioning to civilian life. Consequently, countries have developed policies, processes, and programs focused on addressing these issues.

One recent theoretical development regarding transition stresses the importance of understanding how service leavers carry the cultural imprint of military life with them into the civilian world (Cooper, Caddick, Godier, Cooper, & Fossey, 2017, Cooper et al., 2019). The Model of Transition in Veterans (Cooper et al., 2017) proposes that the cultural legacy of the military endures long into the lives of service leavers and manifests itself in both positive and negative outcomes depending on a range of factors (such as acquisition of transferable skills or qualifications, rank achieved, ability, and experience in negotiating the contrasting "rules" of military and civilian environments). The model also calls for further research into how veterans adapt culturally to civilian life as an important means of understanding successful transition experiences.

A custom survey was developed and distributed to 20 NATO (and five non-NATO) states to determine the nature and extent of transition support provided in each case. Surveys were either completed by subject matter experts (SMEs) or survey respondents who gathered information from SMEs in each country. Survey results were drawn from 11 NATO nations including Australia, Canada, Croatia, New Zealand, Netherlands, Slovenia, Latvia, Estonia, the United States, Norway, and the United Kingdom. The survey asked NATO members to outline their definition of the term "veteran," to give an approximation of the veteran population, and to describe the programs and services offered to former services members, and whether these programs and services had been formally evaluated. Questions on the duration of transition support, whether the support available to service leavers differed according to need or vulnerability, and whether transition outcomes are monitored for a range of service leavers were also included.

The survey revealed that none of the NATO countries have yet produced a formal or official policy on MCT. In lieu of a coordinated and coherent transition policy, however, it is evident that NATO members have been developing particular elements of support for those leaving the military to assist with their preparations for entering civilian life. The level of support provided, along with the elements of support offered, varied among nations with those supporting the largest veteran populations providing the greatest and widest range of support.

Elements of support can be considered in terms of that which is provided by *all* NATO members, that which *most* elect to provide, and that which is provided by *some* or fewer members (Table 4.1).

This chapter delineates the policies, processes, and programs offered within select elements of support by outlining their duration, basis for entitlement, monitoring or follow-up processes, program evaluation, and tracking of their outcomes. The knowledge gaps across countries will also be highlighted.

The ultimate goal of MCT policies, processes, and programs is to provide sufficient support to service leavers and veterans to ensure

TABLE 4.1 Elements of transition support offered by all, most, or some NATO members.

All NATO members	Most NATO members	Some NATO members
• Counseling • Educational assistance • Employment assistance • Disability compensation	• Physical health • Mental health • Substance abuse	• Home care • Housing • Caregiver support • Transportation support • Legal services • Financial support, financial benefits, and financial services

they are fully equipped to succeed in the civilian world. The aim of this chapter is to provide insights about the key elements of support through policies, programs, and processes as well as offer recommendations to countries developing or restructuring their MCT policies, processes, and programs.

Key elements of support

Veterans are resourceful, innovative, highly skilled, and committed. The veteran population has the capacity to make great societal and economic contributions, if given equal opportunity and access to necessary resources. Veterans need adequate medical, emotional, and transitional support to successfully adjust to civilian life and achieve successful outcomes. To ensure that all veterans have access to equitable resources, countries have developed policies, processes, and programs to empower and support veterans during their transition from military to civilian life.

Education and employment assistance

Education and employment programs play a vital role in veterans' transition into civilian life, as these programs help bridge the gap between military service and the civilian workforce. College-educated veterans are predicted to have a somewhat easier time with readjustment when compared with those who only have a high school diploma (Morin, 2011). Because higher education is more likely to lead to financial stability, offering services that provide veterans with tools that strengthen their educational background and employability can potentially lead to positive and sustainable long-term outcomes. The NATO Survey on Transition from Military to Civilian Life (NATO survey) showed that all of the countries surveyed offer educational programs and vocational rehabilitation services to veterans.

Education Assistance

The United States and Canada offer education benefit programs that provide funding for tuition, books, and living expenses. In Canada, for instance, honorably released veterans with at least 6 years of service are eligible for the Education and Training Benefit. Veterans can receive up to $80,000 of funding and have up to 10 years after their release date to receive the funding for their education (VAC, 2017). The US Post-9/11 GI Bill offers educational assistance to veterans who served 90 aggregate days or more on active duty after September 10, 2001, or were honorably discharged from active duty for a service-connected disability after serving 30 continuous days (USDVA, n.d.). Veterans are eligible for benefits for 15 years from their last separation date and can receive up to 36 months of entitlement. For veterans who are interested in private schools, the US Yellow Ribbon Program can provide additional financial assistance. Lastly, the Post-9/11 GI Bill also covers on-the-job training and apprenticeship program expenses (USDVA, n.d.). In 2017, Student Veterans of America, in conjunction with VA, developed the National Veteran Education Success Tracker (NVEST) Project, which aimed to provide a current measure of the Post-9/11 GI Bill's return on investment (ROI) by determining the academic progress and outcomes of recipients (Cate, Lyon, Schmeling, & Bogue, 2017). NVEST proposed that Post-9/11 GI Bill outcome measures should include postsecondary progress and completion, accumulation of education debt, lifetime earnings of recipients, and revenue returned to the national economy (Cate et al., 2017). NVEST results found that students who used the GI Bill were successfully completing degrees in marketable and high demand majors, which in turn will lead to a stronger ROI for the Post-9/11 GI Bill (Cate et al., 2017). The United States recently enforced the Forever GI Bill, which expands several of the Post-9/11 GI Bill's benefits and eligibility. For instance, the 15-year educational benefits expiration date was eliminated for veterans discharged after 2013 (USDVA, n.d.).

Employment assistance provided by departments of defence

Australia's transition management processes and procedures are largely driven by the Military Rehabilitation Compensation Act 2004 (MRCA). Under MRCA, veterans are entitled to a range of benefits, including vocational rehabilitation services. MRCA also emphasizes that the Australian Department of Defence (DoD) and Department of Veterans' Affairs (DVA) are responsible for the rehabilitation of soldiers (DVA, n.d.a, n.d.b). The DoD offers the Career Transition Assistance Scheme (CTAS), which appoints Service Chiefs as the rehabilitation authorities for full-time members. CTAS is offered to both active duty service members 12 months before the completion of their tour date and veterans up to 12 months after their transition date (Australian DoD, n.d.). CTAS eligibility is dependent on years of service, with those who have served 12 years or more receiving more approved absence days and funding for vocational training programs. CTAS offers Job Search Preparation Workshops, Career Transition Trainings, Career Transition Management Coaching, and Curriculum Vitae Coaching (Australian DoD, n.d.).

Similarly, the US DoD, in cooperation with the VA, Department of Labor (DoL), and the Small Business Administration (SBA), administers the Military Transition Assistance Program (TAP) and the Disabled Transition Assistance Program (DTAP), which were established through the National Defense Authorization Act (Congressional Research Service, 2017). TAP is a 5-day program, whereas DTAP includes the 5-day TAP program and additional hours for individual instruction. In 2011, Congress passed the VOW to Hire Heroes Act, which mandates the completion of a pre-separation counseling program to all soldiers during the 24-month period preceding an anticipated retirement date and the 12-month period preceding the anticipated separation date (Congressional Research Service, 2017). Some of the mandated TAP counseling requirements include educational assistance benefits, civilian occupations and related assistance programs, entrepreneurship, DoL's qualified job training programs, etc. Additionally, the DoD-VA Veterans' Employment Initiative Task Force was tasked with revising TAP to more effectively meet the needs of transitioning soldiers, by developing the Transition Goals, Plans, and Successes (GPS). Transition GPS curricula includes topics such as resilient transitions, military occupational code cross walk, personal financial planning, and individual transition plan review (CRS, 2017). TAP's current performance measures include timeliness of TAP attendance, program access and attendance, transition and career readiness preparation, and participant satisfaction and knowledge gain (GAO, 2017a, 2017b). In 2014, the Government Accountability Office (GAO) evaluated TAP by conducting a survey of all military installations (United States and international) that operate TAP to learn about perceptions of accessibility of TAP components, challenges in attending components, and level of commander support for participation. GAO recommended that DoD collaborate with partner agencies to develop an evaluation plan to determine TAP's effectiveness by assessing its impact on post-program outcomes. DoL has an ongoing TAP employment workshop evaluation, and VA is currently developing a survey for veterans that includes questions regarding the effectiveness of TAP (GAO, 2017a, 2017b). An independent national evaluation of TAP found that soldiers who participated in TAP found their first civilian job 3 weeks sooner than those who did not participate (United States Department of Labor. (2017)). VA, DoL, and SBA are currently developing long-term outcome measures to determine the effectiveness of the program.

Employment assistance provided by veterans' affairs

DVA's Veterans' Vocational Rehabilitation Scheme (VVRS) is a free and voluntary rehabilitation program offered to eligible veterans who need additional assistance in finding or retaining civilian employment. Veterans are eligible to apply for VVRS if they have served in the Australian Defence Force and if they have served in the following types of service under the Veterans' Entitlement Act 1986: operational, peacekeeping, hazardous, defense service, and British Nuclear Test Defence (Department of Veterans' Affairs, 2016). VVRS, like many of DVA's rehabilitation programs, uses a Goal Attainment Scaling process, which is a model that determines "client-specific goals, measures the goals against tailor-made scales, and monitors and tracks progress in the clients' functioning, employment, social, and well-being outcomes" (Department of Veterans' Affairs, 2015a, 2015b). VVRS offers services such as a vocational assessment to determine employment opportunities, job-seeking advice, support if current job is at risk, assistance with updating or upgrading skills, etc. VVRS's primary outcome goal is to provide veterans with suitable paid employment (i.e., full-time, part-time, casual, self-employed, traineeship, or apprenticeship). To successfully achieve suitable paid employment, veterans' weekly work hours must either meet that of the related industry standard or the maximum number of hours the veteran can work based other circumstantial factors (Department of Veterans' Affairs, 2016).

The United States offers a vocational program, called the Vocational Rehabilitation and Employment (VR&E) program, which is tailored to meet the needs of veterans with service-connected disabilities. VR&E offers five service tracks that aim to help veterans find sustainable careers and live independently: Reemployment Track, Rapid Access to Employment Track, Self-Employment Track, Employment through Long-Term Services Track, and Independent Living Track (Vets.gov, n.d.). Successful measures for VR&E include completing the program, maintaining a suitable job for 60 days, attaining independent living goals, and achieving maximum independence in daily living. VR&E also takes a cross-sectoral approach by collaborating with DoD, DoL, state vocational rehabilitation agencies, VA's Compensated Work Therapy Program, and employers. In 2009, GAO evaluated VR&E by reviewing relevant agency documents, analyzing data from VA's Corporate WINRS and Benefits Delivery Network data systems, interviewing VA and VR&E staff, and conducting a survey of VR&E officers to follow up on key issues (GAO, 2009). GAO recommended better veteran financial incentives to participate in the program, workforce planning, and performance reporting.

Veterans Affairs Canada (VAC) also offers reimbursement (lifetime maximum of $1000) for its Career Transition Services Program. The program, similar to those in Australia and the United

States, offers resources (e.g., career assessments, aptitude testing, job market analysis, resume writing, job search skills, interview techniques, individual career counseling, and services of a professional recruiter agent) to veterans from both the regular and reserve forces (VAC, n.d. a, n.d.b). VAC's Canadian Veterans Vocational Rehabilitation and Vocational Assistance Program offers similar resources, but only to medically released veterans or veterans with service-related injuries or illness.

Support for physical and mental health conditions

Many mental and physical health conditions are more prevalent among veterans than the civilian population (Olenick, Flowers, & Diaz, 2015). As a result, veterans who are transitioning into civilian life may need greater access to health care, as their health status may be poor. Providing support and necessary resources can help countries efficiently rehabilitate veterans. The NATO survey showed that countries such as the Netherlands, Australia, New Zealand, Norway, the Republic of Croatia, Slovenia, Latvia, the United States, the United Kingdom, Canada, and Estonia offer services such as mental and physical health care benefits, case management or care coordination, and disability compensation to ensure that veterans receive the care they need.

Health care

In most countries, veterans' health care is provided by the civilian system, as most countries do not have separate health care systems for veterans. As a result, the additional benefits that veterans receive are influenced by the type of health system in the country (e.g., single-payer, two-tier, and insurance mandate).

The United Kingdom and New Zealand, for instance, follow the Beveridge Model, a tax-financed National Health Service (NHS) system in which most hospitals and clinics are owned by the government. The United Kingdom provides comprehensive coverage to all citizens, and thus does not offer additional health care funding to veterans (VAC, 2014a, 2014b). Health care coverage in the United Kingdom is offered through the NHS and is free at the point of need (Chang, Peysakhovich, Wang, & Zhu, n.d.). Although the number of services available to veterans and civilians are essentially the same, NHS offers specialized services to veterans to ensure they receive care that is tailored to their unique set of needs. Veterans receive priority access to NHS care (i.e., hospital, primary, and community care) for the treatment of service-related conditions (NHS, 2015). NHS England also offers the Veterans Trauma

Network, which acts as an all-encompassing regional hub for veteran care (NHS, 2015). Specialist teams in the Veterans Trauma Network develop a personalized treatment plan for each veteran. Additionally, veterans must visit dedicated mental health organizations, which focus on early intervention for mental health disorders and therapeutic treatment for complex mental health issues and trauma (NHS, 2015). NHS uses better care impacts such as improved experiences of care, improved outcomes in terms of changes to people's health and well-being (e.g., management of chronic illness, independence, quality of life, reduced hospitalizations), and better use of resources to track the effectiveness of benefits. In 2016, the Organization for Economic Co-operation and Development (OECD) evaluated UK's health care quality and found that each NHS system should focus on a bottom-up approach led by patients and professionals, report regionally aggregated data to provide a more nuanced analysis of quality, and improve cross-regional collaboration in monitoring and improving health care quality (OECD, 2016). The UK's health care model can be beneficial as it provides access to health care coverage to all citizens, is typically low-cost, and does not require copay. However, to fund the health care system, citizens must pay higher taxes, quality of care is entirely dependent on the government, and there are typically long waiting periods for access to care.

New Zealand offers a two-tier health system, which offers both public tax-financed health insurance and private health insurance. Although the public health system covers most costs, it is not inclusive of all health care–related expenses. As a result, veterans are eligible for funding for service-related injuries and illness through Veterans' Affairs New Zealand (VA). Veterans are eligible for treatment funding based on their service; eligible services are listed in the Qualifying Service under the Veterans' Support Act 2014 (VA, 2014). The Veterans' Support Act 2014 ensures that VA "provides appropriate rehabilitation of and support for injured veterans and promotes positive veteran and claimant interactions" (Parliamentary Counsel Office, n.d.). Veterans can receive treatment cards that cover approved treatment that is not funded by other agencies. The VA will also cover 12 months or 12 sessions of long-term treatment, private treatment if waiting time in the public system is too long, and alternative treatments (VA, 2014). The VA determines which treatments will be funded by examining the nature or severity of condition, types of treatments used, quality of the treatment sought, provider's qualifications and experience, coverage by public health system, and potential harm from delay (VA, 2014). In 2015, the Health Quality and Safety Commission evaluated the quality of

New Zealand's health care and found that patients reported that experience of care has been consistent and generally positive over the last 18 months. The evaluation also proposed that New Zealand should use multiple measures to determine the value of health care such as acute hospital bed days per capita (effective use of health resources), patient experience of care (patient-centered care), and amenable mortality (early detection and prevention) (Health Quality & Safety Commission, 2016). In 2008, the Law Commission reviewed the War Pension Act 1954 and assessed the physical and mental health services provided to veterans. The Law Commission proposed that veterans receive continued provision of treatment for accepted disabilities, receive access to comprehensive health care, rather than treatment for accepted injuries and illness, and that the Government offer veterans' health insurance at reduced rates (Law Commission, 2008). Lastly, the Law Commission found that New Zealand does not have a monitoring system and consequently loses track of veterans and their health status. To identify and address health problems more efficiently, the Law Commission proposed that the New Zealand government should keep track of veterans by registering veterans and providing them with a "veteran's card" that can be linked to a centralized database and the veterans' National Health Information number (Law Commission, 2008). New Zealand's two-tier system makes health care more accessible to all veterans but the public health system is not inclusive of all conditions; therefore, it is a possible that veterans who need supplemental care may not be adequately reimbursed for these services.

Canada offers a single-payer health care system, which only allows citizens to use a tax-financed public health system. Although Canada's publicly funded health care, instituted through the Canada Health Act, covers most health care–related costs, some citizens must purchase private supplemental coverage that is not covered under the law. The Canada Health Act aims to "to protect, promote, and restore the physical and mental well-being of residents of Canada and to facilitate reasonable access to health services without financial or other barriers" (Government of Canada, 2017). Some of the services not covered under the Canada Health Act include dental care, prescription drugs, rehabilitation services, home care, and private rooms in hospitals. Veterans are eligible to receive funding for 14 programs of choice that are not covered under Canada's public health system, including aids for daily living, ambulance services, audio (hearing) services, dental services, hospital services, medical services, medical supplies, nursing services, oxygen therapy, prescription drugs, prosthetics and orthotics, related health services, special equipment, and vision care

(VAC, 2014a, 2014b). Veterans who qualify for one or more of VAC's 14 treatment programs receive a VAC Health Care Identification Card (VAC, 2014a, 2014b). Veterans are also eligible to apply for the Public Service Health Care Plan through VAC, which aims to complement medical coverage provided by other sources. Veterans released on or after 2006 who have also been approved for long-term disability and veterans eligible for the Rehabilitation Program qualify to apply for the Public Service Health Care Plan coverage; those who qualify for coverage will be required to pay a monthly contribution depending on the type and level of coverage selected. The outcomes used to measure the performance of veterans' health benefits include access to health care benefits, utilization of health care benefits, and health care needs met. In 2014, an evaluation of VAC's Health Care Benefits and Services Program was conducted. It was recommended that VAC develop more specific measures that will provide comprehensive feedback from veterans regarding program awareness and expectations, provide clearer information on program eligibility and benefits, and include more appropriate measures to assess program performance in the Performance Measurement Strategy (VAC, 2014a, 2014b).

Similarly, countries such as Slovenia, Estonia, and Croatia use single-payer systems that are funded through mandatory social tax of all employed citizens and their employers. The national funds for the three countries include the Health Insurance Institute of Slovenia (HIIS), defined in the Health Care and Health Insurance Act of 1992; Estonia's Health Insurance Fund, defined in its Health Insurance Act 2002; and the Croatian Health Insurance Fund, defined in its Health Insurance Act 1993. Unlike some of the aforementioned countries, Slovenia, Estonia, and Croatia do not provide tailored services to veterans. States and municipalities are required to pay contributions to help war veterans who are unable to contribute to social taxes and access physical and mental health services (Džakula, Sagan, Pavić, Lončarek, & Sekelj-Kauzlarić, 2014). Similar to the aforementioned health care systems, single-payer systems are more cost-effective and ensure that all citizens are covered. However, the funding is typically pulled from taxes and it may take significantly longer to access health care due to long wait times.

In the United States, the Veterans' Health Care Eligibility Reform Act of 1996 enforced the expansion of health benefits and services offered to veterans. Veterans receive more health services than civilians, as the VA provides specialized public insurance programs to veterans under the Veterans Health Administration (VHA). Although most veterans qualify for cost-free services based on a priority system (influenced by service-connected disability, other disability, and income), veterans may be required to pay an out-of-pocket copay for treatment of their non-service-connected conditions (VA, 2018). Veterans who were former prisoners of war have 50% or more compensable service-connected disabilities, and those who were deemed to be "catastrophically disabled" always qualify for free health care and prescriptions. Veterans are also allowed to opt out of veteran health benefits and choose private or publicly funded insurance (VA, 2018). The VA health system covers preventative care services (e.g., immunization), inpatient care services (e.g., traumatic brain injury), ancillary services, specialty care services, emergency care, and specialty inpatient and outpatient mental health care. Veterans are provided with a Veteran Health Identification Card, which allows the VA to retrieve and monitor veteran health records. VA tracks outcomes such as health care–associated infections, readmissions and mortality, patient safety, and ambulatory care–related outcomes (GAO, 2017a, 2017b). In 2017, GAO evaluated VA health care and proposed that VHA should "clearly define the responsibilities of VA medical centers to resolve outstanding enrollment applications; ensure efficient application processing and enrollment determinations by defining oversight responsibilities; develop procedures for collecting reliable system-wide data; and clarify its five-day timeliness standard" (GAO, 2017a, 2017b). Although the VA provides veterans with specialized and tailored care, there are several services that veterans may have to pay for out-of- pocket (e.g., copays).

In 2018, the National Academies of Sciences, Engineering, and Medicine (NASEM) evaluated VA's mental health services by assessing the quality, capacity, and access to mental health care services for veterans who served in Operation Enduring Freedom, Operation Iraqi Freedom, and Operation New Dawn (OEF/OIF/OND). NASEM administered a survey to OEF/OIF/OND veterans, performed site visits, and conducted literature reviews. Some of the key findings of the review include lack of mental health service utilization, lack of awareness of VA services, a challenging process of accessing services, chronic workforce problems, and personal barriers (NASEM, 2018). NASEM recommended that VA should consider developing a strategic plan to ensure veterans receive high quality and accessible integrated mental health services, modifying policies to ensure barriers to accessing mental health care are eliminated, adopting strategies to expand outreach efforts, and addressing workforce issues (NASEM, 2018). Veterans who have non-service-related injuries that are not covered under VA health care may need to explore public and private health insurance options, which can also result in additional costs.

Case management and care coordination

The expansion of veterans' benefits across various countries has led to increasingly complex benefit application and service navigation processes. To help veterans navigate, coordinate, and manage the multitude of services they utilize, countries offer case management and care coordination services. Although case management and care coordination are typically used interchangeably, the two services differ in the ways in which they engage patients. Case management services typically provide patients with single points of contact for activities related to their benefits; case managers typically help balance numerous resources by coordinating all services on behalf of their patients. Care coordination, however, promotes collaboration and information sharing between patients, their family members, and all their health care providers to ensure that patients are receiving appropriate care. Canada, for instance, provides case management services through its Client-Centered Service Approach to ensure veterans receive appropriate care the moment they need it. Veterans can request a case manager during their Transition Interview with VAC representatives. Case managers are typically members of interdisciplinary teams that have access to medical professionals (i.e., doctors, nurses, physiotherapists, occupational therapists, mental health specialists, rehabilitation specialists, and provincial and local programs and service providers). Veterans and case managers will develop a plan after they discuss issues, goals, and barriers. During the course of the case management process, case managers will monitor and evaluate veteran progress and modify the plan as needed. Former members of the Canadian Armed Forces and Royal Canadian Mounted Police are eligible for the case management services if they have significant health issues and are having a difficult time readjusting to civilian life. Veterans may request case management services whenever they need additional support (VAC, n.d.a, n.d. b). New Zealand also offers a complementary one-on-one case management service that helps veterans manage their health and social needs, improve and maintain quality of life, and address questions about claims. Case management is available to all veterans with qualifying service, New Zealand Armed Forces personnel, partners, ex-partners, and children of Vietnam and Operation Grapple veterans (New Zealand VA, 2017).

The United States has recently implemented the Patient Aligned Care Team (PACT), which involves collaboration among veterans and their health care professionals to plan for holistic care that ensures sustainable health and wellness outcomes (USDVA, 2016). PACT uses a team-based approach that empowers veterans to be at the center of their care team. The team includes family members, caregivers, and health care professionals (e.g., primary care provider, nurse care manager, clinical associate, and administrative clerks). The PACT model of care also aims to improve veterans' access to health care by offering educational seminars, group clinics, and pertinent health care information. PACT provides patients with tools such as early detection screenings, preventative or wellness care services, educational materials, and lifestyle coaching (USDVA, 2016). The Center for Evaluation of Patient Aligned Care Teams (CEPACT) was created to evaluate the implementation of the PACT model. The evaluation methodology included site visits, key informant interviews, video observations of clinical appointments, staff surveys, and secondary analysis of medical record data. During its 2010–14 regional evaluation, CEPACT found that intra-team functioning and communication should be strengthened, clinical work schedules should account for the time it takes to create and adjust patient plan changes, and early education to local leadership and across the system should be provided (CEPACT, 2016). Studies have found that although PACT members had positive views of the model, reported that it improved relationships with patients, and increased patient satisfaction, there were several barriers that the teams felt need to be addressed. For instance, PACT members have voiced that the insufficient staffing of teams can act as a barrier, as it reduces individual time with patients, increases participant burnout, and decreases team efficacy due to low-performing team members (Ladebue et al., 2014).

Similarly, DVA offers the Coordinated Veterans' Care Program (CVC), which helps improve chronic disease management and quality of care and assigns each veteran a care team of general practitioners and nurse coordinators. CVC is administered under the "Treatment Principles—Coordinated Veterans' Care Program, the Notes for Providers for the Veterans' Entitlements Act 1986, and the Military Rehabilitation and Compensation Act 2004" (DVA, 2011). Veterans, war widows, war widowers, and dependents who are Gold Card holders and are at risk of being admitted or readmitted to the hospital are eligible to apply to the program, as long as they pass an eligibility assessment. The program focuses on chronic conditions such as congestive heart failure, coronary artery disease, pneumonia, chronic pulmonary disease, and diabetes (DVA, 2011). CVC provides general practitioners who participate in CVC with financial incentives. The efficacy of CVC is dependent on efficient sharing of health information, regular communication, empowerment, and coaching. The CVC also offers a separate Social Assistance service that helps veterans adjust in their communities, expand the type and frequency of social contact, and encourage veterans to proactively engage in their communities (DVA, 2011). The desired long-term outcomes of the program include improved health outcomes, reduced hospital admissions, improved self-management, improved quality of life, enablement of veterans to remain in own homes longer, improved emotional well-being, and reduced isolation (DVA, 2015). In 2015, DVA evaluated CVC by conducting a literature review, administering a survey to general practices, consulting health care professionals and Gold Card holders, analyzing monitoring data, and performing quantitative analysis of health care data. The survey results showed that general practitioners and practice nurses did not believe the eligibility criteria for the CVC program were sufficient and proposed that the program include veterans with mental health disorders (e.g., posttraumatic stress disorder), terminal illness, osteoporosis, rheumatoid and osteoarthritis, and veterans without Gold Cards (DVA, 2015).

Disability

Most countries offer disability compensation to regular or active forces and reserve force veterans. To adequately compensate veterans for their losses due to service-related disabilities, countries such as Canada, the United Kingdom, Latvia, Estonia, New Zealand, and Australia offer compensation for earnings losses and quality of life. These countries provide monthly annuities for earnings losses and allow veterans to select between lump sum and annuity payments for quality of life. The United States, however, does not offer quality of life payments and has recently faced pressure to provide additional compensation to veterans whose quality of life has been significantly impacted by their disabilities. Most countries have also integrated rehabilitation with their disability compensation, and some require veterans to complete vocational rehabilitation programs before providing earnings loss compensation. Countries such as Australia and Canada have recently undergone disability compensation reform to ensure that veterans are able to access services more easily. In recent years, countries have faced criticism for inadequate mental health–related disability compensation, causing a few countries to modify disability policies and adjust the compensation for mental health conditions.

Caregiver Support

Most services offered to veterans use a patient-centered approach to motivate veterans to be proactive about their progress. However, older or severely disabled veterans may not have the capacity to use and capitalize on these services and thus may require additional support from caregivers. However, providing care for patients with chronic illness can lead to caregiver burden as it can be physically, mentally, and financially demanding. Risk factors for caregiver burden include female caregivers, low education, residing with veteran, high numbers of hours spent caregiving, depression, social isolation, financial instability, and lack of choice in being a caregiver (Adelman, Lyubov, Tmanova, & Delgado, 2014). As a result, countries have developed policies and programs to provide caregiver support to those who are at risk of negative outcomes due to caregiving. The NATO survey showed that countries such as the Netherlands, Australia, New Zealand, the United States, the United Kingdom, and Canada offer caregiver support.

Australia enforced the Carer Recognition Act 2010, which aims to "increase recognition and awareness of the role caregivers play in providing daily care and support to people who are older or have disabilities, medical conditions, and mental illness." (DVA, n.d. a, n.d. b). Following the Carer Recognition Act, physicians were provided with the Carer Awareness Training Package, which aimed to ensure that caregivers were receiving the care they need (DVA, n.d. a, n.d. b). Australia offers a myriad of resources and benefits to veteran caregivers through its Veterans' Home Care Program. Caregivers of an entitled person (Gold Card or White Card holders), entitled person who has caregiving responsibilities, and a self-caregiver are all eligible to be assessed for respite care. DVA provides respite in residential aged care facilities, in-home respite care, and emergency short-term home relief. Veterans with caregivers may also receive up to 28 days of in-home and/or residential care (DVA, n.d.a, n.d. b). Veterans and caregivers may also be eligible for domestic assistance (e.g., house cleaning, meal preparation) and safety-related home and garden maintenance (e.g., replacing light bulbs). Canada offers the Family Caregiver Relief Benefit, which offers veterans tax-free lump sum grants to ensure that they are able to get continued support when their caregivers are temporarily unavailable. The purpose of the benefit is to allow caregivers to take well-deserved breaks to attend to their own mental and physical health needs, while veterans receive additional support during their caregivers' absence. Veterans with informal unpaid caregivers who are 18 years or older, with disability award–related injuries and illness, who need ongoing care, and who are not permanent residents of a nursing home or long-term care facility are eligible for this benefit (VAC, 2016).

The United States offers the Comprehensive Assistance for Family Caregivers, and Caregiver Support Service under the Caregivers and

Veterans Omnibus Health Services Act of 2010, which ensures training, services, and assistance for veteran caregivers in need. The Comprehensive Assistance for Family Caregivers provides support for caregivers of eligible veterans who were seriously injured in the line of duty on or after September 11, 2001. The program offers services such as financial stipends, access to health insurance, mental health services and counseling, caregiver training, and respite care (USDVA, 2018). The VA Caregiver Support Service provides caregivers with support lines, peer support mentoring for 6 months, free Building Better Caregivers workshops, mentoring in caregiving, stress management, mood management, and problem-solving through REACH VA, and Caregiver Support Coordinators (USDVA, 2017a, 2017b, 2017c). Additionally, VA offers veterans with caregiver resources such as adult day health care centers, home-based primary care, home hospice care, homemaker and home health aides, home telehealth, respite care, and skilled home care (USDVA, 2017a, 2017b, 2017c). The VA Caregiver Support Program Partnered Evaluation (VA-CARES) Initiative announced that it will evaluate VA's caregiver support services and how they impact veterans and their caregivers. VA-CARES Initiative's goals are to assess the impact caregiver support services have on the health and well-being of family caregivers and veterans by examining health care encounters (acute, primary, and specialty utilization), understand how caregivers use and value various components of both programs, assess the value of the programs to veterans, caregivers, and the VA health care system by developing a profile of the costs and services provided in both programs (USDVA, 2017a, 2017b, 2017c).

Family support

There is a broad acknowledgment across the NATO countries that families are an integral component of the transition process, and this is discussed in more detail elsewhere in this book. Families also "transition" with the service member, and they play a vital role in facilitating successful transitions. The Centre for Social Justice Report on "Military Families and Transition" states "a clear linkage [exists] between a stable, resilient and economically prepared family, and the likelihood that the Service leaver from that family will successfully transition into civilian life after time spent in the Armed Forces. There are also many other benefits of such family resilience that contribute to the effectiveness of serving personnel … So it is in everybody's interests to ensure that issues that could hinder the stability and well-being of the family are evidenced, and that the means whereby they might be addressed are credibly presented."

This acknowledgment is reflected partially in the fact that most countries formally involve families in the transition process. Support for families in the form of programs and services is, however, quite variable across the NATO members.

Most countries offer some form of provision for families, often a derivative form of the services provided for veterans. Commonly provided forms of family support included case management or care coordination, mental health and substance abuse, counseling, and information and referral. A few countries such as New Zealand, Slovenia, the United Kingdom, Canada, and the United States provide support for housing and employment assistance. The United States offers the Marine Gunnery Sergeant John David Fry Scholarship, which provides Post-9/11 GI Bill benefits to the children and surviving spouses of service members who died in the line of duty after September 10, 2001 (USDVA, n.d.). In Canada, children of deceased veterans who died from military service are eligible for VAC's Educational Assistance program, which provides monthly financial support and funding for additional expenses (e.g., tuition) for up to 4 years or 36 academic months (VAC, 2016). Similarly, New Zealand provides education payments for children of qualifying veterans who are studying at a secondary or tertiary level and pensions for the children, spouses, and partners of deceased or severely disabled veterans. New Zealand also provides partners with access to vocational training, childcare payments, and financial advice (New Zealand VA, 2017). In Australia and New Zealand, family members are eligible for case management services. War widows, war widowers, and dependents who are Gold Card holders are eligible for the CVC in Australia (DVA, 2011). In New Zealand, partners, ex-partners, and children of Vietnam and Operation Grapple veterans are eligible to receive case managers. In countries like the United States, New Zealand, the United Kingdom, Norway, the Republic of Croatia, and Canada, family members can also receive disability compensation under varying circumstances. Lastly, many countries offer caregiver support services, which aim to reduce the burden on family caregivers and ensure that family caregivers are given time to take care of their own health and well-being.

In general, programs and services for families are not routinely being evaluated. However, on behalf of the US DoD, Pennsylvania State University (PSU) Clearinghouse for Military Family Readiness provides military family programs with evaluation services such as "evaluability assessments, metrics identification and development, evaluation planning, and program and service evaluation" (PSU, n.d.). Some countries are collecting data on how families are doing following transition, although it is evident that such data are not collected regularly. Barriers to helping families in transition emerged in relation to access, contact, and dissemination of information.

Knowledge gaps

While countries offer several resources to ensure smooth transition for veterans and their families, it is difficult to determine program effectiveness and the long-term impacts of the programs, because most countries do not have a systematic way of tracking success or monitoring veterans after they have completed the programs. Most services and benefits in NATO countries have not been evaluated. Additionally, although most countries reported follow-up or monitoring procedures for wounded, injured, and sick service leavers at a minimum, most do not track veteran progress based on the services that the veteran has used. As a result, most countries do not regularly track long-term program outcomes, so the success rates of each program are based on short-term impacts.

Recommendations

1. Education and Employment Assistance

   Recommendation 1.1: Offer cross-sector programs to help veterans gain a better understanding of the civilian workforce.

   To ensure that veterans are fully prepared for the civilian workforce, countries should utilize a cross-sector approach in their employment assistance programs. Some countries have collaborated with other workforce-related government agencies (e.g., US DoL and SBA) to educate veterans about civilian jobs, entrepreneurship, and policies that are in place to ensure equitable job opportunities for veterans.
2. Physical and Mental Health Support

   Recommendation 2.1: Ensure that veterans are receiving specialized and tailored care that meets their unique set of needs.

   Some countries offer comprehensive and accessible care to all citizens and thus do not provide additional benefits and services to veterans. Countries should acknowledge that veteran populations have needs that significantly differ to those of civilian populations. As a result, countries should offer veterans specialized care tailored to their unique health issues (e.g., services that address service-related mental health disorders or blast injuries).

Recommendation 2.2: Provide case management services to veterans who need additional support when navigating benefits.
To help veterans balance all benefits and services, Veterans' Affairs should consider offering case management services that provide a single point of contact to veterans in cases where a multitude of services are needed. Veterans reported that their under-utilization of services can be attributed to lack of awareness or the complex application process. Care management services can help ensure that veterans are aware of all services available to them and that they do not feel overwhelmed when accessing the services.

Recommendation 2.3: Utilize a patient-centered approach by forming multidisciplinary staff teams and empowering patients to be a part of discussions regarding their conditions and treatments.
Countries should consider utilizing multidisciplinary staff teams, including patients, to ensure regular communication and sharing of information among patients' providers. Ensuring that patients are at the center of these teams can empower them to be more proactive and make informed decisions about their health and treatments.

3. Caregiver Support

Recommendation 3.1: Consider offering funding for respite care to prevent caregiver burnout.
Oftentimes, caregivers experience an immense amount of stress, which can result in negative health and life outcomes. Countries should offer respite care to veterans who have informal caretakers to ensure that veterans still receive the support they need while their caregivers are given time to recharge and take care of their own mental and physical health.

4. Family Support

Recommendation 4.1: Offer additional or similar transition services to family members of veterans.
Countries should acknowledge that families of veterans also go through a transitional period when veterans return from service and should consider offering the family of veterans similar resources (e.g., educational/employment assistance, access to mental and physical health services, case management services) to ensure that family members also feel supported through the MCT.

5. Overarching Recommendations

Recommendation 5.1: Promote cross-sector collaboration, partnership, and engagement to ensure that veterans receive adequate and comprehensive support.

Countries should acknowledge that veteran transition begins before veterans leave service, as the transition process requires planning and preparation. Therefore, the DoD, Veterans' Affairs, and other stakeholders, such as community organizations, should maintain a collaborative partnership to offer services to veterans that begin toward the end of their deployment and continue after they leave service. To ensure smooth transition for veterans, the departments should work together by clearly defining their respective roles in the service to civilian life transition and by developing information sharing and communication strategies to ensure veterans receive appropriate resources during each phase of their transition.

Recommendation 5.2: Regularly evaluate military to civilian programs and monitor veteran progress to ensure program effectiveness.

Transition "outcomes" (including employment status and satisfaction, health, housing, finances, family health and well-being, and life satisfaction) are monitored periodically (e.g., every few years) by a number of countries, with others reporting no systematic tracking of outcomes at all. Evaluation and monitoring processes ensure that countries make evidence-based decisions, which can lead to effective policy and investment decisions, improved service delivery, and positive outcomes for veterans and their families (Lazier, 2017). Countries should monitor veterans and evaluate benefits more frequently and develop systematic monitoring and evaluation processes to ensure that benefits are regularly being improved and modified to meet the needs of veterans. Lastly, countries should clearly define what successful transitioning means by developing a comprehensive list of positive outcomes.

References

Adelman, R. D., Tmanova, L. L., Delgado, D., Dion, S., & Lachs, M. S. (2014). Caregiver burden. A clinical review. *Journal of the American Medical Association, 311*(10), 1052–1060. https://doi.org/10.1001/jama.2014.304.

Ahern, J., Worthern, M., Masters, J., Lippman, S., Ozer, E., & Moos, R. (2015). The challenges of Afghanistan and Iraq veterans' transition from military to civilian life and approaches to reconnection. *PLoS One, 10*, 1–13.

Australian Department of Defence. (n.d.). *Career transition assistance scheme*. Retrieved from http://www.defence.gov.au/DCO/Transition/Employment-support/CTAS.asp/.

Australian Government Department of Veterans' Affairs. (2016). *Overview of the VVRS*. Retrieved from http://clik.dva.gov.au/rehabilitation-library/12-veterans-vocational-rehabilitation-scheme-guidelines/121-overview-vvrs.

Bulmer, S., & Jackson, D. (2016). "You do not live in my skin": Embodiment, voice and the veteran. *Critical Military Studies, 2*(1–2), 25–40.

Cate, C. A., Lyon, J. S., Schmeling, J., & Bogue, B. Y. (2017). *National veteran education success tracker: A report on the academic success of student veterans using the post-9/11 GI Bill*. Washington, DC: Student Veterans of America.

CEPACT. (2016). https://www.visn4.va.gov/VISN4/CEPACT/docs/cepact-frontline-factsheet-20151008single.pdf.

Chang, J., Peysakhovich, F., Wang, W., & Zhu, J. (n.d.). *The UK health care system*. Retrieved from http://assets.ce.columbia.edu/pdf/actu/actu-uk.pdf.

Congressional Research Service. (2017). *Military transition assistance programme (TAP): An overview*. Retrieved from https://fas.org/sgp/crs/natsec/IF10347.pdf.

Cooper, L., Caddick, N., Godier, L., Cooper, A., & Fossey, M. (2017). *Transition from the military into civilian life: An exploration of cultural competence*. Armed Forces & Society.

Cooper, L., Caddick, N., Godier, L., Cooper, A., Fossey, M., & Engward, H. (2017). A model of military to civilian transition: Bourdieu in Action. *Journal of Military, Veteran and Family Health, 3*(2), 53–60.

Danish, S., & Antonides, B. (2013). The challenges of reintegration for service members and their families. *American Journal of Orthopsychiatry, 83*, 550–558.

Department of Veterans' Affairs. (2015a). *Rehabilitation services*. Retrieved from https://www.dva.gov.au/sites/default/files/files/providers/rehabilitation/Rehabilitation_Information_Pack.pdf.

Department of Veterans' Affairs. (2015b). *Factsheet HSV108 - veterans' vocational rehabilitation scheme (VVRS)*. Retrieved from https://www.dva.gov.au/factsheet-hsv108-veterans-vocational-rehabilitation-scheme-vvrs.

DVA. (2011). *Coordinated veterans' care programme*. Retrieved from https://www.dva.gov.au/sites/default/files/files/publications/providers/cvc/GGP.pdf.

DVA. (2015). *Independent monitoring and evaluation of the coordinated veterans' care (CVC) programme*. Retrieved from https://www.dva.gov.au/sites/default/files/files/providers/cvc/Grosvenor–Independent-Monitoring-and-Evaluation–CVC-Programme–Final-Report–Aug2015.pdf.

DVA. (n.d. (a)). *Carers*. Retrieved from https://www.dva.gov.au/health-and-wellbeing/home-and-care/aged-and-community-care/carers.

DVA. (n.d. (b)). *Military Rehabilitation and Compensation Act (MRCA)*. Retrieved from https://www.dva.gov.au/benefits-and-payments/compensation/military-rehabilitation-and-compensation-act-mrca.

Džakula, A., Sagan, A., Pavić, N., Lončarek, K., & Sekelj-Kauzlarić, K. (2014). Croatia: Health system review. *Health Systems in Transition, 16*(3), 1–162.

Federal Benefits for Veterans, Dependents and Survivors, U.S. Department of Veterans Affairs https://www.va.gov/opa/publications/benefits_book/2018_Federal_Benefits_for_Veterans.pdf.

GAO. (2009). *VA vocational rehabilitation and employment*. Retrieved from http://www.nasuad.org/sites/nasuad/files/hcbs/files/154/7693/VR_and_E_report.pdf.

GAO. (2017a). *VA health care quality*. Retrieved from https://www.gao.gov/assets/690/687523.pdf.

GAO. (2017b). *VA health care*. Retrieved from https://www.gao.gov/assets/690/686918.pdf.

Government of Canada. (2017). *Canada Health Act*. Retrieved from https://www.canada.ca/en/health-canada/services/health-care-system/canada-health-care-system-medicare/canada-health-act.html.

Health Quality & Safety Commission. (2016). *A window on the quality of New Zealand's health care 2016*. Retrieved from https://www.hqsc.govt.nz/assets/Health-Quality-Evaluation/PR/window-on-quality-of-NZ-health-care-May-2016.pdf.

Ladebue, A. C., Helfrich, C. D., Gerdes, Z. T., Fihn, S. D., Nelson, K. M., & Sayre, G. G. (2014). The experience of patient aligned care team (PACT) members. *Health Care Management Review, 41*(1), 2–10.

Law Commission. (2008). *Towards a New veterans' entitlements Scheme: A discussion paper on a review of the War Pensions Act 1954*. Retrieved from http://www.lawcom.govt.nz/sites/default/files/projectAvailableFormats/NZLC%20IP7.pdf.

Lazier, R. (2017). A national veteran policy field of study to guide policy development, program investments, and improve outcomes. *PA Times*. Retrieved from https://patimes.org/national-veteran-policy-field-study-guide-policy-development-program-investments-improve-outcomes/.

Morin, R. (2011). The difficult transition from military to civilian life. *Pew Research Social and Demographic Trends*. Retrieved from http://www.pewsocialtrends.org/2011/12/08/the-difficult-transition-from-military-to-civilian-life/.

National Academies of Sciences, Engineering, and Medicine. (2018). *Evaluation of the department of veterans affairs mental health services*. Washington, DC: The National Academies Press. Retrieved from https://www.nap.edu/read/24915/chapter/1.

New Zealand VA. (2017). *Support for families (Scheme two)*. Retrieved from https://www.veteransaffairs.mil.nz/support/family-support/family-support-scheme-two/.

NHS. (2015). *NHS health care for veterans*. Retrieved from https://www.nhs.uk/NHSEngland/Militaryhealthcare/veterans-families-reservists/Pages/veterans.aspx.

OECD. (2016). *OECD reviews of health care quality: United Kingdom 2016: Raising standards*. Paris: OECD Publishing. https://doi.org/10.1787/9789264239487-en.

Olenick, M., Flowers, M., & Diaz, V J. (2015). US veterans and their unique issues: enhancing health care professional awareness. *Advances in Medical Education and Practice, 6*, 635–639.

Parliamentary Counsel Office. (n.d.). *Veterans' Support Act 2014*. Retrieved from http://www.legislation.govt.nz/act/public/2014/0056/latest/DLM5537780.html.

PennState Clearing House for Military Family Readiness. (n.d.). *Services we offer*. Retrieved from https://militaryfamilies.psu.edu/services-we-offer/.

United States Department of Labor. (2017). *Transition assistance programme*. Retrieved from https://www.dol.gov/vets/programmes/tap/tap_fs.htm.

US Department of Veterans Affairs. (2016). *Patient Aligned care team (PACT). Patient care services*. Retrieved from https://www.patientcare.va.gov/primarycare/PACT.asp.

US Department of Veterans Affairs. (n.d. (a)) *Education and training: forever GI Bill - Harry W. Colmery Veterans Educational Assistance Act*. Retrieved from https://benefits.va.gov/gibill/forevergibill.asp.

US Department of Veterans Affairs. (n.d. (b)) *Education and training: Post-9/11 GI Bill*. Retrieved from https://www.benefits.va.gov/gibill/post911_gibill.asp.

USDVA. (2017a). *Caregiver support evaluation (VA-CARES)*. Retrieved from https://www.queri.research.va.gov/about/factsheets/care-PEI.pdf.

USDVA. (2017b). *VA caregiver support: Care for caregivers*. Retrieved from https://www.caregiver.va.gov/Care_Caregivers.asp.

USDVA. (2017c). *VA caregiver support. Care for veterans*. Retrieved from https://www.caregiver.va.gov/Care_Veterans.asp.

USDVA. (2018). *VA caregiver support: Caring for seriously injured post-9/11 veterans*. Retrieved from https://www.caregiver.va.gov/support/support_benefits.asp.

USDVA. (n.d.). *Education and training marine Gunnery Sergent John David fry scholarship*. Retrieved from https://www.benefits.va.gov/gibill/docs/factsheets/fry_scholarship.pdf.

VA Vets.gov. (n.d.). *VR&E rapid access to employment track*. Retrieved from https://www.vets.gov/employment/vocational-rehab-and-employment/service-disabled/job-search-and-counseling/.

VAC. (2014a). *Comparison to other countries*. Retrieved from http://www.veterans.gc.ca/eng/about-us/reports/departmental-audit-evaluation/2009-12-nvc/4-4.

VAC. (2014b). *Evaluation of the health care benefits and services programme*. Retrieved from http://www.veterans.gc.ca/pdf/deptReports/2014-health-care-benefits-evaluation/2014-health-care-benefits-evaluation.pdf.

VAC. (2016). *Educational assistance*. Retrieved from http://www.veterans.gc.ca/eng/services/information-for/families-and-survivors/education-assistance.

VAC. (n.d. (a)). *Career transition services*. Retrieved from https://www.veterans.gc.ca/pdf/publications/career-transition-services/career-transition-services.pdf.

VAC. (n.d. (b)). *Case management*. Retrieved from http://www.veterans.gc.ca/public/pages/publications/system-pdfs/1321f-Case%20Management.pdf.

van Staden, L., Fear, N., Iversen, A., French, C., Dandecker, C., & Wessely, S. (2007). Transition back into civilian life: A study of personnel leaving the U.K. armed forces via "military prison". *Military Medicine, 172*(9), 925–930.

VCA. (2016). *Family caregiver relief benefit*. Retrieved from http://www.veterans.gc.ca/eng/services/health/family-caregiver-relief-benefit.

Veterans Affairs Canada. (2017). *Budget 2017*. Retrieved from http://www.veterans.gc.ca/eng/help/faq/budget#vetb.

Veterans Support Act of 2014 Veterans Support Act of 2014 http://www.legislation.govt.nz/act/public/2014/0056/60.0/DLM5537774.html

CHAPTER

5

Self-assessment of need for assistance with military-to-civilian transition

James M. Thompson[1], *Sanela Dursun*[2], *Jennifer E.C. Lee*[2], *Alla Skomorovsky*[2], *Wendy Lockhart*[3], *Mary Beth MacLean*[3]

[1] Department of Public Health Sciences, Queens University, Kingston, ON, Canada; [2] National Defence Canada, Ottawa, ON, Canada; [3] Veterans Affairs Canada, Charlottetown, PE, Canada

OUTLINE

https://doi.org/10.1016/B978-0-12-815312-3.00005-X

© 2019 Crown Copyright and Elsevier Inc.
All rights reserved.

Introduction

All releasing military members and their families experience some degree of challenge in the process of military-to-civilian transition (MCT) (Pedlar et al. Chapter 3). Many are able to manage with usual administrative, family, and community supports (Forces in Mind Trust, 2013; Thompson et al., 2011; 2014); however, others might require additional help. As demonstrated in other chapters of this book, MCT support services offered by the military and veterans' affairs agencies are evolving in many nations, complemented by a growing array of assistance programs in nongovernmental public and private sectors (e.g., Cramm et al., 2016). The sheer complexity of the array of available support services for serving members, veterans (former members), and their families can be a barrier to service access as they navigate MCT (Auditor General of Canada, 2012), particularly if they are not aware that such services exist, or if they think they do not need additional supports.

There is need for tools that prompt members and veterans to seek and use services. Anecdotal evidence indicates that some transitioning members and veterans who could benefit from support programs present late, when problems are more difficult to manage, or do not present at all (Ashcroft, 2014; Forkin, 2015; Thompson, VanTil et al., 2015; VAC Ombudsman, 2016). Unanticipated or unmet MCT well-being problems could set them up for longer-term difficulties in life after service (Cooper, Caddick, Godier, Cooper, & Fossey, 2018; Thompson & Lockhart, 2015; VAC Ombudsman, 2016). In the 2013 Canadian *Life After Service Studies* (LASS) survey of Regular Force veterans, 60% of the one-quarter who reported difficult transitions had not been released medically but had disproportionate prevalences of chronic health and socioeconomic problems (Thompson, Sweet, VanTil, Poirier, & MacKinnon, 2016). Conversely, 48% of those who had been released medically reported not having a difficult transition (Thompson, MacLean et al., 2015) and so might not have needed intense transition support. The LASS survey found that 37% of Regular Force members and 88% of Reservists who had operational deployment service and were released during 1998–2012 did not participate in VAC transition interviews before release (Thompson, VanTil et al., 2015). Moreover, anecdotal information suggests that some members who did take transition interviews might not have disclosed their situations fully to the military or veterans' affairs system because they assumed that they would do well. The VAC Ombudsman found that CAF members' spouses often are unaware of supports. They called for more direct and proactive communication to explain available programs and services (VAC Ombudsman, 2016).

Worldwide, researchers studying MCT outcomes have noted that inadequate planning and preparation for the challenges of adjusting to civilian life tend to be associated with post-service difficulty (Ashcroft, 2014; Castro, Kintzle, & Hassan, 2014; Forkin, 2015; Shields et al., 2016; Thompson & Lockhart, 2015). People undergoing major life transitions might not reflect sufficiently on their preparedness for aspects of the transition process. For example, military members might become accustomed to ready access to military health services and might not anticipate that access to civilian health care could be difficult after release. Members used to having their needs met by the military might not be prepared to manage their finances or know how to find employment and housing. They might not be aware of useful services that they could access to help them adapt to postservice life. The 2015 CAF *Your Say Survey* showed that about 80% of currently serving CAF members were unaware of the Director Casualty Support Management's publication *The Guide to Benefits, Programs, and Services for Serving and Former Canadian Armed Forces Members and Their Families* (Peach, 2016). Less than half (48%) were aware of VAC Case Management or VAC Career Transition Services (46%), and only about 60% were aware of the CAF Career Transition Assistance Program. These findings are typical of experiences in other nations.

One approach to engaging transitioning members and veterans in needed services is the use of active transition risk assessment screening systems (MacLean et al., 2018). A disadvantage of active screening tools is that members and veterans may choose not to participate, either because they feel they do not need to be screened or owing to the stigma of disclosing themselves to screening agencies. Use of a brief, eye-catching self-assessment tool before screening could improve participation in screening and other forms of outreach. Self-assessment requires introspection, an activity that prior research has shown can be enhanced: self-assessment tools are widely used to prompt people to seek timely assistance for health problems, interpersonal violence, socioeconomic difficulties, and to encourage professionals to think critically (Austin, Gregory, & Chiu, 2008; Banks & Nafukho, 2008, Cooper & Humphreys, 2008; Cowan,

Wilson-Barnett, Norman, & Murrells, 2008; Richy et al., 2004). We found no examples of self-assessment tools that can prompt members and veterans to reflect on their readiness for MCT and help them to determine whether they should seek assistance.

This chapter describes a self-assessment tool that was developed to encourage military members and veterans to reflect on their risk for experiencing MCT difficulties. The tool was designed to prompt them to seek assistance early in their transitions. The objective was to design an inviting, intuitive tool that could easily be disseminated among serving members, veterans, their families, and other supporters to promote self-assessment of risk in MCT. The overall goal was to support efforts to optimize the well-being of transitioned veterans and their families.

Prototype development

The self-assessment tool was developed by a joint VAC–CAF team of researchers with subject matter expertise in MCT. The researchers had expertise in psychology, social science, medicine, public health sciences, knowledge translation, and system management. First, we drafted initial prototypes for serving and veteran members based on a priori design principles, considering expert consensus and published evidence about factors that influence good MCT outcomes. Then, we refined the prototypes in two rounds of interviews with serving members and veterans to test appeal and content. Funding for the project was provided by VAC, the CAF, and DND. The project received ethical approval from the Social Science Research Review Board of the Director General Military Personnel Research and Analysis.

Development of the first prototype

The first step was the development of an initial prototype. The team collaborated to develop the prototype by expert consensus, beginning with a priori development of design criteria (Table 5.1).

The intended primary users are both CAF members and veterans undergoing MCT. Secondary users are spouses or significant others, friends, colleagues, advocates, and staff in agencies such as the CAF and VAC who support CAF members and veterans and their families.

The team sought to develop a simple, easy-to-use tool that would encourage members and veterans to seek assistance in MCT when ordinarily they might not, or to reassure them that they do not need additional assistance. The team decided a priori that a member or

TABLE 5.1 A *priori* design principles.

General principles
- Appealing design to encourage use by busy people.
- Encourage reflection so that users think about their situation in ways they might not have considered.
- Outcome-focused: expected to predict and enhance transition ease/difficulty.
- Accommodate all possible primary user subgroups (e.g., all ranks, all service branches and components, and all release types).
- Participatory: built with significant input from transition service providers with military experience.
- Informed by existing evidence on MCT life courses.
- Not mandatory.
- Preserves anonymity.

Desired properties for the statements
- Based on domains of well-being in MCT.
- Easy to understand and intuitive.
- Contain terms and phrases that are military-specific and accurate.
- Asks for a response to only a single issue.
- Only one sentence long.
- Where appropriate, includes impact on family.

veteran should be able, by reflecting on well-being statements and the offered responses, to infer whether or not they are likely to experience difficulty during MCT and should consider seeking additional assistance.

The design challenge was to find a practical way to operationalize the construct through a self-assessment tool. The prototype was designed to be easy to read and to make the reader want to complete the tool, like a game. The team settled on a green-yellow-red self-assessment continuum to represent self-assessed risk of experiencing difficulty in transition and need for assistance. Green was used to signify that transition was not likely to be difficult, yellow as uncertain, and red as more likely to be difficult. This color scheme was thought to meet several of the design principles listed in Table 5.1, including need for an intuitive self-categorization process and appealing design that encourages reflection and focuses on outcome.

The color continuum was inspired by similar color schemes in the CAF's deployment readiness categories and *Road to Mental Readiness* (R2MR) mental health continuum model (Department of National Defense, 2011, 2013). The US Marine Corps and US Navy Combat and Operational Stress Continuum Model uses similar color categories to reflect increasing risk of psychological distress and injury (Nash, 2011). Military personnel trained in these color schemes think of green as having good mental health or being ready to deploy on operations, and red as needing to seek mental health care or not being ready to deploy. The continuum concept is thought to encourage optimism about being able to move back from yellow or red to green by taking appropriate actions.

In considering the types of well-being statements to use in the tool, the team used the well-being conceptual framework adopted at VAC for defining difficulty and success in transition (Thompson, Maclean et al., 2016). The framework is a superordinate, composite type that is much broader than just psychological or economic well-being. The framework is composite because it incorporates all other well-being measures. It is superordinate because it views health as a subdomain of well-being. In this framework, well-being ranges from poor to good, measured subjectively and objectively in each of seven domains: employment or other main activity, finances, health (physical and mental), life skills and preparedness, social integration, housing/physical environment, and cultural/social environment. The theory states that well-being fluctuates in those domains across the life course in response to determinants of well-being that arise from all the domains (Fig. 3.2). This type of well-being framework therefore accommodates bidirectional causality: just as there are lists of determinants of well-being in the health domain (the "determinants of health"), there are also lists of determinants of well-being for each of the other domains. For example, well-being in the employment domain is influenced by well-being in the health domain, and vice-versa. Studies of military personnel and veterans have confirmed that they variably experience reintegration or MCT difficulties in all of these domains (Cooper et al., 2018; Fear, Wood, & Wessely, 2009; Orazem et al., 2016; Sayer et al., 2010; Thompson, VanTil et al., 2016; Van Staden et al., 2007). This well-being framework is useful for describing how members are doing in transition. For example, a veteran with good well-being in all the domains could be described as having had a successful transition. Good well-being suggests that a person is able to manage independently in all the domains; however, a person is more likely to need assistance if challenged in some domains.

To meet the design specifications of simplicity and compact presentation, the team decided to use two statements for each of the first six of the seven domains of well-being. The seventh domain (cultural/social environment) refers to cultural norms and values, socioeconomic programs and services, and the way members and veterans are viewed by nonmilitary communities—all factors largely beyond their immediate control.

Initial versions of the 12 statements were developed by expert consensus for each of the six domains of well-being by either modifying statements in the existing literature or drafting new statements based on evidence (Adler, Zamorksi, & Britt, 2011; Ahern et al., 2015; Ashcroft, 2014; Brunger, Serrato, & Ogden, 2013; Burkhart & Hogan, 2015; Castro & Kintzle, 2014; CMVH, 2010; Cooper et al., 2019; Fear et al. 2009; Forces in Mind Trust, 2013; Forkin, 2015; Hachey & Sudom, 2013; Hatch et al., 2013; Institute of Medicine, 2013; Iversen, 2005; Jolly, 1996; MacLean et al., 2014; Miltiary-Transition.org, 2016; Orazem et al., 2016; Sayer et al., 2010; Sayer et al., 2011; Sweet & Thompson, 2009; Thompson & Lockhart, 2015; Thompson, MacLean et al., 2015; Thompson, VanTil et al., 2016; U.S. Army, 2018; Van Staden et al., 2007; VanTil, MacLean, Campbell, et al., 2016; Watkins, 2011). The team drafted statements using the rule that a *positive* response to the statements should reassure the member or veteran that they are likely to experience good well-being in MCT, whereas a *negative* response to any single statement should lead the member or veteran to realize that they might have difficulty in MCT and should consider seeking formal assessment or support. A positive answer should lead the user to green (unlikely to experience significant transition difficulty), while a negative answer should lead the user to yellow or red (likely to experience transition difficulty), prompting them to consider seeking assistance.

In the development of the initial prototypes of the statements, evidence from previous research was taken into account, including LASS income studies and surveys. The LASS surveys identified subgroup demographic, military, health, disability, socioeconomic, and stress/coping characteristics associated with good and poor well-being in CAF Regular and Reserve Force Veterans released from 1998, and with perceived ease and difficultly of adjustment to civilian life (MacLean et al., 2014; Thompson & Lockhart, 2015; Thompson et al., 2014; Thompson, MacLean et al., 2015, 2016; Thompson, VanTil et al., 2015, 2016). The team reviewed other published scientific literature, including literature reviews summarized in the R2CL Backgrounder (Thompson & Lockhart, 2015), and findings from consultations with staff who support transition and outreach in various CAF, DND, and VAC programs.

On the basis of the evidence review and consensus process, we had two initial prototypes, one for serving members and one for veterans, each with five main layout components:

1. A title section intended to catch the attention of busy people,
2. Instructions,
3. 12 statements, 2 for each well-being domain,

4. An intuitive process for self-categorizing the member or veteran into likely or unlikely to have MCT difficulty, and
5. A placeholder for follow-up suggestions.

Development of the final prototypes

We refined the initial prototype by testing the wording, usability features, and appeal aspects of the components using cognitive interviewing of both CAF serving members considering release and recently released veterans, in both English and French. Cognitive interviewing is a key first step in designing questionnaires. The process seeks to understand how interviewees interpret and construct answers to statements or questions, how they identify difficulties reacting to the statements, and other reactions that they might have (Collins, 2003; Haeger, Lambert, Kinzie, & Gieser, 2012).

The team designed a structured questionnaire ahead of the interviews with the following components:

1. Introduction and instructions to the interviewees, including consent to proceed.
2. Basic information about demographics and military service.
3. A series of probing questions for each statement, using a combination of the probing and think-aloud cognitive interviewing methods.
4. An emotion-response test instrument for rating the tool.
5. Questions about when in a member's career the tool would be useful for self-assessment, what type of members would find it useful, what directions should be added to the bottom of the tool if the member or veteran feels help is needed, and whether they had any additional suggestions for the tool.

One-to-one interviews were conducted in Ottawa with Regular Force and deployed Reserve Force members and with veterans who had released from service within 10 years. Serving members intending to release from service were recruited at CAF SCAN (Second Career Assistance Network) seminars. Veterans (released members) were recruited with the assistance of the Royal Canadian Legion's Service Bureau. The Reservists had prior Class C (deployment) service. Ten serving members and 10 veterans (7 Anglophones and 3 Francophones in each group) were interviewed in each of the two rounds, for a total of 40 interviews. The majority were men. There were more noncommissioned members than officers. All three service elements were represented, but the majority had Canadian Army service.

The interviews tested all 12 statements, the self-assessment color scheme, and graphic presentation. Findings from the first round of 20 interviews were used by the team in consensus to modify the initial prototype and plan the second-stage interviews. Findings from the second round of 20 interviews were used to decide by consensus on the content and graphic design of the final prototypes (Figs. 5.2 and 5.3).

The cognitive interviews used concurrent probing: (a) the interviewer read the statement, (b) the subject responded to the statement, (c) the interviewer asked a probe question, and (d) the subject answered the probe question. If required, there were cycles of (c) to (d) until the issue was thought to be addressed. The structured interview used the following types of probes:

- Comprehension: How do you understand the words "______"?
- Thinking process: Why did you respond that way?
- Interpretation: What does that mean to you?
- Ease of response: How hard was this to answer?
- Interpretation of the response categories: Is the response category applicable for this statement?

It was anticipated that some terms would not be universally understood, so for some statements an additional probe was used. For example, the probe: "How do you understand the words 'my preferred community'?" was used to ensure consistent understanding of the term "community."

The emotion–response test (Irwansyah, 2015) was adapted from testing developed for the BBC (British Broadcasting Corporation) website redesign process (British Broadcasting Corporation, 2002). The interviewee was asked to rate the tool on eight parameters (Table 5.2) and then invited to elaborate.

TABLE 5.2 Emotion–response test scales.

Confusing	1	2	3	4	5	Clear
Bright	1	2	3	4	5	Dull
Professional	1	2	3	4	5	Amateur
Easy to answer	1	2	3	4	5	Difficult to answer
Dull	1	2	3	4	5	Creative
Boring	1	2	3	4	5	Exiting
Not interesting	1	2	3	4	5	Interesting
Potentially great value	1	2	3	4	5	No value

Fig. 5.1 shows the results of the emotion–response tests after round 2. The round 2 results helped to assess whether changes made after round 1 were acceptable or required further adjustments.

In general, the emotion–response test findings demonstrated acceptability of the design to both serving members and veterans. The sample sizes were very small ($n = 10$ for each group per round of interviews), so statistical testing was not appropriate. Instead, the findings were used to qualitatively inform refinement of wording and graphic design after each of the two rounds of interviews. The average scores tended toward the positive ends of all the scales in both rounds of interviewing, indicating that (a) the initial design was favorable and (b) that only minor adjustments were necessary to fine tune the tool. Following changes made after round 1, some scores decreased. For example, some changes prompted serving members to provide lower ratings of the tool on the "difficult/easy" scale in round 2, revising in the decision to reverse or revise related design features made after round 1.

The lower scoring for the "boring/exciting" scale was not surprising: the interviewees did not see self-assessment as a particularly exciting activity. Nevertheless, responses on that scale tended toward "exciting" rather than "boring," indicating that the tool was engaging. The higher scores on the "not interesting/interesting" scale, particularly for veterans, reflected the interest that members and veterans had in thinking about the MCT process. The scores were generally higher for veterans than serving members, perhaps because the transition experience was more immediate and meaningful for released members.

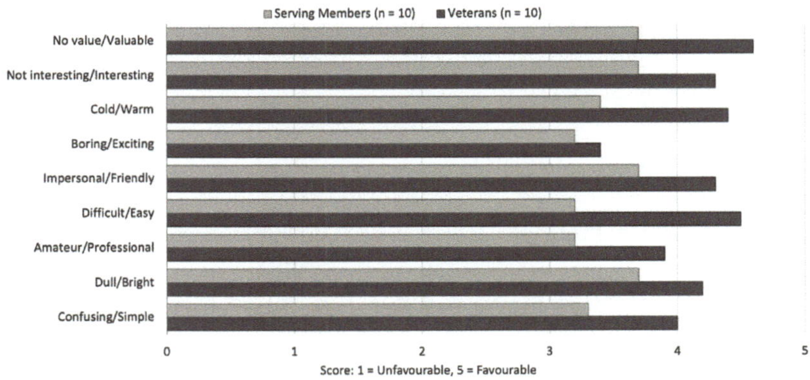

FIGURE 5.1 Emotion–response test results after round 2 interviews.

Final prototypes

Figs. 5.2 and 5.3 show the final prototypes for English-speaking serving members and veterans. French and English prototypes are available from the authors in Microsoft Word format for adaptation to other cultural contexts.

The banner image behind the title wording was constructed for the tool to show CAF soldiers, sailors, and air personnel undergoing MCT. The image can be adapted for other nations. The title wording is specific for serving members or veteran members. Cognitive

Select the response that applies to you for each of the statements below:	**Yes**	**To Some Extent**	**No**
○ If applicable, I know what steps to take to:			
• Secure a good job.	☐	☐	☐
• Enroll in an educational institution.	☐	☐	☐
• Prepare for retirement.	☐	☐	☐
○ I have what I need to find a satisfying job or other meaningful activity.	☐	☐	☐
○ I am financially prepared for civilian life.	☐	☐	☐
○ I will be able to make ends meet.	☐	☐	☐
○ My physical and mental health will allow me to function well in my daily life after release.	☐	☐	☐
○ I know what steps to take to get access to the health care I will need after release.	☐	☐	☐
○ I will get the support that I need from my family and friends after release.	☐	☐	☐
○ I have hobbies and interests outside of the military.	☐	☐	☐
○ I will have suitable housing arrangements after release.	☐	☐	☐
○ I will be able to live in my preferred location.	☐	☐	☐
○ I will adjust well to civilian life.	☐	☐	☐
○ If applicable, my family will adjust well to my transition to civilian life.	☐	☐	☐
If you need help in any of these areas --* Employment, Finances, Health care or Rehabilitation, Social Supports, Housing or Other areas of life – *See __ for services that can help	***Should be good to go***	***Think about it!***	***Consider seeking assistance***

FIGURE 5.2 English-serving member prototype.

Select the response that applies to you for each of the statements below:	**Yes**	**To Some Extent**	**No**
○ I have secured a good job or enrolled in an educational institution or I am prepared for retirement.			
○ I am satisfied with my prospects for a job or other meaningful activity.			
○ I am financially prepared for civilian life.			
○ I am able to make ends meet.			
○ My physical and mental health allow me to function well in my daily life.			
○ I have access to the health care I need.			
○ My family and friends provide me with all the support I need.			
○ I have hobbies and interests outside of the military.			
○ I have suitable housing arrangements.			
○ I am living in my preferred location.			
○ I have adjusted well to civilian life.			
○ If applicable, my family has adjusted well to my transition to civilian life.			
If you need help in any of these areas -- **Employment, Finances, Health care or Rehabilitation, Social Supports, Housing or Other areas of life – *See __ for services that can help***	***Should be good to go***	***Think about it!***	***Consider seeking assistance***

FIGURE 5.3 English veteran prototype.

interview and emotion–response test findings supported the need for different variations of the tool for members before and after release from service. Serving members found it difficult, for example, to answer the initial version of the first statement about post-release employment, school, or retirement when all three outcomes were combined into one statement, possibly owing to their uncertainty about future plans. Conversely, veterans who were already living the released experience found it fairly easy to consider all three options in one statement.

The 12 statements are grouped by domain of well-being using horizontal lines: employment or other meaningful activity (sense of purpose), finances, health, social integration, housing/physical environment, and life skills/preparedness. The three self-assessment agreement/disagreement options for each statement ("yes," "to some extent," or "no") provided a clear sense of choice between no significant risk of difficulty in MCT ("yes," green) to high likelihood of risk ("no," red). The intermediate ("to some extent," yellow) category allowed for cases where the user might have some issues but does not feel at much risk. While two outcome categories (yes or no) have certain theoretical advantages for self-assessment, the interviews indicated that the middle "to some extent" (yellow) option allowed users to feel less intimidated had they picked "no" (red), while still conveying caution and encouraging reflection about whether they should seek assistance.

The wording "Select the response that applies to you for each of the statements below" is the result of several earlier options that did not test well. A more directive style for the three conclusion options at the bottom of the initial prototype did not test well. Some interviewees who realized that they did not meet the full criterion of a statement but felt they were doing reasonably well with their current levels of support in that domain felt stigmatized by being unable to answer "yes" (meaning "should be good to go") when "should consider assistance" was used for yellow and "should seek assistance" was used for red. The final, softer wording "think about it" for yellow and "consider seeking assistance" for red tested well in these Canadian members and veterans.

The last statement, about family adjustment, starts with the preamble "if applicable" to accommodate members and veterans without families during MCT. An earlier version ("My family will adjust [has adjusted] well to transition") emphasized that MCT is a period of adjustment for the families of members and veterans. However, the statement did not test well: members and veterans felt that the challenge for families was to adjust to the member's transition; hence, the wording was changed to "My family will adjust [has adjusted] well to my transition."

Finally, the directions for where to seek help were left blank to allow for adaption to local cultural and support service contexts.

Advantages of the prototype design

The final design of the prototype has several advantages. A self-assessment tool does not require the member or veteran to divulge themselves to an authority but could prompt them to seek assistance. The tool was designed from the ground up to promote reflection and self-assessment by serving or recently released military members about whether they should seek help during MCT. A primary function of the tool would be to engage transitioning military members and veterans who are not reached through transition programs, or who might not realize that they should engage with support services, complementing active risk screening systems.

The tool uses a green/yellow/red color scheme that should be familiar to Canadian and US military personnel who are trained in mental health and deployment readiness. The 12 statements are divided into 6 key domains of well-being with horizontal lines to facilitate linking specific needs with domain-specific services. The interviews with serving members in both English and French indicated that the prototype has good face validity and is perceived to be engaging and useful in both cultures. The cognitive interviews suggested that the tool prompts serving members and veterans to consider seeking additional assistance with transition when they might not have done so, or reassure them that they do not need to seek assistance.

The tool can be used by spouses or partners, family members, friends, advocates, and support services to help members and veterans decide whether they should seek transition supports. Support staff could offer the tool to promote discussions with releasing members and veterans, before a prerelease transition interview, for example. The tool is compact and easy to adapt for distribution in print or electronic forms. The design can be adapted to interactive website or mobile device applications. Finally, the tool can be adapted and deployed by any level of government, nongovernmental organizations, or private sector agencies to leverage whole-of-community engagement in transition support.

Development of follow-up instructions

A service agency that deploys the tool will have to insert appropriate follow-up instructions. Based on lessons learned in the interviews, instructions should be brief but clear, comprehensive, and easy to remember. There should be one set of instructions for serving personnel, and another set for veterans. Depending on the application, suggested follow-up actions could include obtaining a formal screening assessment, attending transition training, contacting an informed peer, seeking medical assistance, calling a referral line, or viewing online information about services specific to the well-being domains that the member or veteran has flagged yellow or red.

Serving members and veterans felt that simply referring users to a single website or 1–800 telephone number would be inadequate. Several felt that users should be directed to the best nongovernmental and government resources, not just military or veterans affairs sources. In print versions, services specific to each well-being domain could be listed on the back side of the paper. In electronic versions, the user could be offered links to direct them to services that could assist with the relevant well-being domain. Serving members and veterans said that once they had decided to seek assistance, they tended to prefer speaking to a person. They emphasized the importance of ensuring that a service request in an online version of the tool should generate immediate electronic acknowledgment, followed by contact with a live service provider within a day or two.

Dissemination of the self-assessment tool

The tool was designed for easy distribution to serving members, veterans, their families, and others through both print and electronic media. Examples of print media distribution include personal contact, mail-outs, bulletin boards, military base stores, bars, sports facilities, service agencies, and health care facilities: anywhere that military members, veterans, and their families might frequent. Examples of electronic media distribution include personal or broadcast emails, postings in social media, postings on military and veterans' affairs websites, release in a smartphone app, or attachment to a military member's release notice.

Strengths and limitations

The tool was designed by researchers at VAC and CAF with expertise in MCT. The expert consensus process was informed by service staff with years of experience working with transitioning members and veterans, and published scientific literature on the characteristics of serving members and veterans who experience difficulty in MCT. The tool permits the user to self-assess their risk across multiple domains of well-being using a documented composite well-being conceptual framework (Thompson, MacLean et al., 2016; Pedlar et al. Chapter 3). Cognitive interviewing and emotion–response testing provided evidence of face validity and potential utility of the tool.

Although the tool is expected to be useful and has evidence of face validity, construct validity and reliability have not been fully evaluated. However, the tool is not intended to be a psychometric instrument for use in risk screening or clinical assessment. Validating a questionnaire or psychometric instrument typically requires more than two statements or question per domain to permit construct validity analysis. A key design objective was to develop a brief tool that could prompt self-assessment in multiple domains. The tool was not developed to generate a single overall score for the risk of transition difficulties. Rather, the intent was to prompt members and veterans to reflect on their needs in specific domains of well-being. The tool was not tested with nondeployed Reserve Force members, and interviews were limited to a single region and so might not be representative of all serving members and veterans across Canada or in other nations. However, as other chapters in this book demonstrate, there appear to be many common features in transition experiences across and within nations. Finally, the tool can be adapted readily to other cultures.

Further research

The tool could be evaluated formally to (1) determine whether the tool promotes self-assessment in CAF members and veterans, (2) assess the tool's effectiveness in promoting help-seeking among those who need it, or reassuring those who do not need specialized supports, and (3) further assess reliability and construct validity. The 12 self-assessment statements were inserted into a recent survey of released CAF members, which will allow further validation. The tool could be adapted to other cultures using the procedures described in this chapter. The finding that several interviewees did not feel that military families also go through MCT and instead needed to adapt to the transitioning member is of interest and could be pursued.

Summary and implementation of the self-assessment tool

This chapter describes the development of a self-assessment tool intended to promote reflection among serving members and veterans about whether they should seek assistance during their transitions to post-military life. The initial prototype was developed using a priori principles including appeal, ability to promote self-reflection, ability to predict transition ease or difficulty, grounding in evidence, and preservation of anonymity. The prototype was refined in two rounds of cognitive interviews with both English- and French-speaking serving and released CAF members. The final prototypes encourage self-assessment of need to access transition support services in six well-being domains: employment or other main activity, finances, health (physical and mental), life skills and preparedness, social integration, housing/physical environment, and cultural/social environment.

Self-assessment assures anonymity, engaging those who might otherwise avoid screening. The self-assessment tool is intended to complement active screening and assessment by service providers. Wording can be adapted to other cultures using the process described in this chapter. Follow-up instructions can be developed that are appropriate to local services and cultures. The tool can be adapted for dissemination in print and electronic formats, reaching transitioning members and veterans who might otherwise wait too late to seek out formal transition support services.

References

Adler, A. M., Zamorksi, M., & Britt, T. W. (2011). The psychology of transition: Adapting to home after deployment. In A. M. Adler, P. D. Bliese, & C. A. Castro (Eds.), *Deployment psychology: Evidence-based strategies to promote mental health in the military*. Washington, DC: American Psychology Association.

Ahern, J., Worthen, M., Masters, J., Lippman, S. A., Ozer, E. J., & Moos, R. (2015). The challenges of Afghanistan and Iraq veterans' transition from military to civilian life and approaches to reconnection. *PLoS One, 10*(7), e0128599.

Ashcroft, M. (2014). *Veterans' transition review*. London, UK: Forces in Mind Trust.

Auditor General of Canada. (2012). *Report of the auditor general of Canada to the house of commons. Chapter 4: Transition of ill or injured military personnel to civilian life*. Retrieved from www.oag-bvg.gc.ca.

Austin, Z., Gregory, P. A., & Chiu, S. (2008). Use of reflection-in-action and self-assessment to promote critical thinking among pharmacy students. *American Journal of Pharmaceutical Education, 72*(3). Art. 48.

Banks, C. H., & Nafukho, F. M. (February 2008). Career transitions across and within organizations: Implications for human resource development. In *Paper presented at the academy of human resource development international research conference in the Americas, Panama city, FL*.

British Broadcasting Corporation. (2002). *The glass wall: The homepage redesign*. Retrieved from www.currybet.net/download/theglasswall.pdf.

Brunger, H., Serrato, J., & Ogden, J. (2013). "No man's land": The transition to civilian life. *Journal of Aggression, Conflict and Peace Research, 5*(2), 86–100.

Burkhart, L., & Hogan, N. (2015). Being a female veteran: A grounded theory of coping with transitions. *Social Work in Mental Health, 13*(2), 108–127.

Castro, C. A., & Kintzle, S. (2014). Suicides in the military: The post-modern combat veteran and the Hemingway effect. *Current Psychiatry Reports, 16*(8), 460. https://doi.org/10.1007/s11920-014-0460-1.

Castro, C. A., Kintzle, S., & Hassan, A. (2014). *The state of the American veteran: The Los Angeles county veterans study*. Los Angeles, CA: University of Southern California School of Social Work.

CMVH. (October 2010). *Readjustment to "normal" – literature review*. Herston, QLD: Centre for Military and Veterans' Health (CMVH), The University of Queensland.

Collins, D. (2003). Pretesting survey instruments: An overview of cognitive methods. *Quality of Life Research, 12*, 229–238.

Cooper, A. A., & Humphreys, K. R. (2008). The uncertainty is killing me: Self-triage decision-making and information availability. *E-Journal of Applied Psychology, 4*, 1–6. https://doi.org/10.7790/ejap.v4i1.124.

Cooper, L., Caddick, N., Godier, L., Cooper, A., & Fossey, M. (2018). Transition from the military into civilian life: an exploration of cultural competence. *Armed Forces & Society, 44*(1), 156–177.

Cowan, D. T., Wilson-Barnett, D. J., Norman, I. J., & Murrells, T. (2008). Measuring nursing competence: Development of a self-assessment tool for general nurses across Europe. *International Journal of Nursing Studies, 45*(6), 902–913.

Cramm, H., Norris, D., Eichler, M., Tam-Seto, L., Mahar, A., & Smith-Evans, K. (2016). *Resources for Canadian armed forces veterans during the military to civilian transition* (Report prepared in contract to the Canadian Institute of Military Veteran Health Research for the Road to Civilian Life Program). Kingston, ON: Canadian Institute of Military Veteran Health Research.

Department of National Defence. (2011). *Road to mental readiness*. Retrieved from http://www.forces.gc.ca/assets/FORCES_Internet/docs/en/caf-community-health-services-r2mr/r2mr-pocket-card.pdf.

Department of National Defence. (2013). *Road to mental readiness aide memoire (Pub. No. DGM-10-07-00285)*. Retrieved from http://www.forces.gc.ca/assets/FORCES_Internet/docs/en/caf-community-health-services-r2mr/r2mr-aide-memoire.pdf.

Fear, N., Wood, D., & Wessely, S. (2009). *Health and social outcomes and health service experiences of UK military service leavers*. London, UK: Academic Centre for Defence Mental Health, King's Center for Military Health Research.

Forces in Mind Trust. (August 2013). *Transition mapping study*. London, UK: Author.

Forkin, K. A. (2015). Transition assistance: Being proactive in the 21st century. *Marine Corps Gazette, 99*(9), 27–34.

Hachey, K. K., & Sudom, K. (2013). *Canadian Forces personnel adjusting to civilian life* (Director General Military Personnel Research and Analysis Technical Memorandum 2013-008). Ottawa, ON: Defence Research and Developmental Canada.

Haeger, H., Lambert, A. D., Kinzie, J., & Gieser, J. (June 2012). Using cognitive interviews to improve survey instruments. In *Paper presented at the annual forum of the association for institutional research, New Orleans, Louisiana*.

Hatch, S. L., Harvey, S. B., Dandeker, C., Burdett, H., Greenberg, N., Fear, N. T., et al. (2013). Life in and after the armed forces: Social networks and mental health in the UK military. *Sociology of Health & Illness, 35*(7), 1045–1064. https://doi.org/10.1111/1467-9566.12022.

Institute of Medicine Committee on the Initial Assessment of Readjustment Needs of Military Personnel, Veterans, and Their Families. (2013). *Returning home from Iraq and Afghanistan: Assessment of readjustment needs of veterans, service members and their families*. Washington, DC: National Academies Press.

Irwansyah. (2015). Bipolar emotional response testing of online news website content: Indonesia case. *International Journal of Social Science and Humanities, 5*(10), 872–878.

Iversen, A. (2005). What happens to British veterans when they leave the armed forces? *The European Journal of Public Health, 15*(2), 175–184.

Jolly, R. (1996). *Changing step*. London, UK: Brassey.

MacLean, M. B., Van Til, L., Thompson, J., Sweet, J., Poirier, A., Sudom, K., et al. (2014). Post-military adjustment to civilian life: Potential risk and protective factors. *Physical Therapy, 94*(8), 1–10.

MacLean, M. B., Campbell, L., Poirier, A., & Sweet, J. (2016). *Military occupation and post-military employment and income outcomes* (Veterans Affairs Canada Research Directorate Technical Report). Charlottetown, PE: Veterans Affairs Canada.

MacLean, M. B., VanTil, L., Murray, R., Ralling, A., Poirier, A., McKinnon, K., et al. (2018). *Development of a risk screening tool for veterans* (Veterans Affairs Canada Research Directorate Technical Report). Charlottetown, PE: Veterans Affairs Canada.

Miltiary-Transition.org. (2016). *Veteran transition survey*. Retrieved from https://docs.google.com/forms/d/e/1FAIpQLSd-ChRvdkwMLQ2B2FGBOmwDeLyItl1lYmTOIVLuvxnneC9Nxg/viewform.

Nash, W. P. (2011). US marine corps and navy combat and operational stress continuum model: A tool for leaders. In E. Ritchie (Ed.), *Combat and operational behavioral health*. Washington, DC: Walter Reed Army Medical Center Borden Institute, Department of Defense Army Medical Department. http://citeseerx.ist.psu.edu/viewdoc/download?doi=10.1.1.222.8091&rep=rep1&type=pdf.

Orazem, R. J., Frazier, P. A., Schnurr, P. P., Oleson, H. E., Carlson, K. F., Litz, B. T., et al. (2016). Identity adjustment among Afghanistan and Iraq War veterans with reintegration difficulty. *Psychological Trauma*. https://doi.org/10.1037/tra0000225. Advance online publication.

Peach, J. (2016). *Fall 2015 Your Say survey results* (DGMPRA Scientific Letter DRDC-RDDC-2016-L061). Ottawa, ON: Defence Research and Development Canada.

Richy, F., Gourlay, M., Ross, P. D., Sen, S. S., Radican, L., De Ceulaer, F., et al. (2004). Validation and comparative evaluation of the osteoporosis self-assessment tool (OST) in a Caucasian population from Belgium. *QJM, 97*(1), 39–46.

Sayer, N. A., Noorbaloochi, S., Frazier, P., Carlson, K., Gravely, A., & Murdoch, M. (2010). Reintegration problems and treatment interests among Iraq and Afghanistan combat veterans receiving VA medical care. *Psychiatric Services, 61*(6), 589–597.

Sayer, N. A., Frazier, P., Orazem, R. J., Murdoch, M., Gravely, A., Carlson, K. F., et al. (2011). Military to civilian questionnaire: A measure of postdeployment community reintegration difficulty among veterans using department of veterans affairs medical care. *Journal of Traumatic Stress, 24*(6), 660–670.

Shields, D. M., Kuh, D., Lutz, K., Frender, J., Baumann, N., & Lopresti, P. (2016). *Mental health and well-being of military veterans during military to civilian transition: Review and analysis of the recent literature (Report prepared for Canadian Institute for Military and Veteran Health Research and Veterans Affairs Canada Road to Civilian Life)*. Retrieved from https://www.cimvhr.ca/documents/R2CL-PVVC-Health-and-Wellbieng.pdf.

Sweet, J., & Thompson, J. M. (2009). *Literature review of military to civilian transition: Results of initial searches* (Veterans Affairs Canada Research Directorate Data Report). Charlottetown, PE: Veterans Affairs Canada.

Thompson, J. M., & Lockhart, W. (2015). *Backgrounder for the road to civilian life (R2CL) program of research into the well-being of Canadian armed forces members/veterans during military–civilian transition* (Veterans Affairs Canada Research Directorate Technical Report). Charlottetown, PE: Veterans Affairs Canada.

Thompson, J. M., MacLean, M. B., Van Til, L., Sudom, K., Sweet, J., Poirier, et al. (2011). *Survey on transition to civilian life: Report on regular force veterans* (Research Directorate, Veterans Affairs Canada and Director General Military Personnel Research and Analysis). Ottawa, ON: Veterans Affairs Canada–Department of National Defence http://publications.gc.ca/site/eng/9.844433/issues.html.

Thompson, J. M., VanTil, L. D., Poirier, A., Sweet, J., McKinnon, K., Van Til, L., et al. (2014). *Health and well-being of Canadian forces veterans: Findings from the 2013 life after service survey* (Veterans Affairs Canada Research Directorate Technical Report). Charlottetown, PE: Veterans Affairs Canada http://publications.gc.ca/site/eng/9.844433/issues.html.

Thompson, J. M., MacLean, M. B., Lockhart, W., Poirier, A., Sweet, J., & Pedlar, D. (2015). *Planning transition supports for Canadian armed forces members/veterans: Findings from the life after service studies* (Research Directorate Brief Report, November 6). Charlottetown, PE: Veterans Affairs Canada.

Thompson, J. M., Pranger, T., Sweet, J., VanTil, L., McColl, M. A., Besemann, M., et al. (2015). Disability correlates in Canadian armed forces regular force veterans. *Disability & Rehabilitation, 37*(10), 884–891.

Thompson, J. M., VanTil, L., Sweet, J., Poirier, A., McKinnon, K., Dursun, S., et al. (2015). *Canadian armed forces veterans: Mental health findings from the 2013 life after service survey* (Research Directorate Technical Report Cat. No. V32-260/2016E-PDF). Charlottetown, PE: Veterans Affairs Canada http://publications.gc.ca/site/eng/9.844433/issues.html.

Thompson, J. M., MacLean, M. B., Roach, M. B., Banman, M., Mabior, J., & Pedlar, D. (2016). *A well-being construct for veterans' policy, programming and research* (Veterans Affairs Canada Research Directorate Technical Report). Charlottetown PE: Veterans Affairs Canada http://publications.gc.ca/site/eng/9.844433/issues.html.

Thompson, J. M., Sweet, J., VanTil, L., Poirier, A., & MacKinnon, K. (2016). *Correlates of mental health problems in Canadian armed forces veterans: 2013 life after service survey* (Veterans Affairs Canada Research Directorate Technical Report). Charlottetown PE: Veterans Affairs Canada http://publications.gc.ca/site/eng/9.844433/issues.html.

Thompson, J. M., VanTil, L., Zamorski, M. A., Garber, B., Dursun, S., Fikretoglu, et al. (2016). Mental health of Canadian armed forces veterans: Review of population studies. *Journal of Military, Veteran and Family Health, 2*(1), 70–86. https://doi.org/10.3138/jmvfh.3258.

U.S. Army Warrior Care and Transition. (2018). *Comprehensive transition plan*. Retrieved from http://www.wct.army.mil/modules/soldier/s1-ctp.html.

VAC Ombudsman. (2016). *Support for military families in transition*. Charlottetown, PE: Author.

Van Staden, L., Fear, N. T., Iversen, A. C., French, C. E., Dandeker, C., & Wessely, S. (2007). Transition back into civilian life: A study of personnel leaving the UK armed forces via "military prison." *Military Medicine, 172*(9), 925–930.

VanTil, L., MacLean, M. B., Poirier, A., McKinnon, K., Keough, J., & Pedlar, D. (2016). *Veterans of the reserve force: Life after service studies 2013* (Veterans Affairs Canada Research Directorate Technical Report No. V32-272/2016E-PDF). Charlottetown, PE: Veterans Affairs Canada http://publications.gc.ca/site/eng/9.844433/issues.html.

Watkins, K. (2011). *Literature review on the mental health and career challenges of the transition from military to civilian life (201)* (Director General Military Personnel Research and Analysis Technical Memorandum DGMPRA TM 2011-027). Ottawa, ON: Defence Research and Development Canada.

CHAPTER

6

Challenging missions: vulnerable veterans leaving the armed forces and promising avenues to support them

Jacco Duel[1], *Lauren Godier-McBard*[2], *Mary Beth MacLean*[3], *Matt Fossey*[2]

[1] Netherlands Veterans Institute, Doorn, the Netherlands; [2] Veterans and Families Institute for Military Social Research, Anglia Ruskin University, Chelmsford, United Kingdom; [3] Veterans Affairs Canada, Charlottetown, PE, Canada

OUTLINE

Military Veteran Reintegration
https://doi.org/10.1016/B978-0-12-815312-3.00006-1 © 2019 Elsevier Inc. All rights reserved.

Across all NATO countries, every year, thousands of service members leave the armed forces for a number of reasons and have to build or rebuild their lives in the civilian world. In general, the international literature on military-to-civilian transition suggests most do well after discharge from the military (Elder, Shanahan, & Clipp, 1994; Iverson et al., 2005; MacLean et al., 2014). However, some veterans may be less fortunate and may experience difficulties during their transition out of the military that result in impaired quality of life due to physical or psychological health problems (Eekhout, Reijnen, Vermetten, & Geuze, 2016; Fear et al., 2010; Hoge et al., 2004), financial problems (Castro, Kintzle, & Hassan, 2014), relationship problems (Makin-Byrd, Gifford, McCutcheon, & Glynn, 2011; Solomon, Deby-Aharon, Zerach, & Horesh, 2011), homelessness (Hamilton, Poza, & Washington, 2011; Metraux, Cusack, Byrne, Hunt-Johnson, & True, 2017), legal issues (MacManus & Wessely, 2011; Wainwright, McDonnell, Lennox, Shaw, & Senior, 2016), difficulties in finding or keeping a new job (Loughran, 2014), or adjusting to civilian culture (Castro et al., 2014; Shields et al., 2016). Despite support often being available, some veterans may be susceptible to such unfavorable outcomes of the military-to-civilian transition because of their background, personal characteristics, experiences, specific circumstances, or the interplay of these factors; these veterans may be regarded as vulnerable.

Several NATO nations acknowledge that some veterans may be vulnerable to poor transition outcomes and attempt to identify those veterans before release to offer them support. For example, an inventory among representatives of the Ministry of Defence for 11 countries revealed that in six nations, service members who may be regarded as vulnerable are identified before release. The representatives mentioned several characteristics that are used to identify vulnerable veterans, such as the "wounded, injured, sick" (named by six countries), "early release" (three countries), "involuntary release" (two countries), "dishonorable release," "low education," "unemployed," and "homeless" (one country).[1] Interestingly, the latter two characteristics are outcomes, which indicate—as was confirmed in the survey—that the identification process extends itself to the time after release in these countries.

This short inventory suggests that while 6 of the 11 countries explicitly make some effort to identify vulnerable veterans before release, the characteristics used to identify them are limited and varied. This raises the question what may constitute vulnerability in the context of military transition. In 2013, UNESCO stated that "the human condition implies vulnerability" (p.13). Accepting this statement, one might think that this chapter on vulnerable veterans concerns all veterans. Obviously it does not. Although we think all humans are vulnerable in one way or another, in the context of military-to-civilian transition, we will refer to vulnerable veterans as those who are at risk of persistent unfavorable transition outcomes, such as those mentioned earlier, leading to poor well-being and quality of life. The timing of these unfavorable outcomes can vary from directly after discharge to years after transition. Furthermore, it may take years for veterans to recognize or report problems or to seek help (Murphy, Weijers, Palmer, & Busuttil, 2015).

[1] The survey will be outlined in the Technical Report (forthcoming) of Research Task Group 263 (The transition of military veterans from active service to civilian life). The Research Task Group is an activity of the Human Factors and Medicine panel which is part of NATO's Science and Technology Organization. See: https://www.sto.nato.int/publications.

Purpose and outline

The purpose of this chapter is twofold. The first is to identify the factors that may contribute to a veteran's vulnerability in the military-to-civilian transition process. The second is, drawing on current models of support in NATO countries, to provide insight into ways to support these vulnerable veterans. Therefore, we will first briefly present a general framework for understanding vulnerability in the military-to-civilian transition. We use this framework to present factors that may contribute to the vulnerability of veterans based on a review of the literature. Next, we discuss some of the issues concerning the support for vulnerable veterans and provide possible ways to support them. We close this chapter by making some conclusions regarding vulnerable veterans and how best to identify and support them.

A general framework for understanding vulnerability in the military-to-civilian transition

The transition out of the military often involves changes in a number of life domains, including relationships, assumptions about self and the world, work environment, and personal and social identities (Castro & Kintzle, 2014; see also Thompson et al., 2017). As a consequence, veterans have to adjust to these changes to be successful in civilian life (Castro et al., 2014; Segal, Lane, & Fisher, 2015). For some, this can be a difficult process. The issue with transition difficulties likely boils down to the mismatch between the demands veterans face in maintaining their general well-being, their health, in finding work or other meaningful activities, in providing income, in establishing or maintaining meaningful relationships with their close relatives and their community in general, and the available resources needed to meet those demands (Adler & Castro, 2013; Castro et al., 2014; Castro, Kintzle, & Hassan, 2015; Kintzle, Rasheed, & Castro, 2016; Schlossberg, 1981; Segal et al., 2015; Spiro, Settersen, & Aldwin, 2016; see also: Bates et al., 2010; Spini, Bernardi, & Oris, 2017; Chapter 3, this volume).

At any given time over the life course of a veteran, various resources and demands may affect how they navigate life (Chapter 3, this volume). Resources and demands may originate before the veteran enters the military, while serving in the military, or after leaving the military. Potential resources may include particular personal characteristics such as a good education, effective coping mechanisms, adequate life skills, and positive life events and experiences such as promotions, being part of a cohesive unit for an extended time, the availability of high quality informal social support by peers, friends, or family, and organizational and public support. Examples of potential demands are adverse childhood experiences, deployments with significant life events, such as combat, and impaired health. Public stigma and negative attitudes toward veterans may also act as a potential demand. The availability of resources and demands may also differ for veterans based on the era in which they are discharged, and the broader historical and national context at the time of discharge. For example, searching for a job after transitioning out of the military in times of economic austerity may be more demanding than in times of economic growth, especially for veterans with specific military skills and knowledge that they feel are difficult to transfer to the civilian context.

Based on a literature review, we will provide an overview of (1) pre-service factors, (2) factors that emerge while in service, (3) factors related to the transition itself, (4) personal characteristics, (5) post-service factors that may contribute to a veteran's vulnerability in the military-to-civilian transition process (see Fig. 6.1).

Vulnerability of veterans when transitioning to civilian life: a review from the literature

Life before service

From a life-course perspective (see Chapter 3, this volume), it is important to consider whether some veterans may already belong to disadvantaged groups when they enter the military. The Transition Mapping study (The Futures Company, 2013) carried out in the United Kingdom suggests that the worst transitions occur as a result of a combination of self-reinforcing factors associated with recruitment from a disadvantaged background: young age on entry to the military, with poor literacy and skill levels. The military may also explicitly focus on recruiting from particular locations and groups considered disadvantaged. Indeed, service members are found to be from a lower socioeconomic background than their civilian counterparts (Booth & Schmiegel, 1998; Ministry of Defense, 2016). Pre-service adversity, such as childhood abuse, is also associated with vulnerability later in life. According to Iversen, Fear et al. (2007), veterans who experienced pre-service adversity may be more prone to adverse outcomes later in life.

In addition, individuals with certain personality traits may be more attracted to a career in the military, and these traits may be

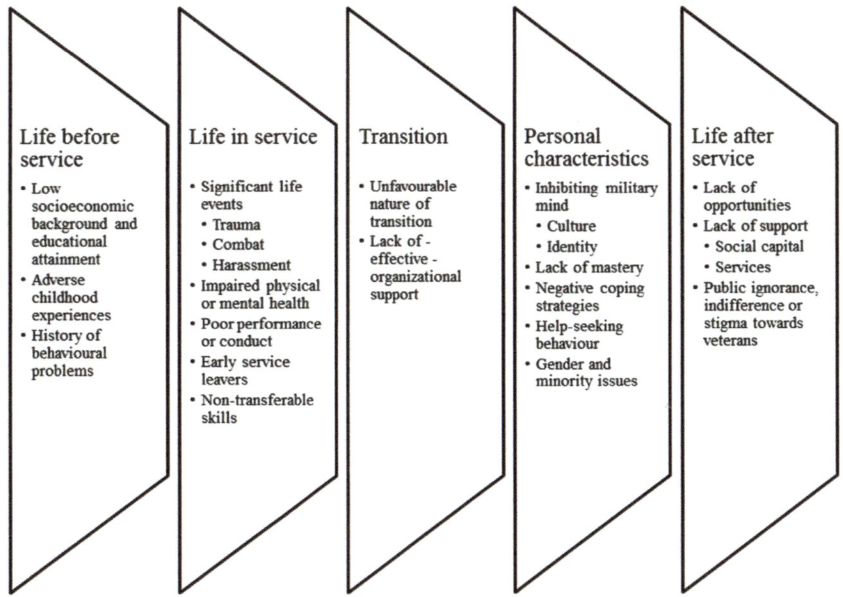

FIGURE 6.1 Five domains with factors that may contribute to a veteran's vulnerability in the military-to-civilian transition process.

linked to pre-service vulnerability to adversity (Iversen, Fear et al., 2007). Background and personality traits such as risk-taking and sensation-seeking may also predispose individuals to situations, such as combat, that are linked to negative outcomes later in life (Iversen, Fear et al., 2007).

Low socioeconomic background and educational attainment

New recruits to the military tend to be young and from low socioeconomic backgrounds. In the United Kingdom, it is reported that noncommissioned recruits tend to have low educational attainment and come from poor communities. For example, the average reading age of trainees at the Infantry Training Centre is 10 (Gee, 2008). Furthermore, survey research suggests that the majority of recruits surveyed came from a broken home, had left school with no academic qualifications, and were classified as being from a deprived background (Ministry of Defense, 2004). Similar results are found in the United States, with Army and Marine Corps recruits shown to come from lower socioeconomic backgrounds than the youths in the general population (Booth & Schmiegel, 1998).

Educational attainment is linked to income and employment status post-discharge, with studies showing those with lower levels of education are more likely to earn less and struggle to find employment (Marshall & Matteo, 2004; Marshall, Matteo, & Mueller, 2000; The Futures Company, 2013). Indeed, being a college graduate in the United States is associated with reporting an easier transition to civilian life (Morin, 2011). In addition, a lower educational level and lower general cognitive abilities appeared to be strong predictors of bad conduct discharges among US Marines (Booth-Kewley, Highfill-McRoy, Larson, & Garland, 2010).

There is also evidence to suggest that UK Army recruiters are more likely to visit the most disadvantaged schools (Gee & Goodman, 2010). This could be related to both the actions of the recruiters and the schools themselves, who may be more likely to approach Army recruiters due to the socio-demographic make-up of their students (Gee & Goodman, 2010). Indeed, disadvantaged groups may be more attracted to the military. For example, individuals from a disadvantaged background may feel the military provides them with an "escape" from adversity at home (Iversen, Fear et al., 2007, p. 509).

The research discussed suggests that factors associated with a disadvantaged background may be related to both poor post-discharge outcomes, and risk factors for vulnerability while in service. Indeed, socioeconomic status in US Marine Corps recruits predicts poor performance on the job (Booth & Schmiegel, 1998), another risk factor for vulnerability discussed in this chapter. Furthermore, armed forces veterans are more likely to be of a lower socioeconomic status in comparison with their civilian counterparts (The Royal British Legion, 2006), suggesting this disadvantage persists.

Adverse childhood experiences

Adverse childhood experiences may contribute to vulnerability later in life, for both veterans and the general population. This may encompass a wide range of experiences, such as physical, mental, and sexual abuse, neglect, exposure to domestic violence, having a household member who was mentally ill, incarceration of a household member, parental separation or divorce, household alcohol abuse, or household drug use.

Research suggests that military personnel have a high prevalence of childhood adversity. For example, in the regular Canadian Armed Forces, the prevalence of any child abuse exposure is higher than in the Canadian general population (48% vs. 33%; Afifi et al., 2016). Likewise, in the United States, 73% of men with a military service history in the all-volunteer era reported having experienced one or more adverse childhood experiences as compared with 58% of the men with no military service history. For females, these numbers were 69% and 63%, respectively (Blosnich, Dichter, Cerulli, Batten, & Bossarte, 2014). In addition, in their study, Montgomery, Cutuli, Evans-Chase, Treglia, and Culhane (2013) found that the prevalence of various adverse childhood experiences was slightly more prevalent among US service members of the regular forces, National Guard, or military reserves than the general population. McCauley, Blosnich, and Dichter (2015) found that on average female US veterans had experienced more childhood adversity than females who never served. Similar results are seen in the United Kingdom, with 76% of male military personnel reporting at least two or more adverse childhood experiences (Iversen, Fear et al., 2007).

Adverse experiences in childhood may affect quality of life and well-being in adulthood. For example, research shows that those who have experienced child abuse are more likely to ideate suicide, make plans for suicide, or attempt suicide. Despite this, the association between abuse and suicidal behaviors was shown to be weaker for military personnel than for the general population (Afifi et al., 2016). However, for service members, there was an additive effect of both child abuse and deployment-related trauma, making individuals who had experienced both particularly vulnerable to suicidal ideation (Afifi et al., 2016). Cabrera, Hoge, Bliese, Castro, and Messer (2007) found that adverse childhood experience was a significant predictor of depression and posttraumatic stress symptoms above and beyond combat exposure among US military personnel. A link between adverse childhood experiences and posttraumatic stress disorder (PTSD) is also a consistent finding in the literature (Bremner, Southwick, Johnson, Yehuda, & Charney, 1993; LeardMann, Smith, & Ryan, 2010; Xue et al., 2015).

There is also evidence to suggest that military service has a mediating effect on some adverse outcomes associated with childhood adversity. US veterans with adverse childhood experiences are more likely to experience homelessness, health problems, or mental health problems in adulthood. However, military service was shown to attenuate the risk of the former two effects and exacerbate the risk of the latter (Montgomery, Cutuli et al., 2013).

A history of behavioral problems

Pre-service behavioral problems may also contribute to someone's vulnerability to poor postdischarge outcomes (see also the section *poor performance or conduct* below). In their study into the effect of childhood adversity on the health of male UK military personnel, Iversen, Fear et al. (2007) found that, besides adverse family relationships that match the adverse childhood experiences mentioned earlier, externalizing behaviors in childhood affected health later in life. These behaviors comprised of being expelled or suspended from school, being involved in fights in school, being in trouble with the police, and playing truant (Iversen, Fear et al., 2007). Childhood externalizing behaviors were associated with a variety of health problems among male UK military personnel, especially high levels of alcohol consumption, having chronic fatigue, or having mental health problems (Iversen, Fear et al., 2007). Furthermore, pre-service violent behaviors or offences and antisocial behavior have been linked to violent offending and incarceration during service and post-discharge (Elbogen et al., 2012a, 2012b; MacManus et al., 2012; MacManus et al., 2013; Rosellini et al., 2016; Wainwright et al., 2016). This highlights the likelihood that for veterans who had behavioral problems before service, a poor life trajectory and outcomes may have occurred regardless of their military service.

Life in service

Life in service may expose service members to certain situations that contribute to vulnerability during transition. Significant life events encountered while in service may impose enduring demands on the veteran that may drain their resources. Furthermore, impaired physical or mental health, associated with significant life events, may contribute to the veteran's vulnerability. Poor performance or conduct, or the inability to adapt to the military culture while in service may be the result of increased demands in the service member's life that may in turn hamper them later in life. For example, those who leave the armed forces before their contracted term may have experienced an insufficient fit with the military. Factors that contribute to service members not being able or willing to function in the military, such as impaired health or a tendency toward poor performance or misconduct, may make it difficult for them to function in other jobs as well or to meet the demands of civilian life. Of course, the military environment can be more demanding than "an ordinary job." But what makes someone unfit for military service obviously does not always translate into difficulties in civilian life. Nevertheless, consideration of the circumstances under which someone is discharged is warranted as that very reason may indicate factors that contribute to vulnerability. Finally, some military personnel with typical military trades, such as rifleman or gunner, may struggle to transfer their work experience or skills to civilian life.

Significant life events

Experiences and significant life events during military service may have an impact on transition outcomes. Deployment may be such a significant life event. However, it is likely that differing personal experiences during deployment are more important than simply deployment itself as a risk factor. For example, exposure to a traumatic event during deployment, such as being seriously injured or witnessing someone else being injured or killed, is associated with difficulty adjusting to civilian life (Morin, 2011). Combat experience during deployment may also have an impact on transition. In the United States, veterans with combat experience report more difficulty in adjusting to civilian life (Morin, 2011). This may also be mediated by experiencing traumatic events during deployment as discussed above. Combat-related deployment as a risk factor for vulnerability has been the focus of a number of studies internationally, and combat is linked to increased levels of health/mental health problems (Buckman et al., 2011), violent behavior and offending (MacManus et al., 2013; MacManus et al., 2015; Elbogen et al., 2012a, 2012b), and lower income post-discharge (Stellman, Stellman, & Sommer, 1988; Engel et al., 1999). Furthermore, sexual harassment and assault are significant life events. Research from the United States suggests that sexual harassment and assault during deployment, or indeed at any point in military service, is associated with vulnerability to poor transition outcomes (Godfrey et al., 2015; Suris & Lind, 2008). In particular, a number of mental health problems are associated with military sexual violence, including increased symptoms of depression, anxiety and PTSD, substance use disorders, and sleep problems (Stander & Thomsen, 2016; Turchik & Wilson, 2010). Individuals who have experienced military sexual violence are more likely to experience difficulties during their transition to civilian life and are at increased risk of homelessness (Pavao et al., 2013; Skinner et al., 2000). Research outside the US context is needed to confirm that these findings can be generalized across NATO countries.

Impaired physical or mental health

A number of research studies in the United States, Canada, and the United Kingdom suggest that experience of combat is linked to PTSD in veterans (Adler, Huffman, Bliese, & Castro, 2005; Hines, Sundin, Rona, Wessely, & Fear, 2014; Hoge et al., 2004; Jones et al., 2013; Sundin et al., 2014; Watkins, Sudom, & Zamorski, 2016). US and Canadian studies suggest high rates of PTSD symptoms in veterans (VanTil et al., 2017). While prevalence estimates in other Western nations such as the United Kingdom and Australia are lower (Hotopf et al., 2006; Hunt, Wessely, Jones, Rona, & Greenberg, 2014; Iverson et al., 2009; Richardson, Frueh, & Aciemo, 2010), PTSD symptoms are associated with vulnerability to poor transition outcomes in veterans. The large (and predominantly United States) literature on PTSD suggests that those who leave the military with PTSD are more vulnerable to a range of adverse post-discharge outcomes, including family relationship problems (Sayers, Farrow, Ross, & Oslin, 2009; Taft, Schumm, Panuzio, & Proctor, 2008), unemployment (Savoca & Rosenheck, 2000), and a number of physical health conditions (Hoge, Terhakopian, Castro, Messer, & Engel, 2007; Richardson, Pekevski, & Elhai, 2009).

More generally, research across NATO countries suggests that poor health in service makes veterans vulnerable to poor transition outcomes. Canadian research indicates a higher likelihood of difficulty adjusting to civilian life in those with chronic physical and/or mental health conditions (MacLean et al., 2014). Poor health or mental health has also been associated with social isolation, homelessness, and unemployment in veterans in the United Kingdom and United States (Dandeker, Thomas, Dolan, Chapman, & Ross, 2005; Iverson et al., 2005; Randall & Brown, 1994; Rosenheck, Frisman, & Chung, 1994).

Poor performance or conduct

Discharge from the military for reasons to do with misconduct and poor performance is related to vulnerability to a number of adverse post-discharge outcomes. For example, in the United States, misconduct and other-than-honorable (OTH) discharges (which are a form of administrative discharge due to misconduct or performance below what is expected) are associated with increased risk of mental health problems, suicide, and incarceration in veterans (Brignone et al., 2017; Noonan & Mumola, 2004; Reger et al., 2015; Tsai & Rosenheck, 2018). OTH discharge has also been associated with younger age, lower income, and lack of health insurance compared with other veterans (Tsai & Rosenheck, 2018). Furthermore, another study from the United States reported that separation from military service as a result of misconduct (related to drugs, alcoholism, offences, infraction, etc.) was associated with a higher risk of homelessness in veterans compared with normal separation (Gundlapalli et al., 2015). These results all indicate that veterans discharged for misconduct or poor performance are vulnerable to a number of adverse outcomes.

It is possible that this association between misconduct in the military and poor post-discharge outcomes are both related to a number of preservice and in-service risk factors, such as criminal behavior pre-service, traumatic experiences during deployment, alcohol, and substance abuse (Gundlapalli et al., 2015). Indeed, research (again from the United States) suggests post-combat psychiatric diagnosis and traumatic brain injury is associated with a higher risk of misconduct-related discharge (Booth-Kewley et al., 2010; Hoge et al., 2005; Ommaya et al., 1996). Individual risk factors found to be associated with misconduct include being of Black race/ethnicity and being younger at time of first combat deployment (Booth-Kewley et al., 2010). While it is clear that veterans discharged for misconduct in the United States represent a vulnerable group, further research is needed to understand the factors that contribute to this. Furthermore, research is needed across other NATO countries to confirm these findings outside the US context.

Early service leavers

Attrition during the early phases of military training is high and many recruits may feel unable to adapt to the extreme change of lifestyle (Cigrang, Carbone, Todd, & Fiedler, 1998; Gee, 2007; Kiernan, Repper, & Arthur, 2015; Klein, Hawes-Dawson, & Martin, 1991). In the United Kingdom, the inability to manage the tough discipline and training regime and the loss of freedom and separation from friends and family has been described as "Culture Shock"

(Gee, 2007; Kiernan et al., 2015). A mismatch between recruit's expectations and the reality of the military environment has also been described in the literature (Gee, 2007; Kiernan et al., 2015). Indeed, both US and UK research has found a high proportion of early discharges are recorded in terms of the serving person being unmotivated to continue or unable to cope or adjust for emotional or social reasons (Cigrang et al., 1998; Kiernan et al., 2015; Klein et al., 1991).

Those who leave the services early because they are unable to adapt to military life may be vulnerable for a number of reasons. They are often not entitled to the same level of organizational support during transition back to civilian life as those who have long service histories, and as such may be vulnerable to poor transition outcomes (Godier, Caddick, Kiernan, & Fossey, 2018). Furthermore, they will not have had the time to develop job-related skills that may have helped them in the civilian job market. Indeed, research in the United Kingdom and United States suggests that those who leave the services early are more at risk of physical and mental health problems and poor employment outcomes (Booth-Kewley, Larson, & Ryan, 2002; Buckman et al., 2013; Iversen et al., 2005; Staal, Cigrang, & Fiedler, 2000). Furthermore, research has shown that those who separate early are more likely to represent already vulnerable groups, and vulnerability may also be related to preservice risk factors. For example, early attrition is associated with lower levels of educational attainment, and having been in trouble with the police before enlistment (Kiernan et al., 2015).

Nontransferable skills

Those who join the military with low skills and educational levels and leave without having built on these are more likely to have difficulties in civilian employment (Forces in Mind Trust, 2013; Keeling, Kintzle, & Castro, 2018). This often includes those who release at lower ranks, with few years of service, or who served in occupations unique to the military (Ashcroft, 2014; Forces in Mind Trust, 2013; MacLean, Campbell, Poirier, & Sweet, 2016; MacLean, VanTil, Sweet, Poirier, & McKinnon, 2019; Prigerson, Maciejewski, & Rosenheck, 2002). These unique military occupations, often combat positions, such as infantryman and tank operators, may have few or no equivalent occupations in the civilian world (Kleykamp, 2013b). The transferability of skills from military to civilian life is suggested to be a particularly important factor in gaining meaningful employment post-discharge (MacLean, Campbell et al., 2016; The Futures Company, 2013; Thompson et al., 2011). As such, individuals in these unique military trades may experience a "skills mismatch" in the civilian labor market, in that they find their skills to be untransferable to civilian life (MacLean, 2017). Indeed, some research suggests that those trained for combat positions are vulnerable to poor employment outcomes in civilian life, and that employers do not value military experience to the same extent as experience in the civilian labor market (Barley, 1998; Kleykamp, 2013b). However, pre-service education and attainment should be considered in this context, as these individuals may have self-selected into these lower skilled military roles and may have been vulnerable to poor employment outcomes regardless of their military service. Veterans in these types of unique military trades may need additional help in gaining employment and support in recognizing how their skills translate to the civilian workplace (MacLean, 2017).

The transition

The nature of the transition itself can be unfavorable, leading to additional demands for the veteran or prohibiting them from gaining or exploiting resources to meet these demands. These additional demands may put veterans at risk of poor transition outcomes. A lack of effective organizational support for veterans transitioning out of the armed forces may contribute to veterans having insufficient resources to meet the demands of transition.

An unfavorable nature of the transition

The nature of the transition itself is shown to have an effect on its outcomes. Veterans may transition out of the armed forces voluntarily or involuntarily, and they may perceive the transition as positive or negative, or as a gain or loss. Veterans may also perceive the transition as predictable or unpredictable (Castro & Kintzle, 2014; Kintzle et al., 2016). These different perspectives of the transition process are likely to have an effect on their veterans experience and transition outcomes.

An untimely transition may, for example, result in insufficient time to prepare oneself for life after service. In addition, veterans who are involuntarily released may remain focused on staying in the military and they may use their resources—such as time and energy—in attempting to prevent what might become inevitable: the transition out of the military. This may in turn cause resentment toward the military, resulting in veterans not optimally using the support that the organization can provide them during transition. Research from Canada and the United Kingdom has suggested that medical and involuntary discharge is associated with difficulty adjusting to civilian life (MacLean et al., 2014; The Futures Company, 2013). Veterans with injuries and disabilities are likely to face a number of additional demands and challenges to their daily lives (Resnik & Allen, 2007). For those veterans who experience their discharge as unpredictable, i.e., for medical or disciplinary reasons, the lack of psychological preparation is suggested to be particularly tough during transition (The Futures Company, 2013). Furthermore, an unpredictable transition such as this may lead to feelings of identity loss and betrayal by the military (Thompson et al., 2017).

Lack of effective organizational support

The lack of effective organizational support such as that provided by the military or other governmental organizations may affect the veteran's transition to civilian life. In several countries, there are programs provided by the government that are available to all discharged personnel (see Chapter 4, this volume). However, programs may have issues with reach, accessibility, and effectiveness.

The accessibility of support also determines its effectiveness. In the United Kingdom, the Veteran's Transition Review (Ashcroft, 2014) suggested that while there is a large amount of resettlement support available from the Ministry of Defence, it is often hard to find, poorly presented, and confusing to service leavers. Furthermore, in the United Kingdom, access to support is dependent on time served, with early service leavers unable to access the full resettlement support available (Ministry of Defense, 2015). In the United Kingdom, early service leavers receive the least amount of support and yet are considered to be particularly vulnerable as a group (Ashcroft, 2014; Forces in Mind Trust, 2013). The same is seen in the United States, with those discharged dishonorably or not having been on active duty unable to access the same benefits, health care, and employment support as other veterans (U.S. Department of Veterans Affairs, 2015). As mentioned above, those who leave the military early are more at risk of poor transition outcomes (Booth-Kewley et al., 2002; Buckman et al., 2013; Iversen et al., 2005; Staal et al., 2000), and as such these individuals would likely benefit from enhanced, rather than reduced, access to transition support.

Finally, despite organizational support being available, veterans may not be able to receive the support they need because—for whatever reason—they do not qualify or are not provided the opportunity to participate in programs or activities, such as taking transition preparation classes. Not receiving the support they need from the armed forces or the veterans administration might generate or exacerbate a feeling of alienation among veterans when they transition to civilian life. Ahern et al. (2015) found that many US veterans they interviewed did not feel as though they had received the support they deserved in recognition of their service. This resulted in poor transition outcomes, such as leaving mental health problems undiagnosed and untreated. This highlights the importance of effective support from the military institution itself in supporting veterans through their transition to civilian life.

Personal characteristics

Personal characteristics may create further challenges and place additional demands on veterans when transitioning out of the armed forces. First, military training and military life may instil a "military mind," based on a strong military identity and a specific set of values and norms associated with the military culture. This may make transition difficult because such a "military mind" may deviate significantly from the prevailing civilian culture. This instilled military identity may be necessary to function effectively in the military. However, the unwillingness or inability in adjusting the "military mind" may hamper veterans in their transition as it makes it difficult to connect to civilian life. In addition, military life may restrict veterans from developing basic life skills such as finding accommodation, managing finances, accessing personal medical care, or obtaining and maintaining employment, as the military provides these services. As such, following discharge, a veteran may not feel able to use these basic life skills to succeed in civilian life. Furthermore, poor coping mechanisms and help-seeking behavior may exacerbate the impact of these challenges and lead to poor transition outcomes for these veterans. In addition, gender and minority issues may represent additional demands.

Inhibiting military mind

The military culture itself, and the strength with which service personnel identify with the military at the point of discharge, is likely to have an impact on the ease with which they adjust to civilian life (Brunger, Serrato, & Ogden, 2013; Cooper, Caddick, Godier, Cooper, & Fossey, 2018). The military and civilian worlds represent two very different cultures with different rules and expectations. The rigid, hierarchical, and masculine nature of the military is ingrained in service personnel from basic training and is very different from the more relaxed style of most civilian work environments (Cooper et al., 2018). Some have suggested that those who view the armed forces as a job rather than a way of life are more likely to adapt better to civilian life (Higate, 2001; The Futures

Company, 2013). In addition, veterans who feel superior toward civilians and who do not want to change may have difficulties in forming successful relationships with civilians (Castro et al., 2014). While identity issues are being increasingly highlighted as central in adjustment to civilian life (Thompson et al., 2017), there is little empirical research investigating the effect of identity on military-to-civilian transition. In the United Kingdom, it has been suggested that successful transition hinges on the ability to shift identity from military to civilian and successfully remobilize military skills for civilian life (Cooper et al., 2017, 2018). Indeed, qualitative research in the United States suggests that problems adjusting the contrasting military and civilian expectations for identity can cause poor mental health post-discharge (Smith & True, 2014). Those who have deeply invested military identities and struggle to adapt post-discharge may also develop negative attitudes and beliefs in regard to civilian life. For example, they may feel that civilians do not understand them (Smith & True, 2014), or they may feel frustrated in civilian working environments which may appear to be less efficient than the military (Demers, 2011; The Futures Company, 2013). In the United Kingdom, Hatch et al. (2013) found that veterans who were less integrated in society were more likely to have mental health problems. In Canada, veterans who have a stronger sense of community belonging had lower rates of reporting difficulty in adjusting to civilian life (MacLean et al., 2014).

Mastery

The Veteran's Transition Review (Ashcroft, 2014) in the United Kingdom highlighted the lack of "life skills" training provided to veterans before discharge. As such, some veterans may feel unprepared to face the realities of civilian life. Evidence suggests that personal preparation for transition out of the workforce is an important factor in determining how successful an individual's transition is (Glass & Flynn, 2000). Those who have prepared themselves the least are more likely to find transition difficult (The Futures Company, 2013). However, research in the civilian populations indicates that mastery, or the sense of control one has over their life, mediates the effect of preparedness on ease of adjustment (Donaldson, Earl, & Muratore, 2010). Furthermore, mastery is found to buffer the effects of stress on health. Indeed, high levels of mastery have been found to ease adjustment to civilian life in Canadian veterans (Hachey, Sudom, Sweet, MacLean, & VanTil, 2016). This suggests that for those who experience difficulties during their transition to civilian life, high levels of mastery may mitigate the detrimental effect of this on adverse outcomes. Relatedly, realistic expectations of civilian employment and life are also shown to be predictors of satisfaction and successful transition in US veterans (Taylor, Shultz, Spiegel, Morrison, & Greene, 2007).

Negative coping strategies

For those who do struggle with adjustment to civilian life, risky behaviors and negative coping strategies may exacerbate the negative effects of this. Some veterans may abuse alcohol and other substances when struggling to adjust to civilian life (Demers, 2011). These behaviors may represent negative coping strategies that result from a lack of preparation or adjustment to the civilian world. Furthermore, this may be exacerbated by the drinking culture evident in the military. Research in the United Kingdom suggests hazardous levels of drinking in the armed forces that is much higher than the general population (Fear et al., 2007), and heavy/binge drinking in the US Armed Forces is shown to be increasing (Bray, Brown, & Williams, 2013). This drinking culture may make veterans more vulnerable to developing dependence post-discharge (The Futures Company, 2013). Indeed, alcohol abuse has been found to be the most common diagnosis in UK service and ex-service personnel (Iversen et al., 2009). Alcohol and substance abuse problems in veterans have been linked to deployment in the United Kingdom, United States, Germany, Australia, and Canada (Kelsall et al., 2015). An association with PTSD has also been reported (Petrakis, Rosenheck, & Desai, 2011). Across NATO countries, alcohol and substance abuse have also been linked to a number of other poor outcomes such as poor mental and physical health, homelessness, unemployment, and criminal behavior in veterans (Anderson & Mitchell, 1992; Iversen, Waterdrinker et al., 2007; National Association of Probation Officers, 2009, 2008; Ray & Forchuk, 2011; Thompson & Goodall Associates, 2009).

Help-seeking behavior

When veterans have experienced problems during their transition to civilian life, research suggests that they are less likely to ask for help than the general population. For example, in the United Kingdom, early service leavers have been highlighted as a group who are both particularly vulnerable to poor transition outcomes and the least likely to ask for help (Ashcroft, 2014; Godier et al., 2018). In addition, veterans who have mental health problems are much less likely to ask for help than those who do not (Hoge et al., 2004; Pietrzak, Johnson, Goldstein, Malley, & Southwick, 2009). Furthermore, Kintzle et al. (2016) report that most US veterans prefer to handle their own problems rather than ask for help. The authors go on to suggest that while this may be positive in the sense of self-reliance and resiliency, many veterans may not possess the necessary skills or engage in behaviors that improve their situation. As such this may be concerning, as many vulnerable veterans are choosing not to ask for help. Furthermore, studies in the United Kingdom and United States have highlighted the stigma associated with mental health and a reluctance to ask for help among veterans with mental health problems (Iversen et al., 2011, 2010; Pietrzak et al., 2009). This lack of help-seeking presents a barrier for service providers in providing care to those veterans who need it and is likely to result in further problems adjusting to civilian life.

Gender and minority issues

Most western militaries are predominantly populated by white, heterosexual men. For those who deviate from this stereotype, such as female service members, lesbian, gay, bisexual, or transgender service members, or service members from a specific racial or ethnic background, life in service may be more difficult, which may add to their vulnerability for adverse transition outcomes. They may be more likely to experience bullying and harassment during their service. For example, females, sexual and gender minorities, and racial and ethnic minorities are more likely to experience military sexual trauma in the United States (Buchanan, Settles, & Woods, 2008; Gurung et al., 2018; Suris & Lind, 2008).

Moreover, people who belong to these groups may have been disadvantaged in society already before they entered the armed forces and they may well be after leaving it, also adding to their vulnerability. For example, sexual and gender minority civilians in the United States are at an elevated risk of a number of health concerns, such as obesity, exposure to traumatic events, substance abuse, suicidality, and mental health problems. These vulnerabilities are also seen in sexual and gender minorities in veterans (Mattocks et al., 2014). Furthermore, belonging to an ethnic or racial minority is associated with increased risk of homelessness and disproportionate experience of chronic diseases in veterans (a result again similarly seen in civilians belonging to ethnic and racial minorities) (Aponte et al., 2017). Female veterans are also more at risk of certain difficulties post-discharge compared to their male counterparts. In the United States, female veterans are more likely to develop symptoms of PTSD, service-related disabilities, and homelessness (Baechtold & De Sawal, 2009, pp. 35–43; DiRamio & Jarvis, 2011; Mattocks et al., 2012). In the United Kingdom, female veterans are more frequently diagnosed with common mental health disorders such as anxiety (other than PTSD) and mood disorders, but less likely to be diagnosed with PTSD (Rona, Fear, Hull, & Wessely, 2006). This is supported by research with veterans of the Australian Defence Force, which has also found women are more likely to suffer from depression and panic attacks than their male counterparts (Neuhaus & Crompvoets, 2013).

On the other hand, compared with civilians with specific gender and minority backgrounds, veterans from the same background may do better on transition to civilian life because the armed forces may have acted as a bridging environment to a better future because it provided them opportunities. For example, to gain work experience or to attain a better educational level than they otherwise may have had. Although it is beyond the scope of this chapter to outline the many complexities and nuances concerning how gender and minority issues may affect a veteran's vulnerability in each country's specific context, it is paramount to realize that gender and minority issues may affect a veteran's vulnerability (see, e.g., Aponte et al., 2017; Burkhart & Hogan, 2015; Cochran, Balsam, Flentje, Malte, & Simpson, 2013; Crompvoets, 2011; Demers, 2013; Eichler, 2017; Hachey, Sudom, Sweet, Thompson et al., 2016; Hoglund & Schwartz, 2014; McCauley et al., 2015; Padavic & Prokos, 2016; Peterson et al., 2018; Woodhead, Wessely, Jones, Fear, & Hatch, 2012).

Life after service

Finally, the context into which the veteran transitions may introduce demands that contribute to the veteran's vulnerability. First, the area and environment they transition into may lack resources (e.g., housing) and/or opportunities (e.g., jobs). Furthermore, social and community support may be inadequate or lacking. Public support initiatives, such as programs delivered by charities and nongovernmental organizations, can help veterans in making a smooth transition out of the military. However, a lack of such public support initiatives or perceived barriers to care may place demands on veterans and contribute to their vulnerability. Finally, public ignorance toward veterans or stigma toward the veteran's background or health status may add to the vulnerability of veterans.

Lack of opportunities

The context into which veterans are released can have an impact on their employment opportunities and outcomes. For example, veterans discharged in the years following the 2008 financial crisis and recession in the United States and United Kingdom may have faced difficult economic times. Research suggests that employment rates have reduced in recent US veterans in the wake of the recession (Faberman & Foster, 2013). In both Canada and the United States, veterans of more recent missions had higher unemployment rates following release (MacLean, Keough, Poirier, McKinnon, & Sweet, 2018; U.S. Bureau of Labor Statistics, 2014). However, after an initial period of job search, the impact does not appear to be persistent (Kleykamp, 2013a; Loughran, 2014). In Canada, employment and work satisfaction rates have been found to increase over time (MacLean et al., 2018).

Furthermore, in the United Kingdom, employment rates vary by location, indicating that the area of relocation following discharge may have an impact on opportunity for employment (Ministry of Defence, 2017). Indeed research in the United States emphasizes the lack of employment opportunities in veterans transitioning to rural areas (Szelwach, Steinkogler, Badger, & Muttukumaru, 2011).

Lack of support

The military is an institution in which a high level of social integration is required (Hatch et al., 2013). Research suggests that veterans may feel a sense of loss post-discharge as they no longer feel the camaraderie and social embeddedness they felt while in the military (Brunger et al., 2013; Dandeker, Iversen, Ross, & Wessely, 2003). Indeed, Canadian veterans have been found to have a lower sense of community belonging than the general population (Thompson et al., 2011; VanTil et al., 2014). Research suggests that a lack of social support may make veterans more vulnerable to problems during transition. It is well known that social support can play an important role in providing social capital and such capital can be a valuable resource (e.g., Albertson, Irving, & Best, 2015; Kwon & Adler, 2014). Indeed, social support has been shown to act as an important buffer against mental health problems such as PTSD in veterans (Hatch et al., 2013). Low social support has been associated with increased rates of anxiety, addiction, and depression post-discharge (Boscarino, 1995). Furthermore, social support is reported to reduce stress and ease adjustment to civilian life (Hachey, Sudom, Sweet, MacLean et al., 2016). These findings highlight the importance of maintaining social networks post-discharge, as the support provided by these networks helps ease the transition to civilian life.

Social support and integration has a protective effect on veterans' mental health, and community support is likely to be important in the management of transition. In a study looking at the transition experiences of US veterans, Demers (2011) highlights the importance of community transition support groups for veterans with family, friends, and the local community to enable veterans to reintegrate. Furthermore, military cultural training for professionals is recommended to allow them to address the unique needs of the military which in turn may help veterans feel more understood by their community (Coll, Weiss, & Yarvis, 2011; Cooper, Andrew, & Fossey, 2016).

In addition to governmental programs, there are a growing number of programs in the nonprofit sector, providing various types of services for veterans who transitioned out of the military. The tangible public support programs for veterans often only address needs when veterans' problems have become chronic, whereas support in an earlier stage to prevent chronic problems from developing are much needed (Chapter 10, this volume). Despite public services for veterans in several countries (Chapter 10, this volume), veterans may have difficulties in crossing the barriers they find between them and those services. This may be associated with personal characteristics mentioned earlier, as well as self-imposed stigma and lack of trust in service providers (Sharp et al., 2015), or an unwarranted trust in one's ability to solve one's problems (Kintzle et al., 2016). Veterans may also experience practical barriers to support such as local availability, or difficultly attending because of personal obligations (Farmer, Hosek, & Adamson, 2016; Kintzle et al., 2016), or the sheer problem of not seeing the forest for the trees when it comes to available support (Chapter 10, this volume). Moreover, it has been suggested that further research is needed to identify gaps in the support available and duplication in services and to identify which types of services are effective (Cramm et al., 2016; MacLean, Keough et al., 2016).

Public ignorance, indifference, or stigma toward veterans

Another factor that may affect a veteran's vulnerability in the military-to-civilian transition is the public attitude toward veterans. A positive view on veterans among the general public may help veterans in transitioning out of the military (Chapter 10, this volume). If the general public are ignorant or indifferent toward veterans' needs or if they hold a negative view of veterans (for example, seeing veterans as "mad, bad, and sad" (The Royal British Legion, 2014, p. 4; see also, e.g., Mahar et al., 2017), this may hamper a veteran's transition to civilian life (see, e.g., Chapter 10, this volume).

Employer perceptions of the military may also reduce veterans' opportunities for employment. Organizations may lack an understanding of the military culture and have a negative attitude toward hiring veterans (Veteran Transition Advisory Committee, 2013).

A survey of employers in Canada found that less than half agreed that veterans make good employees (Veteran Transition Advisory Committee, 2013). As discussed above, employers may not see military experience as equivalent to civilian workplace experience (Kleykamp, 2013a).

Another example is that "employers may have the perception that military members are accustomed to operating within a structured, rigid, "do as your told" culture and unable to 'fit' within a less rule-bound, less directive, less compliance-based setting found in many civilian organizations" (Rishe, 2016; see also, e.g., Kintzle et al., 2015). Especially for those veterans who are vulnerable already, a community being ignorant or indifferent to veterans' needs and their abilities or the public negatively labeling veterans may be especially demanding when trying to transition into civilian life.

Summary: what makes veterans vulnerable?

Although a wealth of factors emerge from the literature, as summarized above, several qualitative studies (e.g., Hamilton et al., 2011; Mellotte, Murphy, Rafferty, & Greenberg, 2017; Wainwright et al., 2016) indicate that pathways into unfavorable outcomes after transition may differ by outcome and context. These studies make clear that vulnerabilities interact with each other and form a "web of vulnerability" in which a veteran can become entangled, leading to long-term negative outcomes; these outcomes may emerge sometimes up to 10 years or more after transitioning (Hamilton et al., 2011, p. s205). Thus, although research finds support for all factors being linked to veterans who are vulnerable, identifying the specific factor or combination of factors that make an individual veteran susceptible to pervasive poor transition outcomes is not straightforward.

While it may not be possible to determine the origin of a number of factors associated with vulnerability (i.e., pre-service, developed during or after service), or how factors interact to create vulnerability, certain factors and groups of factors are consistently found to be associated with poor post-discharge outcomes. It may be possible to identify some of these before discharge and provide support to prevent challenges during transition. We feel that the following groups of veterans consistently show vulnerability to poor transition outcomes and should be identified for additional support:

- *Early service leavers.* Those who leave early, before they are able to gain experience and qualifications, may need additional support to gain employment, to find housing and to manage their day-to-day lives as civilians. As the majority of young recruits are from disadvantaged backgrounds, this may add a further layer of vulnerability to those who leave early, who also tend to fall into this demographic profile. Rather than reduced support, these individuals should be identified and receive enhanced support in these areas.

- *Unpredictable discharge.* Those who experience an unpredictable discharge (i.e., for reasons associated with misconduct or medical discharge) are unlikely to be prepared for civilian life and may need support in a number of areas to support their day-to-day life in a similar way to early service leavers, including employment and education, housing and managing finances, and signposting to health and social care services.
- *Impaired physical or mental health.* Those with physical and mental health problems are shown to have a number of challenges and poor outcomes following discharge. This may include issues with substance abuse and negative coping strategies. They may require specific health care support and signposting to the relevant support and health services at discharge.
- *Significant life events.* Those who experience significant life events during service, for example, traumatic experiences during deployment or sexual violence, should also be identified (if possible) as individuals particularly at risk of mental health problems and subsequently poor transition outcomes. Again, these individuals may benefit from specific support and signposting to services in the civilian world.
- *Behavioral problems and misconduct.* Those with a history of behavioral and conduct problems, including those released early for misconduct as discussed above, are shown to experience poor transition outcomes. These service members may again require additional support in their transition.

It may be possible to identify these factors in service personnel before discharge and provide them with or signpost them to help and support to avoid adverse outcomes. It should be noted that this list is not final or exhaustive. Further research is required across NATO countries to confirm the importance of these and other factors associated with vulnerability. There are a number of other factors identified in this review that may affect vulnerability, but are more difficult to identify in personnel unless explicitly divulged. These include pre-service factors such as childhood adversity and pre-service behavioral problems, as well as personal characteristics that may develop before or during service, such as a strong military identity, a lack of mastery, negative coping strategies, and poor help-seeking behavior. Furthermore, certain demographic groups, such as ethnic minorities and gender and sexual minorities, may be more at risk of adverse outcomes. It may be that identifying specific factors for which they feel they need support, such as impaired health, lack of planning for transition, poor education and employment skills, difficulty transferring skills to civilian life, or behavioral problems, etc., will be more important in supporting these individuals and mitigating the impact of additional vulnerabilities. Additionally, it is important to consider the balance between stigmatizing and targeting help to these individuals when needed. With this in mind, we will now turn to avenues for supporting vulnerable veterans.

Avenues for supporting vulnerable veterans

As mentioned above, it is key to prevent groups of veterans feeling stigmatized by targeting specific programs or services to "vulnerable groups." While vulnerability does not refer to all veterans, as mentioned in the introduction, vulnerability may be very difficult to discern as—the interplay of—numerous factors may contribute to a veteran's vulnerability. Therefore, a support program to prevent vulnerability should typically include an assessment of all service members who will be discharged. This will allow the identification of service members with specific risk factors outlined above (leaving the services early, unpredictable/involuntary discharge, impaired health and mental health, significant life events, and behavioral and conduct problems), while enabling all service personnel to highlight areas in which they feel they need support.

A promising avenue that would enable this is to provide for a general "stepped-care" program (see for principles of stepped-care programs, e.g., Australian Government, n.d.; Bower & Gilbody, 2005; Franx, Oud, De Lange, Wensing, & Grol, 2012; Sobell & Sobell, 1999); every veteran participates in the program but support is provided based on veteran's needs. A typical "stepped-care" program could start with timely information provided to veterans. This information should raise awareness among veterans that a transition is about to take place, what difficulties may accompany that transition, what actions are needed by the veteran, and what support is available for them—while in service and afterward—and how they can get access to that support.

The next step could be a transition scan, which could take the form of an exit interview for each veteran. The aim of the scan is to map the resources and demands for each veteran and to highlight any risk factors or specific challenges they might be facing. Veterans can be screened for the risk factors identified above, as well as consulted to discuss any support they feel they need. This scan provides insight to both the veteran and the armed forces. Veterans gain a good overview of their personal situation that provides them with a starting point for how to better prepare themselves for the transition and life afterward. For the armed forces, this scan provides insights on how the organization can support veterans in making the transition and to prepare them for civilian life. The scan should be scheduled in such a way that both the veteran and the armed forces have ample time to prepare for the transition. In the case of an unpredictable transition, this should take place as soon as possible before discharge.

The factors discussed in this chapter provide for a good starting point for what to scan for. However, the relevance and importance of factors may vary from nation to nation. As such it will be important to delineate the relevant factors for each specific context and country. Longitudinal research will be needed to answer this question by monitoring former service-members over time. This will also enable the identification of factors that emerge over time following transition. Moreover, unrealistic expectations, or unwillingness or inability among veteran to acknowledge problems and to seek help, may cause problems to arise over time. Therefore, monitoring former service-members over time may provide periodic insights on how former service members are doing and what needs they have.

The next steps concern the support provided. The chapters in this volume provide an overview of the possible ways to support veterans and the effectiveness of support programs (see, e.g., Chapter 4, this volume; Chapter 8, this volume). As advocated elsewhere in this volume (see e.g., Chapter 11, this volume) support should be based on needs, not entitlement. Additionally, it must be noted that the aforementioned "web of vulnerability" indicates that the needs of vulnerable veterans are multiple and complex and may require holistic rather than specific support programs.

We would like to make two closing remarks concerning the support for vulnerable veterans. First, the initial two steps of the stepped-care program underscore the importance of prevention in the process of supporting vulnerable veterans. Forewarned is forearmed. They also underscore the inclusiveness of all veterans in the program because vulnerability may be difficult to discern and an all-inclusive program may help to find the "not that obvious" vulnerable veterans among the many veterans who leave the armed forces in each country, every year.

Second, our review makes clear that our knowledge about vulnerability among veterans almost exclusively comes from American, British, or Canadian research. However, how military personnel are selected, recruited, and trained, how armed forces function, under what circumstances veterans leave the armed forces, what support is available for veterans while in service, when transitioning out of the armed forces, or as a veteran, how society in the broader sense supports veterans may differ remarkably between countries (Chapter 10, this volume). And with that, the factors that affect vulnerability may differ from country to country. To be better able to understand vulnerability among veterans and to be better able to prevent it, we need more insights from other countries as well. In addition, vulnerability is more complex than the mere outlining of a list of factors that may affect a veteran's vulnerability. We need a better understanding how factors interact over time and how they eventually form a "web of vulnerability" around the veteran so we can prevent it or support veterans who become entangled in it.

Conclusions

Veterans may be vulnerable for pervasive negative transition outcomes because of pre-service factors, factors that emerged while serving, an unfavorable transition situation or environment, inhibiting personal characteristics, or the interplay of some or all of these factors. Indeed, for these vulnerable veterans, transitioning out of the military can be a challenging mission.

We have identified risk factors that are consistently shown to be associated with poor transition outcomes and suggest these should be identified before discharge to target support. However, vulnerability is complex and difficult to grasp for both the veteran and those who want to support them. For some, vulnerabilities may not be so obvious. It is clear from the literature that those who come from a disadvantaged background (and as such were likely to be vulnerable to adverse outcomes anyway) are more likely to experience poor transition outcomes. Additionally, strong adherence to the military culture itself presents difficulties when adjusting to civilian life. It may not be possible to identify these issues immediately on discharge, and associated demands may take time to emerge. Support for vulnerable veterans typically requires a continuous, comprehensive, and long-term approach. Therefore, addressing vulnerability and supporting vulnerable veterans who transition out of the military can be a challenging mission for those involved in providing the support as well. We suggest that a holistic "stepped care" approach be used in which veteran's demands and resources are mapped to determine the support they require. For those veterans whose discharge is planned, this should take place early in the process. However, for veterans whose discharge is unplanned, this will need to take place as soon as possible, and follow-up will be imperative to identify emerging issues. It is emphasized that, considering the evidence reviewed, support should be based on need rather than the current model of entitlement.

Besides the armed forces, other organizations, initiatives, and of course society in general in which the veteran transitions may be involved in supporting vulnerable veterans. It will be necessary to carry out a mapping exercise of the available support for veterans to enable the armed forces to signpost to other avenues of support where they are unable to provide it. How support for vulnerable veterans actually takes place will vary from nation to nation taking into account each nation's specific context of possibilities and constraints to support its citizens in general and veterans in particular.

Acknowledgment

The authors would like to thank Ryan Murray, Veterans Affairs Canada, for his help in the literature review.

References

Adler, A. B., & Castro, C. A. (2013). An occupational mental health model for the military. *Military Behavioral Health, 1*, 41–51. https://doi.org/10.1080/21635781.2012.721063.

Adler, A. B., Huffman, A. H., Bliese, P. D., & Castro, C. A. (2005). The impact of deployment length and experience on the well-being of male and female soldiers. *Journal of Occupational Health Psychology, 10*(2), 121–137. https://doi.org/10.1037/1076-8998.10.2.121.

Afifi, T. O., Taillieu, T., Zamorksi, M. A., Turner, S., Cheung, K., & Sareen, J. (2016). Association of child abuse exposure with suicidal ideation, suicide plans, and suicide attempts in military personnel and the general population in Canada. *Journal of the American Medical Association Psychiatry, 73*(3), 229–238. https://doi.org/10.1001/jamapsychiatry.2015.2732.

Ahern, J., Worthen, M., Masters, J., Lippman, S. A., Ozer, E. J., & Moos, R. (2015). The challenges of Afghanistan and Iraq veterans' transition from military to civilian life and approaches to reconnection. *PLoS One, 10*(7), e0128599. https://doi.org/10.1371/journal.pone.0128599.

Albertson, K., Best, D., & Irving, J. (2015). A social capital approach to assisting veterans through recovery and desistance transitions in civilian life. *The Howard Journal of Criminal Justice, 54*(4), 384–396. https://doi.org/10.1111/hojo.12138.

Anderson, K., & Mitchell, J. (1992). Effects of military experience on mental health problems and work behaviour. *Medical Care, 30*(6), 554–563. https://doi.org/10.1097/00005650-199206000-00008.

Aponte, M., Garin, T., Glasgow, D., Lee, T., Newsom, E., III, Thomas, E., et al. (2017). *Minority veterans report. Military service history and VA benefit utilization statistics.* Washington, DC: Department of Veterans Affairs, Data Governance and Analytics.

Ashcroft, M. A. (2014). *The veterans' transition review.* Lord Ashcroft KCMG PC. Retrieved from http://www.veteranstransition.co.uk/vtrreport.pdf.

Australian Government. (n.d.). *Stepped care.* See: http://www.health.gov.au/internet/main/publishing.nsf/content/2126B045A8DA90FDCA257F6500018260/%24File/1PHN%20Guidance%20-%20Stepped%20Care.PDF.

Baechtold, M., & De Sawal, D. M. (2009). *Meeting the needs of women veterans.* New Directions for Student Services.

Barley, S. R. (1998). Military downsizing and the career prospects of youths. *The Annals of the American Academy of Political and Social Science, 559,* 141–157.

Bates, M. J., Bowles, S., Hammermeister, J., Stokes, C., Pinder, E., Moore, M., et al. (2010). Psychological fitness. *Military Medicine, 175*(8), 21–38.

Blosnich, J. R., Dichter, M. E., Cerulli, C., Batten, S. V., & Bossarte, R. M. (2014). Disparities in adverse childhood experiences among individuals with a history of military service. *Journal of the American Medical Association Psychiatry, 71*(9), 1041–1048. https://doi.org/10.1001/jamapsychiatry.2014.724.

Booth-Kewley, S., Highfill-McRoy, R. M., Larson, G. E., & Garland, C. F. (2010). Psychosocial predictors of military misconduct. *The Journal of Nervous and Mental Disease, 198*(2), 91–98. https://doi.org/10.1097/NMD.0b013e3181cc45e9.

Booth-Kewley, S., Larson, G. E., & Ryan, M. A. K. (2002). Predictors of naval attrition. I. Analysis of 1 year attrition. *Military Medicine, 167*(9), 760–769. https://doi.org/10.1093/milmed/167.9.760.

Booth, S. J., & Schmiegel, K. M. (1998). *Socioeconomic status and performance in the US Army and US marine Corps.* Monterey, California: Naval Postgraduate School. Retrieved from http://www.dtic.mil/dtic/tr/fulltext/u2/a345037.pdf.

Boscarino, J. A. (1995). Post-traumatic stress and associated disorders among Vietnam veterans: The significance of combat exposure and social support. *Journal of Traumatic Stress, 8*(2), 317–336. https://doi.org/10.1007/BF02109567.

Bower, P., & Gilbody, S. (2005). Stepped care in psychological therapies: Access, effectiveness and efficiency. Narrative literature review. *British Journal of Psychiatry, 186,* 11–17.

Bray, R. M., Brown, J. M., & Williams, J. (2013). Trends in binge and heavy drinking, alcohol-related problems, and combat exposure in the US military. *Substance Use & Misuse, 48*(10), 799–810. https://doi.org/10.3109/10826084.2013.796990.

Bremner, J. D., Southwick, S. M., Johnson, D. R., Yehuda, R., & Charney, D. S. (1993). Childhood physical abuse and combat-related posttraumatic stress disorder in Vietnam veterans. *The American Journal of Psychiatry, 150*(2), 235–239. https://doi.org/10.1176/ajp.150.2.235.

Brignone, E., Fargo, J. D., Blais, R. K., Carter, M. E., Samore, M. H., & Gundlapalli, A. V. (2017). Non-routine discharge from military service: Mental illness, substance use disorders, and suicidality. *American Journal of Preventive Medicine, 52*(5), 557–565. https://doi.org/10.1016/j.amepre.2016.11.015.

Brunger, H., Serrato, J., & Ogden, J. (2013). "No man's land": The transition to civilian life. *Journal of Aggression, Conflict and Peace Research, 5*(2), 86–100. https://doi.org/10.1108/17596591311313681.

Buchanan, N. T., Settles, I. H., & Woods, K. C. (2008). Comparing sexual harassment subtypes among Black and White women by military rank: Double jeopardy, the jezebel, and the cult of true womanhood. *Psychology of Women Quarterly, 32*(4), 347–361.

Buckman, J. E., Forbes, H. J., Clayton, T., Jones, M., Jones, N., Greenberg, N., et al. (2013). Early service leavers: A study of the factors associated with premature separation for the UK armed forces and the mental health of those that leave early. *The European Journal of Public Health, 23*(3), 410–415. https://doi.org/10.1093/eurpub/cks042.

Buckman, J. E., Sundin, J., Greene, T., Fear, N. T., Dandeker, C., Greenberg, N., et al. (2011). The impact of deployment length on the health and well-being of military personnel: A systematic review of the literature. *Occupational and Environmental Medicine, 68*(1), 69–76. https://doi.org/10.1136/oem.2009.054692.

Burkhart, L., & Hogan, N. (2015). Being a female veteran: A grounded theory of coping with transitions. *Social Work in Mental Health, 13*, 108–127. https://doi.org/10.1080/15332985.2013.870102.

Cabrera, O. A., Hoge, C. W., Bliese, P. D., Castro, C. A., & Messer, S. C. (2007). Childhood adversity and combat as predictors of depression and post-traumatic stress in deployed troops. *American Journal of Preventive Medicine, 33*(2), 77–82. https://doi.org/10.1016/j.amepre.2007.03.019.

Castro, C. A., & Kintzle, S. (2014). Suicides in the military: The post-modern combat veteran and the Hemingway effect. *Current Psychiatry Reports, 16*, 460. https://doi.org/10.1007/s11920-014-0460-1.

Castro, C. A., Kintzle, S., & Hassan, A. (2014). *The state of the American veteran: The Los Angeles County veterans study.* Los Angeles, CA: USC School of Social Work, Center for Innovation and Research on Veterans & Military Families.

Castro, C. A., Kintzle, S., & Hassan, A. (2015). *The state of the American veteran: The Orange County veterans study.* Los Angeles, CA: USC School of Social Work, Center for Innovation and Research on Veterans & Military Families.

Cigrang, J. A., Carbone, E. G., Todd, S., & Fiedler, E. (1998). Mental health attrition from Air Force basic military training. *Military Medicine, 163*(12), 834.

Cochran, B. N., Balsam, K., Flentje, A., Malte, C. A., & Simpson, T. (2013). Mental health characteristics of sexual minority veterans. *Journal of Homosexuality, 60*, 419–435. https://doi.org/10.1080/00918369.2013.744932.

Coll, J. E., Weiss, E. L., & Yarvis, J. S. (2011). No one leaves unchanged: Insights for civilian mental health care professionals into the military experience and culture. *Social Work in Health Care, 50*(7), 487–500. https://doi.org/10.1080/00981389.2010.528727.

Cooper, L., Andrew, S., & Fossey, M. (2016). Educating nurses to care for military veterans in civilian hospitals: An integrated literature review. *Nurse Education Today, 47*, 68–73. https://doi.org/10.1016/j.nedt.2016.05.022.

Cooper, L., Caddick, N., Godier, L., Cooper, A., & Fossey, M. (2018). Transition from the military into civilian life: An exploration of cultural competence. *Armed Forces & Society, 44*(1), 156–177. https://doi.org/10.1177/0095327X16675965.

Cooper, L., Caddick, N., Godier, L., Cooper, A., Fossey, M., & Engward, H. (2017). A model of military to civilian transition. Bourdieu in action. *Journal of Military, Veteran and Family Health, 3*(2), 53–60. https://doi.org/10.3138/jmvfh.4301.

Cramm, H., Norris, D., Eichler, M., Tam-Seto, L., Mahar, M., & Smith-Evans, E. (2016). *Resources for Canadian armed forces veterans during the military to civilian transition.*

Crompvoets, S. (2011). The health and wellbeing of female veterans: A review of the literature. *Journal of Military and Veterans' Health, 19*(2), 25–31. Retrieved from http://jmvh.org/article/the-health-and-wellbeing-of-female-veterans-a-review-of-the-literature/.

Dandeker, C., Iversen, A., Ross, J., & Wessely, S. (2003). *Improving the delivery of cross departmental support and services for veterans.* London, United Kingdom: The King's Centre for Military Health Research. Retrieved from http://www.veterans-uk.info/pdfs/publications/misc/kings_college_report_jul_03.pdf.

Dandeker, C., Thomas, S., Dolan, M., Chapman, F., & Ross, J. (2005). *Feasibility study on the extent, causes, impact and costs of rough sleeping and homelessness amongst ex-service personnel in a sample of local authorities in England*. London, United Kingdom: The King's Centre for Military Health Research. Retrieved from https://www.kcl.ac.uk/kcmhr/publications/assetfiles/veterans/Dandeker2005-feasabilitystudyhomeless.pdf.

Demers, A. (2011). When veterans return: The role of community in reintegration. *Journal of Loss & Trauma, 16*(2), 160–179. https://doi.org/10.1080/15325024.2010.519281.

Demers, A. L. (2013). From death to life: Female veterans, identity negotiation, and reintegration into society. *Journal of Humanistic Psychology, 53*(4), 489–515. https://doi.org/10.1177/0022167812472395.

DiRamio, D., & Jarvis, K. (2011). Veterans in higher education: When Johnny and Jane come marching to campus. *ASHE Higher Education Report, 37*. John Wiley & Sons.

Donaldson, T., Earl, J. K., & Muratore. A. M. (2010). Extending the integrated model of retirement adjustment: Incorporating mastery and retirement planning. *Journal of Vocational Behavior, 77*(2), 279–289.

Eekhout, I., Reijnen, A., Vermetten, E., & Geuze, E. (2016). Post-traumatic stress symptoms 5 years after military deployment to Afghanistan: An observational cohort study. *The Lancet Psychiatry, 3*(1), 58–64. https://doi.org/10.1016/S2215-0366(15)00368-5.

Eichler, M. (2017). Add female veterans and stir? A feminist perspective on gendering veterans research. *Armed Forces & Society, 43*(4), 674–694. https://doi.org/10.1177/0095327X16682785.

Elbogen, E. B., Johnson, S. C., Newton, V. M., Straits-Troster, K., Vasterling, J. J., Wagner, H. R., et al. (2012). Criminal justice involvement, trauma, and negative affect in Iraq and Afghanistan war era veterans. *Journal of Consulting and Clinical Psychology, 80*(6), 1097.

Elbogen, E. B., Johnson, S. C., Wagner, H. R., Newton, V. M., Timko, C., Vasterling, J. J., et al. (2012). Protective factors and risk modification of violence in Iraq and Afghanistan war veterans. *The Journal of Clinical Psychiatry, 73*(6), e767–e773. https://doi.org/10.4088/JCP.11m07593.

Elder, G. H., Shanahan, M. J., & Clipp, E. C. (1994). When war comes to men's lives: Life-course patterns in family, work, and health. *Psychology and Aging, 9*(1), 5–16. https://doi.org/10.1037/0882-7974.9.1.5.

Engel, C. C., Jr., Ursano, R., Magruder, C., Tartaglione, R., Jing, Z., Labbate, L. A., et al. (1999). Psychological conditions diagnosed among veterans seeking Department of Defense care for Gulf War-related health concerns. *Journal of Occupational and Environmental Medicine, 41*(5), 384–392. https://doi.org/10.1097/00043764-199905000-00006.

Faberman, R. J., & Foster, T. (2013). Unemployment among recent veterans during the great recession. In *Economic perspectives* (Vol. 37, pp. 1–13). Chicgo, Il: Federal Reserve Bank of Chicago. https://www.chicagofed.org/publications/economic-perspectives/2013/1q-faberman-foster.

Farmer, C. M., Hosek, S. D., & Adamson, D. M. (2016). Balancing demand and supply for veterans' health care. A summary of three RAND assessments conducted under the Veterans Choice Act. *Rand Health Quarterly, 6*(1), 12. Retrieved from https://www.ncbi.nlm.nih.gov/pmc/articles/PMC5158276/.

Fear, N. T., Iversen, A., Meltzer, H., Workman, L., Hull, L., Greenberg, N., et al. (2007). Patterns of drinking in the UK armed forces. *Addiction, 102*(11), 1749–1759. https://doi.org/10.1111/j.1360-0443.2007.01978.x.

Fear, N. T., Jones, M., Murphy, D., Hull, L., Iversen, A. C., Coker, B., et al. (2010). What are the consequences of deployment to Iraq and Afghanistan on the mental health of the UK armed forces? A cohort study. *Lancet, 375*, 1783–1797. https://doi.org/10.1016/S0140-6736(10)60672-1.

Forces in Mind Trust. (2013). *The Transition Mapping Study: Understanding the transition process for Service personnel returning to civilian life*. London, United Kingdom: Forces in Mind Trust. Retrieved from http://www.fim-trust.org/wp-content/uploads/2015/01/20130810-TMS-Report.pdf.

Franx, G., Oud, M., De Lange, J., Wensing, M., & Grol, R. (2012). Implementing a stepped-care approach in primary care: Results of a qualitative study. *Implementation Science, 7*(8).

Gee, D. (2007). Informed choice? Armed forces recruitment practice in the United Kingdom. Retrieved from https://www1.essex.ac.uk/armedcon/story_id/000733.pdf.

Gee, D. (2008). *Informed choice? Armed forces recruitment practice in the United Kingdom*. Retrieved from https://www1.essex.ac.uk/armedcon/story_id/000733.pdf.

Gee, D., & Goodman, A. (2010). *Army recruiters visit London's poorest schools most often*. Retrieved from http://www.informedchoice.org.uk/armyvisitstoschools.pdf.

Glass, C., & Flynn, D. K. J. (2000). Retirement needs and preparation of rural middle-aged persons. *Educational Gerontology, 26*(2), 109–134.

Godfrey, K. M., Mostoufi, S., Rodgers, C., Backhaus, A., Floto, E., Pittman, J., et al. (2015). Associations of military sexual trauma, combat exposure, and number of deployments with physical and mental health indicators in Iraq and Afghanistan veterans. *Psychological Services, 12*(4), 366–377. https://doi.org/10.1037/ser0000059.

Godier, L. R., Caddick, N., Kiernan, M. D., & Fossey, M. (2018). Transition support for vulnerable service leavers in the UK: Providing care for early service leavers. *Military Behavioral Health, 6*(1), 13–21. https://doi.org/10.1080/21635781.2017.1325804.

Gundlapalli, A. V., Fargo, J. D., Metraux, S., Carter, M. E., Samore, M. H., Kane, V., et al. (2015). Military misconduct and homelessness among US veterans separated from active duty, 2001–2012. *Journal of the American Medical Association, 314*(8), 832–834. https://doi.org/10.1001/jama.2015.8207.

Gurung, S., Ventuneac, A., Rendina, H. J., Savarese, E., Grov, C., & Parsons, J. T. (2018). Prevalence of military sexual trauma and sexual orientation discrimination among lesbian, gay, bisexual, and transgender military personnel: A descriptive study. *Sexuality Research and Social Policy, 15*(1), 74–82.

Hachey, K. K., Sudom, K., Sweet, J., MacLean, M. B., & VanTil, L. D. (2016). Transitioning from military to civilian life: The role of mastery and social support. *Journal of Military, Veteran and Family Health, 2*(1), 9–18. https://doi.org/10.3138/jmvfh.3379.

Hachey, K. K., Sudom, K., Sweet, J., Thompson, J. M., MacLean, M. B., & VanTil, L. (2016). *Differences in adjustment to civilian life between male and female Canadian armed forces veterans*. Res Militaris, ERGOMAS issue, no 2. Retrieved from http://resmilitaris.net/index.php?ID=1022317.

Hamilton, A. B., Poza, I., & Washington, D. L. (2011). "Homelessness and trauma go hand-in-hand": Pathways to homelessness among women veterans. *Women's Health Issues, 21*(4S), S203–S209. https://doi.org/10.1016/j.whi.2011.04.005.

Hatch, S. L., Harvey, S. B., Dandeker, C., Burdett, H., Greenberg, N., Fear, N. T., et al. (2013). Life in and after the armed forces: Social networks and mental health in the UK military. *Sociology of Health & Illness, 35*(7), 1045–1064. https://doi.org/10.1111/1467-9566.12022.

Higate, P. R. (2001). Theorizing continuity: From military to civilian life. *Armed Forces & Society, 27*(3), 443–460. https://doi.org/10.1177/0095327X0102700306.

Hines, L. A., Sundin, J., Rona, R. J., Wessely, S., & Fear, N. T. (2014). Posttraumatic stress disorder post Iraq and Afghanistan: Prevalence among military subgroups. *Canadian Journal of Psychiatry, 59*(9), 468–479. https://doi.org/10.1177/070674371405900903.

Hoge, C. W., Castro, C. A., Messer, S. C., McGurk, D., Cotting, D. I., & Koffman, R. L. (2004). Combat duty in Iraq and Afghanistan, mental health problems, and barriers to care. *The New England Journal of Medicine, 351*(1), 13–22. https://doi.org/10.1056/NEJMoa040603.

Hoge, C. W., Terhakopian, A., Castro, C. A., Messer, S. C., & Engel, C. C. (2007). Association of posttraumatic stress disorder with somatic symptoms, health care visits, and absenteeism among Iraq war veterans. *American Journal of Psychiatry, 164*(1), 150–153. https://doi.org/10.1176/ajp.2007.164.1.150.

Hoge, C. W., Toboni, H. E., Messer, S. C., Bell, N., Amoroso, P., & Orman, D. T. (2005). The occupational burden of mental disorders in the U.S. military: Psychiatric hospitalizations, involuntary separations, and disability. *American Journal of Psychiatry, 162*(3), 585–591. https://doi.org/10.1176/appi.ajp.162.3.585.

Hoglund, M. W., & Schwartz, R. M. (2014). Mental health in deployed and nondeployed veteran men and women in comparison with their civilian counterparts. *Military Medicine, 179*, 1–19. https://doi.org/10.7205/MILMED-D-13-00235.

Hotopf, M., Hull, L., Fear, N. T., Browne, T., Horn, O., Iversen, A., et al. (2006). The health of UK military personnel who deployed to the 2003 Iraq war: A cohort study. *The Lancet, 367*(9524), 1731–1741. https://doi.org/10.1016/S0140-6736(06)68662-5.

Hunt, E. J. F., Wessely, S., Jones, N., Rona, R. J., & Greenberg, N. (2014). The mental health of the UK armed forces: Where facts meet fiction. *European Journal of Psychotraumatology, 5*, 23617. https://doi.org/10.3402/ejpt.v5.23617.

Iversen, A. C., Fear, N. T., Simonoff, E., Hull, L., Horn, O., Greenberg, N., et al. (2007). Influence of childhood adversity on health among male UK military personnel. *British Journal of Psychiatry, 191*, 506–511. https://doi.org/10.1192/bjp.bp.107.039818.

Iversen, A., Nikolaou, V., Greenberg, N., Unwin, C., Hull, L., Hotopf, M., et al. (2005). What happens to British veterans when they leave the armed forces? *The European Journal of Public Health, 15*(2), 175–184. https://doi.org/10.1093/eurpub/cki128.

Iversen, A. C., Van Staden, L., Hughes, J. H., Browne, T., Greenberg, N., Hotopf, M., et al. (2010). Help-seeking and receipt of treatment among UK service personnel. *The British Journal of Psychiatry, 197*(2), 149–155. https://doi.org/10.1192/bjp.bp.109.075762.

Iversen, A. C., Van Staden, L., Hughes, J. H., Browne, T., Hull, L., Hall, J., et al. (2009). The prevalence of common mental disorders and PTSD in the UK military: Using data from a clinical interview-based study. *BMC Psychiatry, 9*(1), 68. https://doi.org/10.1186/1471-244X-9-68.

Iversen, A. C., Van Staden, L., Hughes, J. H., Greenberg, N., Hotopf, M., Rona, R. J., et al. (2011). The stigma of mental health problems and other barriers to care in the UK armed forces. *BMC Health Services Research, 11*(1), 31. https://doi.org/10.1186/1472-6963-11-31.

Iversen, A., Waterdrinker, A., Fear, N., Greenberg, N., Barker, C., Hotopf, M., et al. (2007). Factors associated with heavy alcohol consumption in the UK armed forces: Data from a health survey of Gulf, Bosnia, and era veterans. *Military Medicine, 172*(9), 956–961.

Jones, M., Sundin, J., Goodwin, L., Hull, L., Fear, N. T., Wessely, S., et al. (2013). What explains post-traumatic stress disorder (PTSD) in UK service personnel: Deployment or something else? *Psychological Medicine, 43*(8), 1703–1712. https://doi.org/10.1017/S0033291712002619.

Keeling, M., Kintzle, S., & Castro, C. A. (2018). Exploring U.S. veterans' post-service employment experiences. *Military Psychology, 30*(1), 63–69. https://doi.org/10.1080/08995605.2017.1420976.

Kelsall, H. L., Wijesinghe, M. S. D., Creamer, M. C., McKenzie, D. P., Forbes, A. B., Page, M. J., et al. (2015). Alcohol use and substance use disorders in Gulf War, Afghanistan, and Iraq War veterans compared with nondeployed military personnel. *Epidemiologic Reviews, 37*(1), 38–54. https://doi.org/10.1093/epirev/mxu014.

Kiernan, M. D., Repper, J., & Arthur, A. (2015). Why do they fail? A qualitative follow up study of 1000 recruits to the British army infantry to understand high levels of attrition. *Work, 52*(4), 921–934. https://doi.org/10.3233/WOR-152208.

Kintzle, S., Keeling, M., Xintarianos, E., Taylor-Diggs, K., Munch, C., Hassan, A. M., et al. (2015). *Exploring the economic & employment challenges facing U.S. veterans: A qualitative study of volunteers of America service providers & veteran clients*. Los Angeles, CA: USC School of Social Work, Center for Innovation and Research on Veterans & Military Families.

Kintzle, S., Rasheed, J. M., & Castro, C. A. (2016). *The state of the American veteran: The Chicagoland veterans study.* Los Angeles, CA: USC School of Social Work, Center for Innovation and Research on Veterans & Military Families. Retrieved from http://cir.usc.edu/wp-content/uploads/2016/04/CIR_ChicagoReport_double.pdf.

Klein, S. P., Hawes-Dawson, J., & Martin, T. (1991). *Why recruits separate early.* Santa Monica, CA: RAND Corporation. Retrieved from https://www.rand.org/pubs/reports/R3980.html.

Kleykamp, M. (2013a). Unemployment, earnings and enrollment among Post 9/11 veterans. *Social Science Research, 42*(3), 836–851. https://doi.org/10.1016/j.ssresearch.2012.12.017.

Kleykamp, M. (2013b). Labour market outcomes among veterans and military spouses. In M. Wilmoth, & A. S. London (Eds.), *Life-course perspectives on military service* (pp. 144–164). New York, NY: Routledge.

Kwon, S. W., & Adler, P. S. (2014). Social capital: Maturation of a field of research. *Academy of Management Review, 39*(4), 412–422. https://doi.org/10.5465/amr.2014.0210.

LeardMann, C. A., Smith, B., & Ryan, M. A. K. (2010). Do adverse childhood experiences increase the risk of postdeployment posttraumatic stress disorder in US marines? *BMC Public Health, 10*, 437. https://doi.org/10.1186/1471-2458-10-437.

Loughran, D. S. (2014). *Why is veteran unemployment so high?* Santa Monica, CA: RAND Corporation. Retrieved from https://www.rand.org/content/dam/rand/pubs/research_reports/RR200/RR284/RAND_RR284.pdf.

MacLean, A. (2017). Skills mismatch? Military service, combat occupations, and civilian earnings. *Sociological Perspectives, 60*(2), 229–250.

MacLean, M. B., Campbell, L., Poirier, A., & Sweet, J. (2016). *Military occupation and post-military employment and income outcomes.* Charlottetown, Canada: Veterans Affairs Canada, Research Directorate.

MacLean, M. B., Keough, J., Poirier, A., McKinnon, K., & Sweet, J. (2016). *Labour-market outcomes of veterans.* Charlottetown, PE, Canada: Veterans Affairs Canada.

MacLean, M. B., Keough, J., Poirier, A., McKinnon, K., & Sweet, J. (2018). *Labour-market outcomes of veterans.* Manuscript submitted for publication.

MacLean, M. B., VanTil, L., Sweet, J., Poirier, A., & McKinnon, K. (2019). Factors associated with work satisfaction among veterans. *Journal of Military, Veteran and Family Health.*

MacLean, M. B., VanTil, L., Thompson, J. M., Sweet, J., Poirier, A., Sudom, K., et al. (2014). Postmilitary adjustment to civilian life: Potential risks and protective factors. *Physical Therapy, 94*(8), 1186–1195. https://doi.org/10.2522/ptj.20120107.

MacManus, D., Dean, K., Iversen, A. C., Hull, L., Jones, N., Fahy, T., et al. (2012). Impact of pre-enlistment antisocial behaviour on behavioural outcomes among UK military personnel. *Social Psychiatry and Psychiatric Epidemiology, 47*(8), 1353–1358.

MacManus, D., Dean, K., Jones, M., Rona, R. J., Greenberg, N., Hull, L., et al. (2013). Violent offending by UK military personnel deployed to Iraq and Afghanistan: A data linkage cohort study. *The Lancet, 381*(9870), 907–917. https://doi.org/10.1016/S0140-6736(13)60354-2.

MacManus, D., Rona, R., Dickson, H., Somaini, G., Fear, N., & Wessely, S. (2015). Aggressive and violent behavior among military personnel deployed to Iraq and Afghanistan: Prevalence and link with deployment and combat exposure. *Epidemiologic Reviews, 37*(1), 196–212. https://doi.org/10.1093/epirev/mxu006.

MacManus, D., & Wessely, S. (2011). Why do some ex-armed forces personnel end up in prison? *British Medical Journal, 342*, d3898. https://doi.org/10.1136/bmj.d3898.

Mahar, A. L., Gribble, R., Aiken, A. B., Dandeker, C., Duffy, B., Gottfried, G., et al. (2017). Public opinion of the armed forces in Canada, U.K. and the U.S. *Journal of Military, Veteran and Family Health, 3*(2), 2–3. https://doi.org/10.3138/jmvfh.3.2.002.

Makin-Byrd, K., Gifford, E., McCutcheon, S., & Glynn, S. (2011). Family and couples treatment for newly returning veterans. *Professional Psychology: Research and Practice, 42*(1), 47–55. https://doi.org/10.1037/a0022292.

Marshall, V. W., & Matteo, R. A. (2004). *Canadian Forces clients of veterans Affairs Canada: Risk factors for post-release socioeconomic well-being*. Charlottetown, PE, Canada: Veterans Affairs Canada.

Marshall, V. W., Matteo, R. A., & Mueller, M. M. (2000). *Canadian Forces clients of veterans Affairs Canada: Employment status, career and retirement planning issues*. Charlottetown, PE, Canada: Veterans Affairs Canada.

Mattocks, K. M., HaskelL, S. G., Krebs, E. E., Justice, A. C., Yano, E. M., & Brandt, C. (2012). Women at war: Understanding how women veterans cope with combat and military sexual trauma. *Social Science & Medicine, 74*, 537–545.

Mattocks, K. M., Kauth, M. R., Sandfort, T., Matza, A. R., Sullivan, J. C., & Shipherd, J. C. (2014). Understanding health-care needs of sexual and gender minority veterans: How targeted research and policy can improve health. *LGBT Health, 1*(1), 50–57.

McCauley, H. L., Blosnich, J. R., & Dichter, M. E. (2015). Adverse childhood experiences and adult health outcomes among veteran and non-veteran women. *Journal of Women's Health, 24*(9), 723–729. https://doi.org/10.1089/jwh.2014.4997.

Mellotte, H., Murphy, D., Raferty, L., & Greenberg, N. (2017). Pathways into mental health care for UK veterans: A qualitative study. *European Journal of Psychotraumatology, 8*, 1389207. https://doi.org/10.1080/20008198.2017.1389207.

Metraux, S., Cusack, M., Byrne, T. H., Hunt-Johnson, N., & True, G. (2017). Pathways into homelessness among post-9/11-era veterans. *Psychological Services, 14*(2), 229–237. https://doi.org/10.1037/ser0000136.

Ministry of Defence. (2004). 'Analysis of socio-economic and educational background of non-officer recruits' [memorandum to the house of commons defence committee, 2004], cited in house of commons defence committee (2005) (Third Report of Session 2004-05) *Duty of Care*, 2. Ev 255-257.

Ministry of Defence. (2015). *JSP 534: The tri-service resettlement and employment support manual*. London, United Kingdom: Ministry of Defence. Retrieved from https://www.gov.uk/government/uploads/system/uploads/attachment_data/file/465794/20151001-JSP_534_Issue_14_TESRR_FINAL-O__3_.pdf.

Ministry of Defence. (2016). *UK Armed Forces monthly service personnel statistics 1 April 2016*. Retrieved from https://www.gov.uk/government/uploads/system/

uploads/attachment_data/file/522121//Monthly_service_personnel_statistics-_Apr_2016.pdf.

Ministry of Defence. (2017). *Annual population survey: UK armed forces veterans residing in Great Britain 2016*. Retrieved from https://www.gov.uk/government/statistics/annual-population-survey-uk-armed-forces-veterans-residing-in-great-britain-2016.

Montgomery, A. E., Cutuli, J. J., Evans-Chase, M., Treglia, D., & Culhane, D. P. (2013). Relationship among adverse childhood experiences, history of active military service, and adult outcomes: Homelessness, mental health, and physical health. *American Journal of Public Health, 103*(S2), S262–S268. https://doi.org/10.2105/AJPH.2013.301474.

Montgomery, A. E., Hill, L. L., Kane, V., & Culhane, D. P. (2013). Housing chronically homeless veterans: Evaluating the efficacy of a housing first approach to HUD-VASH. *Journal of Community Psychology, 41*(4), 505–514. https://doi.org/10.1002/jcop.21554.

Morin, R. (2011). *The difficult transition from military to civilian life*. Washington, DC: Pew Research Center. Retrieved from http://assets.pewresearch.org/wp-content/uploads/sites/3/2011/12/The-Difficult-Transition-from-Military-to-Civilian-Life.pdf.

Murphy, D., Weijers, B., Palmer, E., & Busuttil, W. (2015). Exploring patterns in referrals to combat stress for UK veterans with mental health difficulties between 1994 and 2014. *International Journal of Emergency Mental Health and Human Resilience, 17*(3), 652–658. https://doi.org/10.4172/1522-4821.1000250.

National Association of Probation Officers. (2008). *Ex-armed forces personnel and the criminal justice system*. London, United Kingdom: National Association of Probation Officers. Retrieved from http://www.napo.org.uk/publications/Briefings.cfm.

National Association of Probation Officers. (2009). *Armed forces and the criminal justice system*. London, United Kingdom: National Association of Probation Officers. Retrieved from http://www.napo.org.uk/publications/Briefings.cfm.

Neuhaus, S. J., & Crompvoets, S. L. (2013). Australia's servicewomen and female veterans: Do we understand their health needs? *The Medical Journal of Australia, 199*, 530–532.

Noonan, M. E., & Mumola, C. J. (2004). *Veterans in state and federal prison*. From the Bureau of Justice Statistics Special Report. Washington, DC: US Department of Justice. Retrieved from https://www.prisonpolicy.org/scans/bjs/vsfp04.pdf.

Ommaya, A. K., Salazar, A. M., Dannenberg, A. L., Ommaya, A. K., Chervinsky, A. B., & Schwab, K. (1996). Outcome after traumatic brain injury in the U.S. Military medical system. *The Journal of Trauma, 41*(6), 972–975.

Padavic, I., & Prokos, A. (2016). Aiming high: Explaining the earnings advantage for female veterans. *Armed Forces & Society, 43*(2), 368–386. https://doi.org/10.1177/0095327X16682044.

Padgett, D. K. (2007). There's no place like (a) home: Ontological security in the third decade of the 'homelessness crisis' in the United States. *Social Science & Medicine, 64*(9), 1925–1936. https://doi.org/10.1016/j.socscimed.2007.02.011.

Pavao, J., Turchik, J. A., Hyun, J. K., Karpenko, J., Saweikis, M., McCutcheon, S., et al. (2013). Military sexual trauma among homeless veterans. *Journal of General Internal Medicine, 28*(suppl. 1), S536–S541. https://doi.org/10.1007/s11606-013-2341-4.

Peterson, K., Anderson, J., Boundy, E., Ferguson, L., McCleery, E., & Waldrip, K. (2018). Mortality disparities in racial/ethnic minority groups in the veterans health adminsitration: An evidence review and map. *American Journal of Public Health, 108*(3), e1–e11. https://doi.org/10.2105/AJPH.2017.304246.

Petrakis, I. L., Rosenheck, R., & Desai, R. (2011). Substance use comorbidity among veterans with posttraumatic stress disorder and other psychiatric illness. *The American Journal on Addictions, 20*(3), 185–189. https://doi.org/10.1111/j.1521-0391.2011.00126.x.

Pietrzak, R. H., Johnson, D. C., Goldstein, M. B., Malley, J. C., & Southwick, S. M. (2009). Perceived stigma and barriers to mental health care utilization among OEF-OIF veterans. *Psychiatric Services, 60*(8), 1118–1122. https://doi.org/10.1176/ps.2009.60.8.1118.

Prigerson, H. G., Maciejewski, P. K., & Rosenheck, R. A. (2002). Population attributable fractions of psychiatric disorder and behavioral outcomes associated with combat exposure among US men. *American Journal of Public Health, 92*(1), 59–63.

Randall, G., & Brown, S. (1994). *Falling out: Research study of homeless ex-service people.* Crisis.

Ray, S. L., & Forchuk, C. (2011). *The experience of homelessness among Canadian Forces and allied forces veterans (Research Report submitted to HRSDC Canada).* Retrieved from http://www.homelesshub.ca/sites/default/files/Homelesss%20Vets%20Article.

Reger, M. A., Smolenski, D. J., Skopp, N. A., Metzger-Abamukang, M. J., Kang, H. K., Bullman, T. A., … Gahm, G. A. (2015). Risk of suicide among US military service members following operation enduring freedom or operation Iraqi freedom deployment and separation from the US military. *Journal of the American Medical Association Psychiatry, 72*(6), 561–569. https://doi.org/10.1001/jamapsychiatry.2014.3195.

Resnik, L. J., & Allen, S. M. (2007). Using international classification of functioning, disability and health to understand challenges in community reintegration of injured veterans. *Journal of Rehabilitation Research and Development, 44*(7), 991–1006.

Richardson, L. K., Frueh, B. C., & Acierno, R. (2010). Prevalence estimates of combat-related post-traumatic stress disorder: Critical review. *Australian and New Zealand Journal of Psychiatry, 44*(1), 4–19. https://doi.org/10.3109/00048670903393597.

Richardson, J. D., Pekevski, J., & Elhai, J. D. (2009). Post-traumatic stress disorder and health problems among medically ill Canadian peacekeeping veterans. *Australian and New Zealand Journal of Psychiatry, 43*(4), 366–372. https://doi.org/10.1080/00048670902721061.

Risher, P. (October 31, 2016). *What employers say about hiring veterans – behind closed doors* [Still Serving Veterans' website]. Retrieved from https://ssv.org/blog/what-employers-say-about-hiring-veterans.

Rona, R. J., Fear, N. T., Hull, L., & Wessely, S. (2006). Women in novel occupational roles: Mental health trends in the UK armed forces. *International Journal of Epidemiology, 36*, 319–326.

Rosellini, A. J., Monahan, J., Street, A. E., Heeringa, S. G., Hill, E. D., Petukhova, M., et al. (2016). Predicting non-familial major physical violent crime perpetration in the U.S. army from administrative data. *Psychological Medicine, 46*(2), 303–316. https://doi.org/10.1017/S0033291715001774.

Rosenheck, R., Frisman, L., & Chung, A. M. (1994). The proportion of veterans among homeless men. *American Journal of Public Health, 84*(3), 466–469.

Savoca, E., & Rosenheck, R. (2000). The civilian labor market experiences of Vietnam-era veterans: The influence of psychiatric disorders. *The Journal of Mental Health Policy and Economics, 3*(4), 199–207. https://doi.org/10.1002/mhp.102.

Sayers, S. L., Farrow, V. A., Ross, J., & Oslin, D. W. (2009). Family problems among recently returned military veterans referred for a mental health evaluation. *Journal of Clinical Psychiatry, 70*(2), 163.

Schlossberg, N. K. (1981). A model for analyzing human adaptation to transition. *The Counseling Psychologist, 9*(2), 2–18. https://doi.org/10.1177/001100008100900202.

Segal, M. W., Lane, M. D., & Fisher, A. G. (2015). Conceptual model of military career and family life course events, intersections, and effects on well-being. *Military Behavioral Health, 3*, 95–107. https://doi.org/10.1080/21635781.2015.1009212.

Sharp, M. L., Fear, N. T., Rona, R. J., Wessely, S., Greeenberg, N., Jones, N., et al. (2015). Stigma as a barrier to seeking health care among military personnel with mental health problems. *Epidemiologic Reviews, 37*, 144–162. https://doi.org/10.1093/epirev/mxu012.

Shields, D. M., Kuhl, D., Lutz, K., Frender, J., Baumann, N., & Lopresti, P. (2016). *Mental health and well-being of military veterans during military to civilian transition: Review and analysis of the recent literature*. Vancouver, Canada: University of British Columbia. Retrieved from https://cimvhr.ca/documents/R2CL-PVVC-Health-and-Wellbieng.pdf.

Skinner, K. M., Kressin, N., Frayne, S., Tripp, T. J., Hankin, C. S., Miller, D. R., et al. (2000). The prevalence of military sexual assault among female Veterans' Administration outpatients. *Journal of Interpersonal Violence, 15*(3), 291–310. https://doi.org/10.1177/088626000015003005.

Smith, R. T., & True, G. (2014). Warring identities: Identity conflict and the mental distress of American veterans of the wars in Iraq and Afghanistan. *Society and Mental Health, 4*(2), 147–161. https://doi.org/10.1177/2156869313512212.

Sobell, M. B., & Sobell, L. C. (1999). Stepped care for alcohol problems: An efficient method for planning and delivering clinical services. In J. A. Tucker, D. M. Donovan, & G. A. Marlatt (Eds.), *Changing addictive behavior: Bridging clinical and public health strategies* (pp. 331–343). New York, NY, US: Guilford Press.

Solomon, Z., Debby-Aharon, S., Zerach, G., & Horesh, D. (2011). Marital adjustment, parental functioning, and emotional sharing in war veterans. *Journal of Family Issues, 32*(1), 127–147. https://doi.org/10.1177/0192513X10379203.

Spini, D., Bernardi, L., & Oris, M. (2017). Toward a life course framework for studying vulnerability. *Research in Human Development, 14*, 5–25. https://doi.org/10.1080/15427609.2016.1268892.

Spiro, A., III, Settersen, R. A., & Aldwin, C. M. (2016). Long-term outcomes of military service in ageing and the life course: A positive re-envisioning. *The Gerontologist, 56*(1), 5–13. https://doi.org/10.1093/geront/gnv093.

Staal, M. A., Cigrang, J. A., & Fiedler, E. (2000). Disposition decisions in U.S. air force basic trainees assessed during mental health evaluations. *Military Psychology, 12*(3), 187–203. https://doi.org/10.1207/S15327876MP1203_2.

Stander, V. A., & Thomsen, C. J. (2016). Sexual harassment and assault in the U.S. military: A review of policy and research trends. *Military Medicine, 181*(1), 20–27. https://doi.org/10.7205/MILMED-D-15-00336.

Stellman, J. M., Stellman, S. D., & Sommer, J. F. (1988). Utilization, attitudes, and experiences of Vietnam era veterans with veterans administration health facilities: The American legion experience. *Environmental Research, 47*(2), 193–209. https://doi.org/10.1016/S0013-9351(88)80041-0.

Sundin, J., Herrell, R. K., Hoge, C. W., Fear, N. T., Adler, A. B., Greenberg, N., et al. (2014). Mental health outcomes in US and UK military personnel returning from Iraq. *British Journal of Psychiatry, 204*(3), 200–207. https://doi.org/10.1192/bjp.bp.113.129569.

Suris, A., & Lind, L. (2008). Military sexual trauma: A review of prevalence and associated health consequences in veterans. *Trauma, Violence, & Abuse, 9*(4), 250–269. https://doi.org/10.1177/1524838008324419.

Szelwach, C. R., Steinkogler, J., Badger, E. R., & Muttukumaru, R. (2011). Transitioning to the civilian workforce: Issues impacting the reentry of rural women veterans. *Journal of Rural Social Sciences, 26*(3), 83–112.

Taft, C. T., Schumm, J. A., Panuzio, J., & Proctor, S. P. (2008). An examination of family adjustment among operation desert storm veterans. *Journal of Consulting and Clinical Psychology, 76*(4), 648–656. https://doi.org/10.1037/a0012576.

Taylor, M. A., Shultz, K. S., Spiegel, P. E., Morrison, R. F., & Greene, J. (2007). Occupational attachment and met expectations as predictors of retirement adjustment of naval officers. *Journal of Applied Social Psychology, 37*(8), 1697–1725. https://doi.org/10.1111/j.1559-1816.2007.00234.x.

The Futures Company. (2013). *The transition mapping study.* Retrieved from http://www.fim-trust.org/wp-content/uploads/2015/01/20130810-TMS-Report.pdf.

The Royal British Legion. (2006). *Profile and needs: Comparison between ex-service community and the UK population.* London, United Kingdom: The Royal British Legion. https://media.britishlegion.org.uk/Media/2272/2005-household-survey.pdf?_ga=2.120557768.1956156387.1526388009-521527159.1516099496.

The Royal British Legion. (2014). *The UK ex-service community: A household survey.* London, United Kingdom: The Royal British Legion. https://media.britishlegion.org.uk/Media/2275/2014householdsurveyreport.pdf?_ga=2.98236447.1611296855.1516099496-521527159.1516099496.

Thompson, J. M., Lockhart, W., Roach, M. B., Atuel, H., Bélanger, S., Black, T., et al. (2017). *Veterans' identities and well-being in transition to civilian life — a resource for policy analysts, program designers, service providers and researchers.* Report of the Veterans' Identities Research Theme Working Group, *Canadian Institute for Military and Veteran Health Research Forum 2016* [Research Directorate Technical Report. 01 June 2017]. Charlottetown, PE, Canada: Research Directorate, Veterans Affairs Canada. Retrieved from https://cimvhr.ca/documents/Thompson%202017%20Veterans%20Identities%20Technical%20Report.pdf.

Thompson, J. M., MacLean, M. B., Lockhart, W., Poirier, A., Sweet, J., & Pedlar, D. (2015). *Planning transition supports for Canadian armed forces members/veterans: Findings from the life after service studies.* Charlottetown, Canada: Veterans Affairs Canada, Research Directorate.

Thompson, J. M., MacLean, M. B., VanTil, L., Sudom, K., Poirier, A., Adams, J., et al. (2011). *Survey on transition to civilian life: Report on regular force veterans.* Charlottetown, PE, Canada: Veterans Affairs Canada, Research Directorate Technical Report and Ottawa, Canada: Department of National Defence, Director General Military Personnel Research and Analysis. Retrieved from http://publications.gc.ca/collections/collection_2011/acc-vac/V32-231-2011-eng.pdf.

Thomson & Goodall Associates. (2009). *Veterans at risk.* Brisbane, Australia: Australian Department of Veterans' Affairs. Retrieved from www.dva.gov.au/aboutDVA/publications/social_research/vets_at_risk/Pages/index.aspx.

Tsai, J., & Rosenheck, R. A. (2018). Characteristics and health needs of veterans with other-than-honorable discharges: Expanding eligibility in the veterans health administration. *Military Medicine* https://doi.org/10.1093/milmed/usx110.

Tsemberis, S., & Eisenberg, R. F. (2000). Pathways to housing: Supported housing for street-dwelling homeless individuals with psychiatric disabilities. *Psychiatric Services, 51*(4), 487–493. https://doi.org/10.1176/appi.ps.51.4.487.

Turchik, J. A., & Wilson, S. M. (2010). Sexual assault in the U.S. Military: A review of the literature and recommendations for the future. *Aggression and Violent Behavior, 15*(4), 267–277. https://doi.org/10.1016/j.avb.2010.01.005.

UNESCO. (2013). *The principle of respect for human vulnerability and personal integrity.* Report from the international bioethics committee of UNESCO (IBC). Paris, France: United Nations Educational, Scientific and Cultural Organization. Retrieved from http://unesdoc.unesco.org/images/0021/002194/219494E.pdf.

U.S. Bureau of Labor Statistics. (2014). *Employment situation of veterans. Summary.* Washington, DC: US Department of Labor.

U.S. Department of Veterans Affairs. (2015). *M21-1, Part III, Subpart II, Chapter 6. Determining veteran status and eligibility for benefits.* Washington, DC: Veterans Benefits Administration. Retrieved from http://www.benefits.va.gov/WARMS/docs/admin21/m21_1/mr/part3/subptii/ch06/M21-1III_ii_6.docx.

VanTil, L., Macintosh, S., Thompson, J. M., MacLean, M. B., Campbell, L., Sudom, K., et al. (2014). *2013 Synthesis of life after service studies.* Charlottetown, PE, Canada: Veterans Affairs Canada, Research Directorate. Retrieved from http://www.veterans.gc.ca/pdf/about-us/research-directorate/2013-life-after-service-studies.pdf.

VanTil, L., Sweet, J., Thompson, J. M., Poirier, A., McKinnon, K., Sudom, K., et al. (2017). *Well-being of Canadian regular force veterans.* Findings from the LASS 2016 survey [Research Directorate Technical Report. June 2017]. Charlottetown, PE, Canada: Research Directorate, Veterans Affairs Canada. Retrieved from http://publications.gc.ca/collections/collection_2017/acc-vac/V32-340-2017-eng.pdf.

Veteran Transition Advisory Committee. (2013). *Veteran transition advisory council: 2013 interim report.* VTAC group meeting, fall 2013.

Wainwright, V., McDonnell, S., Lennox, C., Shaw, J., & Senior, J. (2016). Soldier, civilian, criminal: Identifying pathways to offending of ex-armed forces personnel in prison. *Psychology, Crime and Law, 22*(8), 741–757. https://doi.org/10.1080/1068316X.2016.1181175.

Watkins, K., Sudom, K., & Zamorski, M. (2016). Association of combat experiences with post-traumatic stress disorder among Canadian military personnel deployed in support of the mission in Afghanistan. *Military Behavioral Health, 4*(3), 285–292. https://doi.org/10.1080/21635781.2016.1153538.

Woodhead, C., Wessely, S., Jones, N., Fear, N. T., & Hatch, S. L. (2012). Impact of exposure to combat during deployment to Iraq and Afghanistan on mental health by gender. *Psychological Medicine, 42*(9), 1985–1996. https://doi.org/10.1017/S003329171100290X.

Xue, C., Ge, Y., Tang, B., Liu, Y., Kang, P., Wang, M., et al. (2015). A meta-analysis of risk factors for combat-related PTSD among military personnel and veterans. *PLoS One, 10*(3), e0120270. https://doi.org/10.1371/journal.pone.0120270.

Yanos, P. T., Felton, B. J., Tsemberis, S., & Frye, V. A. (2007). Exploring the role of housing type, neighborhood characteristics, and lifestyle factors in the community integration of formerly homeless persons diagnosed with mental illness. *Journal of Mental Health, 16*(6), 703–717. https://doi.org/10.1080/09638230701496378.

CHAPTER

7

Development of a Medical Release Transition Framework

Jennifer E.C. Lee, Kimberley Watkins, Sanela Dursun

National Defence Canada, Ottawa, ON, Canada

OUTLINE

Individuals undergo a number of transitions over the course of their lives. Whether it be entering high school, marriage, or parenthood to changing careers or leaving the workforce, life transitions represent critical periods of self-reflection and growth, yet

Military Veteran Reintegration
https://doi.org/10.1016/B978-0-12-815312-3.00007-3

© 2019 Crown Copyright and Elsevier Inc.
All rights reserved.

result in considerable degrees of stress (Bauer & McAdams, 2004). Not surprisingly, life transitions have received a great deal of attention in the scholarly literature (Kralik, Visentin, & Van Loon, 2006). Indeed, the topic has been explored in a range of ways and across multiple disciplines, and is generally recognized as representing more than change alone, but rather "the psychological processes involved in adapting to the change event or disruption" (Kralik et al., 2006, p. 322).

Most recently, the topic of transition has garnered interest from military researchers. This has especially been the case in relation to the experiences of military personnel as they exit military service, with many studies conducted on the topic over the past two decades (e.g., Binks & Cambridge, 2018; Higate, 2001; Morin, 2011; Thompson et al., 2011). While the transition to civilian life is a relatively smooth process for the majority of veterans, an important minority may experience psychosocial problems, including homelessness, alcohol and drug addiction, poverty, unemployment, suicide, criminality, incarceration, or mental illness (e.g., Bergman, Burdett, & Greenberg, 2014; Brenner & Barnes, 2012; Fossey, 2010; Pease, Billera, & Gerard, 2015). Among those at greatest risk of experiencing difficult adjustment following their release from the military are ill or injured service members[1] (MacLean et al., 2014). Results of a Canadian study on veterans suggest that medically released personnel generally fare worse in their transition to civilian life compared with veterans released for other reasons[2] (MacLean et al., 2014).

Findings presented above are of concern in light of recent trends in the proportion of service members being released medically across militaries. While the majority of military members voluntarily release from service, the percentage of medical releases[3] has

[1] The term ill or injured is commonly used to refer to military personnel with one or more health condition(s) that may prevent them from remaining in uniform in Canada (National Defence and the Canadian Armed Forces, 2018a), while the term wounded, injured, and sick (WIS) has been used in the United Kingdom (Ministry of Defence, 2017b).

[2] It is acknowledged that members who release *voluntarily* with health conditions and related impairments may also experience difficult adjustment, and that a significant proportion of veterans who are released voluntarily may experience a health condition.

[3] Medical releases are defined as releases from service with medical limitations rendering members unable to meet military service requirements. In the Canadian military, for example, the principle of "universality of service" provides guidelines for minimal operational standards in terms of physical fitness, employability, and deployability (National Defence and the Canadian Armed Forces, 2018b).

been on the rise in a number of countries. In Canada, for example, the percentage of Regular Force members who were medically released increased from 24% in 2012 to 40% in 2016/2017. Similar trends were observed across services in the United Kingdom in 2017 (Ministry of Defence, 2017a).

Such trends underline the growing importance of finding appropriate ways to support service members during medical release and increase their likelihood of a successful transition to civilian life. This chapter takes an in-depth look at the military-to-civilian transition (MCT) process for ill/injured service members. That process is a pivotal time in a member's transition that can span anywhere from several months to several years. The aim is to present an injury transition trajectory and identify the key barriers that impact this process. In particular, the Medical Release Transition Framework is proposed for understanding the process of transition to civilian society for ill/injured service members, taking into account psychosocial and institutional barriers that can influence this transition.

Military-to-civilian transition frameworks

The transition from military to civilian life has been described as a "complex, multifaceted process with variable institutional, health, psychological, work, family, and community dimensions" (Thompson et al., 2013, p. e15). Different theoretical approaches have been used to describe the concept of transition for service members leaving the military. Borrowing from psychosocial theory on adult development, DiRamio and his colleagues (DiRamio, Ackerman, & Mitchell, 2008) developed a conceptual framework for understanding the experiences of military personnel as they enter college life. Specifically, they found that the transition of US military veterans from combat to college could be explained using Schlossberg, Lynch, and Chickering's (1989) "Moving In, Moving Through, Moving Out" model, which posits that there are challenges associated with each of these stages of transition. For instance, on joining the military, individuals may experience difficulties associated with the "Moving In" phase of this initial transition, such as the requirement to learn the rules and expectations of their new position in a short period of time. Later, they may encounter "Moving Through" obstacles, such as traumatic combat events. Finally, when preparing to leave the military, members are often faced with "Moving Out" challenges, including difficulties in relationships due to differing experiences and the failure of transition programs to meet all their needs. As the veterans enter college, the transition cycle restarts, with potentially new "Moving In" issues related to college, such as socialization with other students, dealing with faculty and administration, and coping with any service-related physical or mental health problems. Although transition is an ongoing process, with challenges at each stage, modifiable resources, such as social support and coping strategies, can make it more manageable (Schlossberg et al., 1989, as cited in DiRamio et al., 2008).

More recently, Castro and his colleagues proposed Military Transition Theory (MTT) to describe notable transitions that may occur through a service member's entire military career (Castro & Kintzle, 2016). From their perspective, the process of leaving the military can be seen as comprising three interacting and overlapping phases that are each influenced by a number of individual, interpersonal, community, and organizational factors. The first phase—Approaching the Military Transition—describes the various factors that provide the foundation for the transition trajectory, such as personal or cultural factors and the nature of the transition itself (e.g., whether it is expected). In Managing the Transition, factors that influence individuals' progression from military to civilian life are outlined. These span individual attributes (e.g., coping styles, attitudes, beliefs) and transition management factors (e.g., support programs and services) to community-level supports which may ultimately influence their adjustment to the transition. Finally, Assessing the Transition refers to the outcomes experienced by individuals who have gone through the transition process.

While MTT has received empirical support and has been applied to a range of military-related issues (e.g., suicide and sexual assault; Castro & Kintzle, 2014; Castro, Kintzle, Schuyler, Lucas, & Warner, 2015), the theory is meant to be comprehensive by describing the transition process, regardless of the type of release. As is the premise in MTT, the specific circumstances leading to release from the military play a role in setting the stage for the process. Hence, there may be value in developing a framework that recognizes the unique needs of specific subgroups of military personnel during this transition. Building on MTT, the Medical Release Transition Framework (MRTF) was developed to address this gap and characterize MCT among service members who are being medically released from the military.

There are a number of reasons to believe that the transition of ill/injured service members to civilian society is uniquely challenging. In many cases, being released may not be a matter of choice, but rather a question of no longer being able to meet the requirements for military service. As a result, the transition back to civilian life may be abrupt, complicated, and unexpected, resulting in little to no time or few resources to psychologically prepare oneself for the change. An additional challenge is the loss of identity that service members experience when they transition out of uniform. Experiencing this loss while also dealing with a health condition might exacerbate difficulties during this adjustment. Indeed, injured veterans may need to negotiate the concept of themselves as disabled and face uncertainty concerning the activities in which they will be able to engage in the longer term (Messinger, 2010). The MRTF, illustrated in Fig. 7.1, identifies the three consecutive, interconnected phases that may characterize the trajectories of ill or injured service members, specifically, during MCT.

As illustrated in Fig. 7.1, the first phase of the MRTF, the *Injury/ Illness Diagnosis Process,* begins with the identification of medical issues and initial medical interventions. During this phase, the condition is fully assessed to obtain diagnosis and treatment. Some service members may be able to return to duty following their rehabilitation and recovery. However, this phase may also end once a formal decision is made by medical professionals to medically release the service member (i.e., due to a medical employment limitation).

At the *Pre-Release Preparation* phase, preparation for the actual release is initiated. The duration of this phase depends on a number of factors, including information about the illness or injury, functional limitations, mental health, psychosocial factors, and the adequacy of the health care system for meeting the service member's needs after release. In some military organizations, this period can last up to 3 years, ending on the actual day of release.

Finally, representing the start of civilian life and transition into veteran status, *Post-Release Adaptation* is the period during which newly released ill/injured veterans learn to adapt to their illness/

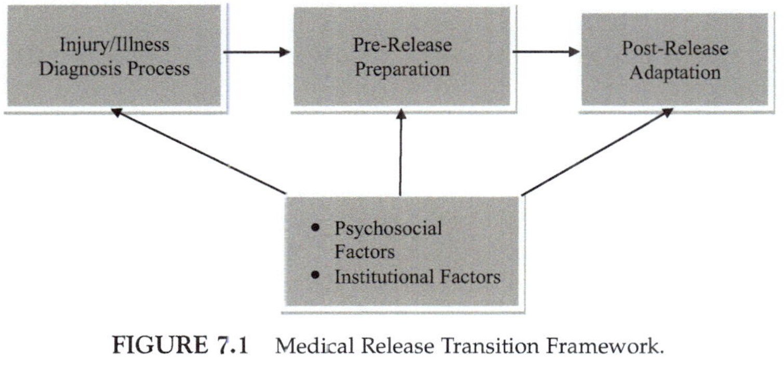

FIGURE 7.1 Medical Release Transition Framework.

injury and settle into their new lives—sometimes in a new community. They must also adapt to a new health care system in addition to new health care providers. While each veteran proceeds through this phase at his/her own pace, based on a number of factors, it has been suggested that this transition may last up to 2 years (Thompson & Lockhart, 2015).

At each of these interconnected phases, a number of individual, interpersonal, community, and military organizational factors come into play. In broad terms, these may be categorized into two categories of determinants of MCT: those that are psychosocial and those that are institutional in nature. The following section provides a review of the manner in which these factors may shape the transition trajectories of ill/injured veterans.

Transition trajectories within a Medical Release Transition Framework

While there is no clear consensus on how to define successful transition (Thompson et al., 2013; Veterans Ombudsman, 2017), it is acknowledged that the trajectories characterizing MCT can vary widely, from smooth to tenuous (Thompson & Lockhart, 2015). Thompson and Lockhart (2015) outlined some of the trajectories that may characterize mental health during MCT. In some cases, mental health may flourish, with veterans only experiencing transient and normal responses to the stressors they encounter. In other cases, veterans who are normally free of diagnosed mental health conditions may experience heightened distress in response to specific transition-related challenges, but improve once these difficulties are resolved. Alternatively, veterans with preexisting mental health conditions may find that their symptoms become exacerbated in response to the increased demands they face during this transition. In turn, this may place them at risk of relapse or enduring degradation in mental health (Thompson & Lockhart, 2015).

In the extant literature, some indicators of successful transition include stable levels of psychological and physical health, satisfying work or other meaningful activities, a post-military identity and sense of purpose, and positive relationships with one's spouse and other family members. These are important components of well-being at each phase of the MRTF. Moreover, at any of the phases, these components will be determined by the psychosocial and institutional contexts within which individuals are embedded.

Psychosocial factors

Psychosocial determinants of health and well-being can be seen as factors that either mediate the effects of social structural factors on individual processes or are shaped by the social context (Martikainen, Bartley, & Lahelma, 2002). Throughout MCT, such factors may influence outcomes at any of the phases outlined in the MRTF. A few examples are described below, although this list is by no means exhaustive.

Nature of the injury/illness

Notwithstanding the fact that health status is in and of itself one of the indicators of well-being during MCT, there is ample evidence suggesting that the type and severity of medical conditions have important psychosocial implications and can influence the MCT trajectories of service members. In terms of the *Injury/Illness Diagnosis Process* while in uniform, marked differences in trajectories may be observed depending on whether the medical condition is primarily mental, physical, or a combination of both.

One broad distinction that has been made is between "visible" health conditions, such as amputations or musculoskeletal injuries, and "invisible" health conditions, such as mental health or cognitive problems (Cathcart, 2018; Manser, 2015). Oftentimes, visible health conditions involve a much clearer onset, diagnosis, and prognosis than mental health conditions. In contrast, "invisible wounds" (Tanelian et al., 2008) resulting from military operations may not be diagnosed and treated as early as other medical conditions. This lag in diagnosis and treatment is problematic, given the importance of early treatment in the prevention of chronic mental health problems (Maguen, Madden, Cohen, Bertenthal, & Seal, 2012).

The complexity of administrative processes involved in decisions regarding the possibility of continued service also depends on the nature of a service member's illness or injury. Because of their clear implications on suitability for service, decisions favoring release from the military may be relatively clear for some health conditions. However, it may be more difficult to assess suitability for service in relation to mental health conditions, as the severity and prognosis of such conditions may vary widely both between service members and for a given service member over time. Consequently, service members with mental health conditions may experience uncertainty regarding the future of their career for an extended period of time before receiving a release order.

Experiences during the *Pre-Release Preparation* phase may also vary depending on the type of health condition, given the complexity of the transition process (Office of the Auditor General of Canada, 2012). Service members' and veterans' perceptions of being overwhelmed by the large number of programs and services for ill or injured military personnel during release have been noted in several studies based on in-depth interviews (Cathcart, 2018; Silins, Coulthard, & Lee, 2017). Such perceptions may be exacerbated among those facing serious health problems. As well, service members with mental health conditions may be less willing to share information about available family support programs and services with their spouse or other family members because of the stigma associated with their condition. In turn, spouses may not become aware of and, thus, benefit from these programs (Silins et al., 2017).

Certain health conditions may place veterans at risk of poorer outcomes during *Post-Release Adaptation*. For example, in the United States, veterans released because of depression, bipolar disorder, or schizophrenia have been found to underutilize needed mental health services (Mojtabai, Rosenheck, Wyatt, & Susser, 2003). In addition, veterans with posttraumatic stress disorder (PTSD) have been found to be at greater risk of a range of unfavorable postservice outcomes, including victimization through physical or sexual violence, homelessness, and poorer quality of life (O'Connell, Kasprow, & Rosenheck, 2008; Schnurr, Hayes, Lunney, McFall, & Uddo, 2006; Taft et al., 2009). They have also been found to be more likely to develop substance use disorders, which may further increase their risk of homelessness (O'Connell et al., 2008). In addition, families have been shown to be more resilient to the impacts of physical injuries compared with the impacts of psychological injuries (Gorman, Fitzgerald, & Blow, 2010).

Mental health conditions have been found to be associated with an elevated risk for many physical health problems (De Hert et al., 2011). Conversely, veterans with severe "visible" combat injuries may also be at risk of developing mental health conditions in the longer term. Dutch military members who had sustained a physical combat–related injury in Afghanistan, for example, reported significantly greater levels of traumatic and other types of psychological distress than their non-injured peers 5 years postdeployment (Hoencamp et al., 2015). In the United Kingdom, not only have injuries, such as traumatic brain injuries, been associated with an increased risk of later mental health problems (Murphy et al., 2015), but illnesses (most commonly gastrointestinal illnesses contracted on deployment) have also been linked to mental health problems, including PTSD, years later (Forbes et al., 2012). Comorbid mental and physical illnesses/injuries have also been found to be more strongly associated with activity limitations than physical or mental health conditions alone (Thompson et al., 2015). In a study of treatment-seeking Canadian military personnel, somatic symptom severity was found to independently contribute to health-related quality of life (St. Cyr, McIntyre-Smith, Contractor, Elhai, & Richardson, 2014).

Stigma

Particularly in the case of mental illnesses, stigma may be a significant barrier to successful transition at each stage of the trajectory. Indeed, stigma may prevent the transition process from even beginning, as beliefs about the negative social connotations of receiving mental health services have been shown to be a powerful barrier to seeking treatment in United States, United Kingdom, Canadian, Australian, New Zealand (Gould et al., 2010; Greene-Shortridge, Britt, & Castro, 2007), and German (Siegel et al., 2017) militaries. Moreover, this perceived association with seeking mental health care tends to be strongest among military members who report symptoms consistent with diagnostic criteria for a mental illness and, thus, would most benefit from diagnosis and treatment (Gould et al., 2010; Hoge et al., 2004; Jones, Keeling, Thandi, & Greenberg, 2015; Warner et al., 2011). Concerns about career repercussions are common stigma-related barriers at this transition phase and include fears of being deemed unsuitable for promotion, deployment, and, ultimately, service entirely (Coleman, Stevelink, Hatch, Denny, & Greenberg, 2017; Gould et al., 2010; Hoge et al., 2004; Sharp et al., 2015). The UK Naval Forces and Army showed a significant increase in the proportion of predominantly mental health–related medical releases from 2013/2014 to 2017/2018, suggesting that recent stigma reduction campaigns may have been effective (Ministry of Defence, 2018). Indeed, in the US Army, mental health services use increased and mental health–related stigma decreased over the course of Operation Enduring Freedom and Operation Iraqi Freedom (2002–11). Yet, more than half of US soldiers with mental health problems did not seek treatment, indicating that stigma is likely still a barrier to receiving psychological care (Quartana et al., 2014).

Stigma can also negatively affect the ill and injured at the rehabilitation stage. The Australian Defence Force's (ADF) Rehabilitation Program, for example, aims to provide medical and occupational rehabilitation using a case management model to optimally treat their ill and injured members (Australian Government, n.d.). Transfer of service members to this program, however, may be perceived as a disruption to unit cohesion, possibly resulting in negative attitudes from other unit members

(Dunt, 2009). The Canadian Armed Forces (CAF) Transition Centres provide similar support services for ill or injured personnel (National Defence and the Canadian Armed Forces, 2018a). Members receiving these services, too have reported feelings of judgment and isolation from their former unit members (Compton, 2016). In an effort to reduce this stigma, the CAF and Veterans Affairs Canada (VAC) created the Operational Stress Injury Social Support peer support program, which regards service-related mental disorders as psychological "injuries" comparable to the less-stigmatized physical injuries (Heber, Grenier, Richardson, & Darte, 2006).

It is possible that the stigma associated with seeking treatment for mental health difficulties in the military may persist to the end of the process of transition to civilian life. US veterans with PTSD not receiving care for the disorder in the Veterans Health Administration (VHA) cite stigma-related concerns, such as embarrassment asking for help and worry about the social repercussions of PTSD treatment, as the strongest barriers to seeking care in the VHA; this perceived stigma is greatest among those with the most severe PTSD symptoms. PTSD avoidance symptoms were the most strongly related to both stigma and institutional barriers, including perceptions of VHA staff sensitivity, logistical access barriers, and low feelings of integration (Ouimette et al., 2011). German (Schuy et al., 2018) and British (Iversen et al., 2011; Mellotte, Murphy, Rafferty, & Greenberg, 2017) veterans have reported similar stigma-related mental health care seeking barriers. With the separation of services pre- and post-transition in many militaries (e.g., the DoD and VA in the United States, the CAF and VAC in Canada, the Ministry of Defence and National Health Service in the United Kingdom), veterans may need to seek new mental health services at the postrelease organization. This may be particularly difficult for veterans with mental disorders, who may experience substantial barriers related to stigma, as well as feelings of isolation and confusion, which may lead to avoidance and, as a result, exacerbation of psychological symptoms.

Relationship with friends and family

The impact of military life on families has been increasingly recognized over the past decades (Burrell, Adams, Durand, & Castro, 2006). At the same time, family or other close relationships play an important role in the *Illness/Injury Diagnosis Process*. While support from family members may help mitigate some of the stress surrounding the illness or injury, it may also influence whether service members seek help. On the one hand, reliance on family support may delay treatment seeking. Indeed, service members and veterans identified as having a possible need for services have reported the perception that family members would provide better care as one of the top reasons for not seeking care (Tanelian et al., 2008). On the other hand, friends and family may also enable service members to seek treatment earlier. Failure to recognize the symptoms of mental health conditions often results in delays in seeking mental health care (Kelly, Jorm, & Wright, 2007). For instance, a UK study found that a number of soldiers who met probable diagnostic criteria for a mental health condition did not believe that they had any psychological difficulties (Jones et al., 2015). Often, friends and family are among the first to identify signs and symptoms of mental health problems and, thus, serve as the catalyst for seeking treatment. In addition, a desire to improve relationships with family and friends has been identified as a top reason for seeking care among ill or injured military personnel and veterans (Lee, Silins, & Coulthard, 2017). Ultimately, receiving earlier treatment can result in better health outcomes and a smoother adjustment to civilian life.

Given the complexity of the transition process, ill or injured service members must often rely on friends and family for help with navigating the system. Throughout the *Pre-Release Preparation* phase, friends and family may thus play an important role in helping service members as they prepare for their release. Among married veterans, spouses have been perceived as an integral part of the transition process, and greater involvement of family members in transition planning has been identified as one of the key strategies to improve transition (Veterans Ombudsman, 2017).

During *Post-Release Adaptation*, additional issues may surface, such that veterans may continue to be at risk of developing mental health problems. It has been suggested that veterans might not recognize or respond to the need for mental health care after being released (Shields, White, & Egan, 2009). Again, family and friends continue to be important in enabling veterans to seek care. In a survey of ADF members, veterans who had a probable mental health condition identified their partner as the primary individual who both suggested and assisted in their help seeking (Van Hooff et al., 2018). UK veterans' likelihood of having a mental health condition has been found to increase as the size of their social network decreases, and those not in a relationship have been found to report greater social isolation (Hatch et al., 2013). Moreover, veterans without family connections have been found to be at risk of some poorer outcomes, including unlawful behavior (Larson & Norman, 2014).

Identity

Individuals' social identity may influence their well-being by way of their attitudes, behaviors, or coping strategies (Haslam, Jetten, Postmes, & Haslam, 2009). An important aspect of socialization at the start of the military career involves the formation of a military identity during basic training. This is accomplished by separating recruits from their civilian lives to allow them to identify with military culture and values (Cooper, Caddick, Godier, Cooper, & Fossey, 2016). Norwegian research has provided support for these efforts, finding that military identity is associated with increased perceived occupational engagement and competence (Bandlitz Johansen, Laberg, & Martinussen, 2013; Bandlitz Johansen, Martinussen, & Kvilvang, 2015). One important characteristic of military culture is the emphasis placed on strength, courage, and stoicism (Hall, 2011; Knutson, 2015). Hall (2011) argued that this stoicism, in turn, may result in greater reluctance of service members to seek treatment when faced with psychological issues. During the *Illness/Injury Diagnosis Process*, military identity and culture may therefore begin to influence transition trajectories by impacting service members' propensity to seek care and, possibly, result in delayed treatment seeking. In the *Pre-Release Preparation* phase, this culture of strength and stoicism may also make it difficult for service members to accept any physical or psychological limitations that interfere with their ability to perform their military duties as they once did.

As much as social identity continuity may contribute to better functioning, its loss may negatively impact well-being (Haslam et al., 2009). In a study of former CAF members with peacekeeping and combat experiences, veterans described their experience of being released from the military as an initial sense of freedom, followed by a great sense of loss (Knutson, 2015). This sense of loss may result in significant stress for veterans as they must adapt to civilian life and find a new sense of identity or purpose. Indeed, losing one's military identity was identified as one of the top challenges in the transition from military to civilian life in a survey of newly released ill or injured CAF veterans, with about a third of veterans reporting it as having been very or extremely challenging (Statistics Canada, 2018). British ill and injured veterans with traumatic experiences have described similar feelings of identity loss, including diminished self-confidence and vitality. At the same time, they have reported a polarization of their military identity and increased alienation after transition to civilian life. Estrangement and isolation from civilians, and feelings of superiority and contempt for their norms and culture—sometimes due to a perceived lack of gratitude for their health sacrifices in service—are not uncommon (Brewin, Garnett, & Andrews, 2011). Difficulties negotiating and reconstructing their identity in light of their new postservice life may interfere with successful transition for newly released ill or injured service members.

While basic training or boot camp aids in shaping the military identity, it has been noted that "there is no equivalent civilian camp to assist veterans with successful reintegration" (Demers, 2011, p. 176). It is generally recognized that the ability to find new purpose and meaning can result in a smoother transition process for veterans. Research has found that involvement in activities, such as adaptive sport, recreation, school, work or volunteering, could help injured veterans develop the personal and social resources needed to support their community reintegration (Hawkins, McGuire, Linder, & Britt, 2015). For many veterans, participation in the labor force can contribute to greater life satisfaction and well-being, and help form a new identity. However, veterans who have been medically released have been found to be less likely to participate in the labor force (MacLean, Keough, Poirier, McKinnon, & Sweet, 2016). Having had their careers managed and administered by the military, many service members may not be prepared for the civilian workforce, where they will have to manage their own career.

The availability of programs and services to help prepare ill or injured service members with adjustment to the civilian workforce or other important elements of transition are examples of institutional factors that may influence transition trajectories and are discussed in the following subsection.

Institutional factors

Notwithstanding the idiosyncratic nature of transition trajectories and the role that psychosocial factors play in shaping them, it is important to recognize the role that military institutions can play in easing MCT for ill or injured service members during the *Pre-Release Preparation* and *Post-Release Adaptation* phases.

Policies

The policies that military institutions adopt regarding fitness for duty and flexibility in making accommodations for military employment limitations can influence transition trajectories by determining the duration and capacity in which ill or injured members may remain in uniform. Generally, service members with health conditions that may impact their ability to perform their duties will be subjected to a medical evaluation and be graded against criteria used to define fitness for duty. In both the United Kingdom and Canada, for example, service members who clearly do not meet the criteria for retention will be recommended for medical discharge. However, in many cases, the service member will first be downgraded to allow time for recovery and rehabilitation (Ministry of Defence, 2017b; National Defence and the Canadian Armed Forces, 2018b). Hence, the policies used to guide this process across military organizations will play a role in determining outcomes during the *Illness/Injury Diagnosis Process*, by stipulating the amount of time that service members have to prepare for their release.

Programs and services

At the *Pre-Release Preparation* and *Post-Release Adaption* phases, the availability and accessibility of programs and services can be vital to facilitating MCT. In the United Kingdom, service members undergoing medical discharge are able to access a wide range of services, including the Individual Resettlement Training Costs grant, which can be used to cover costs for training at the Resettlement Training Center or a range of other training suppliers (Ministry of Defence, 2017b). Similar services are offered in other nations, including the United States, Australia, and New Zealand (Gottschall & Urban, 2018). In addition to providing various transition workshops (e.g., career transition and job search strategies) through the Secondary Career Assistance Network, the CAF offers service members with an impending medical release the Vocational Rehabilitation Program for Serving Members. This program allows them to participate in nonmilitary vocational rehabilitation training up to 6 months before their release (National Defence and the Canadian Armed Forces, 2018c). A scoping review of vocational rehabilitation interventions for veterans with severe mental illnesses suggested that individual placement and support (IPS; Bond, 1998), a form of supported employment based on clients' desire to work, rather than on their perceived readiness by leaders and health care providers, is very successful in securing competitive employment (Van Til et al., 2013). This finding suggests that vocational rehabilitation may be most effective when implemented as soon as the member or veteran with a psychological condition wants to return to work, rather than waiting for symptoms to improve. Recent US Veterans Affairs research has produced similar findings (Davis et al., 2018) and the VHA plans to implement IPS at more VHA centers (Horrom, 2018).

While the majority of military institutions offer programs and services to help facilitate MCT, challenges may exist regarding the extent that service members are aware of and able to access these services. A review by the Auditor General in Canada (Office of the Auditor General of Canada, 2012) found that the transition process was complex and hard to navigate despite the wide range of support programs, benefits, and services offered by the Department of National Defence (DND) and VAC to help ill or injured members with MCT. In addition, challenges were outlined with accessing some of the available services in a timely manner because of difficulties with understanding and assessing eligibility criteria. It was recommended that the DND and VAC coordinate efforts to ensure a more seamless process and coordination of benefits and services, and this remains a key strategic priority for the departments.

Governance

In recent years, there has been increasing recognition that the governance structure under which service members' MCT is administered is an important factor in the smoothness of the process. In many cases (e.g., Australia, Canada, the United States), the transition process is the responsibility of two separate federal government departments (Australian Government Department of Veterans' Affairs, 2013; Gottschall & Urban, 2018). Once they are released from military service, service members are no longer eligible for programs and services for military personnel but may be eligible to receive a number of services and benefits from veteran or community organizations. To prevent gaps in services received, it is essential that efforts of the various bodies governing these services be coordinated.

In the case of ill or injured service members, a key issue involves access to medical care. Indeed, an important source of stress for service members before release relates to uncertainty regarding the medical coverage and benefits they will be able to access once released. In a recent survey, finding a health care provider was identified as the top challenge by new ill or injured CAF veterans (Statistics Canada, 2018). In a series of focus groups held with US military veterans with self-identified disabilities, participants reported that the wait time for veteran services had a significant impact on their eventual access and adherence to medical and psychological health care. Specific problems included poor communication from the service agencies, which resulted in distrust and confusion about available services (Lee, VanLooy, Young, & Stern, 2016). For veterans with serious health problems requiring intensive treatment, delays in medical coverage can give rise to treatment gaps or financial strain related to having to personally cover medical bills. In turn, this can negatively impact the health and financial well-being of veterans and their families.

Concluding remarks

The growing body of work on MCT over the past two decades has emphasized the significant consequences of this stage on the well-being of military members and their families. From this research, it is evident that ill or injured military members face unique challenges that may place them at greater risk for poor outcomes in this process. This underscores the value of understanding critical points at which military and veteran organizations can intervene to improve the experiences of service members undergoing medical release. To this end, this chapter has presented a review of various psychosocial and institutional factors that have been linked with well-being during MCT and described the MRTF as a tool that may be used to illustrate how these key factors shape the MCT experiences of service members at different phases of medical release. While it is recognized that this list of factors is by no means exhaustive, it is hoped that the MRTF can help military and veteran organizations be more efficient in developing initiatives and interventions to facilitate MCT among ill or injured service members and veterans.

References

Australian Government (n.d.). The Australian defence force rehabilitation program. http://www.defence.gov.au/Health/DRC/ADFRehabilitationProgram.asp.

Australian Government Department of Veterans' Affairs. (2012-2013). *The relationship between DVA and Defence*. Retrieved from https://www.dva.gov.au/about-dva/accountability-and-reporting/veterans-affairs-portfolio-annual-reports/annual-reports-2-10.

Bandlitz Johansen, R., Laberg, J. C., & Martinussen, M. (2013). Military identity as predictor of perceived military competence and skills. *Armed Forces & Society, 40*(3), 521–543.

Bandlitz Johansen, R., Martinussen, M., & Kvilvang, N. (2015). The influence of military identity on work engagement and burnout in the Norwegian army rapid reaction force. *Journal of Military Studies, 6*(1), 36–46.

Bauer, J. J., & McAdams, D. P. (2004). Personal growth in adults' stories of life transitions. *Journal of Personality, 72*(3), 573–602.

Bergman, B. P., Burdett, H. J., & Greenberg, N. (2014). Service life and beyond—institution or culture? *The RUSI Journal, 159*(5), 60–68.

Binks, E., & Cambridge, S. (2018). The transition experiences of British military veterans. *Political Psychology, 39*(1), 125–142.

Bond, G. R. (1998). Principles of the individual placement and support model: Empirical support. *Psychiatric Rehabilitation Journal, 22*(1), 11–23.

Brenner, L. A., & Barnes, S. M. (2012). Facilitating treatment engagement during high-risk transition periods: A potential suicide prevention strategy. *American Journal of Public Health, 102*(Suppl. 1), S12–S14.

Brewin, C. R., Garnett, R., & Andrews, B. (2011). Trauma, identity, and mental health in UK military veterans. *Psychological Medicine, 41*, 1733–1740.

Burrell, L. M., Adams, G. A., Durand, D. B., & Castro, C. A. (2006). The impact of military lifestyle demands on well-being, army, and family outcomes. *Armed Forces & Society, 33*(1), 43–58.

Castro, C. A., & Kintzle, S. (2014). Suicides in the military: The post-modern combat veteran and the Hemingway effect. *Current Psychiatry Reports, 16*(8), 460.

Castro, C. A., & Kintzle, S. (June 3, 2016). *Military matters: The military transition theory: Rejoining civilian life*. Available at http://www.istss.org/education-research/traumatic-stresspoints/2016-june/military-matters-the-military-transition-theory-re.aspx.

Castro, C. A., Kintzle, S., Schuyler, A. C., Lucas, C. L., & Warner, C. H. (2015). Sexual assault in the military. *Current Psychiatry Reports, 17*(54), 1–13.

Cathcart, D. (2018). *Mandatory career change: Transition experiences of Canadian Armed Forces veterans* (Doctoral dissertation). Kingston, Ontario, Canada: Queen's University.

Coleman, S. J., Stevelink, S. A. M., Hatch, S. L., Denny, J. A., & Greenberg, N. (2017). Stigma-related barriers and facilitators to help seeking for mental health issues in the armed forces: A systematic review and thematic synthesis of qualitative literature. *Psychological Medicine, 47*(11), 1880–1892.

Compton, L. A. (2016). *Accessing mental health care in the Canadian Armed Forces: Soldiers' stories* (Master's thesis). Ottawa, Ontario, Canada: University of Ottawa.

Cooper, L., Caddick, N., Godier, L., Cooper, A., & Fossey, M. (2016). Transition from the military into civilian life: An exploration of cultural competence. *Armed Forces & Society, 44*(1), 156–177.

Davis, L. L., Kyriakides, T. C., Suris, A. M., Ottomanelli, L. A., Mueller, L., Parker, P. E., et al. (2018). Effect of evidence-based supported employment vs transitional work on achieving steady work among veterans with posttraumatic stress disorder: A randomized clinical trial. *Journal of the American Medical Association Psychiatry, 75*(4), 316–324.

De Hert, M., Correll, C. U., Bobes, J., Cetkovich-Bakmas, M., Cohen, D., Asai, I., et al. (2011). Physical illness in patients with severe mental disorders. I. Prevalence, impact of medications and disparities in health care. *World Psychiatry, 10*(1), 52–77.

Demers, A. (2011). When veterans return: The role of community in reintegration. *Journal of Loss & Trauma, 16*(2), 160–179.

DiRamio, D., Ackerman, R., & Mitchell, R. L. (2008). From combat to campus: Voices of student-veterans. *Journal of Student Affairs Research and Practice, 45*(1), 73–102.

Dunt, D. (2009). *Review of mental health care in the ADF and transition through discharge*. Retrieved from https://www.dva.gov.au/sites/default/files/files/consultation%20and%20grants/healthstudies/ReviewofMentalHealth1May2009.pdf.

Forbes, H. J., Jones, N., Woodhead, C., Greenberg, N., Harrison, K., White, S., et al. (2012). What are the effects of having an illness or injury on post deployment mental health? A population based record linkage study of UK army personnel who have served in Iraq or Afghanistan. *BioMed Central Psychiatry, 12*, 178.

Fossey, M. (2010). *Across the wire. Veterans, mental health and vulnerability*. London: Centre for Mental Health.

Gorman, L. A., Fitzgerald, H. E., & Blow, A. J. (2010). Parental combat injury and early child development: A conceptual model for differentiating effects of visible and invisible injuries. *Psychiatric Quarterly, 81*(1), 1–21.

Gottschall, S., & Urban, S. (2018). *Military to civilian life transition: An examination across the technical cooperation Program nations* (DRDC-RDDC-2018-R244). Ottawa, Ontario, Canada: Defence Research and Development Canada.

Gould, M., Adler, A., Zamorski, M., Castro, C., Hanily, N., Steele, N., et al. (2010). Do stigma and other perceived barriers to mental health care differ across Armed Forces? *Journal of the Royal Society of Medicine, 103*, 148–156.

Greene-Shortridge, T. M., Britt, T. W., & Castro, C. A. (2007). The stigma of mental health problems in the military. *Military Medicine, 172*(2), 157–161.

Hall, L. K. (2011). The importance of understanding military culture. *Social Work in Health Care, 50*(1), 4–18.

Haslam, S. A., Jetten, J., Postmes, T., & Haslam, C. (2009). Social identity, health and well-being: An emerging agenda for applied psychology. *Applied Psychology: An International Review, 58*(1), 1–23.

Hatch, S. L., Harvey, S. B., Dandeker, C., Burdett, H., Greenberg, N., Fear, N. T., et al. (2013). Life in and after the Armed Forces: Social networks and mental health in the UK military. *Sociology of Health & Illness, 35*(7), 1045–1064.

Hawkins, B. L., McGuire, F. A., Linder, S. M., & Britt, T. W. (2015). Understanding contextual influences of community reintegration among injured servicemembers. *Journal of Rehabilitation Research and Development, 52*(5).

Heber, A., Grenier, S., Richardson, D., & Darte, K. (2006). Combining clinical treatment and peer support: A unique approach to overcoming stigma and delivering care. In *Human dimensions in military operations – military leaders' strategies for addressing stress and psychological support* (pp. 23-1–23-14). France: RTO. Meeting Proceedings RTO-MP-HFM-134, Paper 23. Neuilly-sur-Seine.

Higate, P. R. (2001). Theorizing continuity: From military to civilian life. *Armed Forces & Society, 27*(3), 443–460.

Hoencamp, R., Idenburg, F. J., van Dongen, T. T. C. F., de Kruijff, L. G. M., Huizinga, E. P., Plat, M.-C. J., et al. (2015). Long-term impact of battle injuries; five-year follow-up of injured Dutch servicemen in Afghanistan 2006-2010. *PLoS One, 10*(2), e0115119.

Hoge, C. W., Castro, C. A., Messer, S. C., McGurk, D., Cotting, D. I., & Koffman, R. L. (2004). Combat duty in Iraq and Afghanistan, mental health problems, and barriers to care. *New England Journal of Medicine, 351*(1), 13–22.

Horrom, T. (2018). *Individual placement and support more effective than transitional work for veterans with PTSD*. Retrieved from https://www.research.va.gov/currents/0218-Individual-Placement-and-Support-more-effective-than-transitional-work.cfm.

Iversen, A. C., van Staden, L., Hacker Hughes, J., Greenberg, N., Hotopf, M., Rona, R. J., et al. (2011). The stigma of mental health problems and other barriers to care in the UK Armed Forces. *BioMed Central Health Services Research, 11*, 31.

Jones, N., Keeling, M., Thandi, G., & Greenberg, N. (2015). Stigmatisation, perceived barriers to care, help seeking and the mental health of British military personnel. *Social Psychiatry and Psychiatric Epidemiology, 50*(12), 1873–1883.

Kelly, C. M., Jorm, A. F., & Wright, A. (2007). Improving mental health literacy as a strategy to facilitate early intervention for mental disorders. *Medical Journal of Australia, 187*(7), S26–S30.

Knutson, D. (2015). *Yukon veterans in transition: Factors affecting post-service transition and reintegration processes of ex-Canadian Armed forces service members with peacekeeping and combat experiences* (Unpublished Master's thesis). University of Nordland, Bodo, Norway.

Kralik, D., Visentin, K., & Van Loon, A. (2006). Transition: A literature review. *Journal of Advanced Nursing, 55*(3), 320–329.

Larson, G. E., & Norman, S. B. (2014). *Prospective prediction of functional difficulties among recently separated Veterans* (No. NHRC-12-51). San Diego, CA: Naval Health Research Center.

Lee, J. E. C., Silins, S., & Coulthard, J. (2017). *Operational stress injury social support (OSISS) peer support program study: Summary of key findings and recommendations* (DRDC-RDDC-2017-R173). Ottawa, Ontario, Canada: Defence Research and Development Canada.

Lee, K., VanLooy, S., Young, J., & Stern, L. (2016). *Strategies for gaining insight to the employment challenges of veterans with disabilities: Final report to the Bob Woodruff Foundation*. Ithaca, NY: Yang-Tan Institute on Employment and Disability.

MacLean, M. B., Keough, J., Poirier, A., McKinnon, K., & Sweet, J. (2016). *Labour-market outcomes of veterans*. Charlottetown, Prince Edward Island, Canada: Veterans Affairs Canada Research Directorate.

MacLean, M. B., Van Til, L., Thompson, J. M., Sweet, J., Poirier, A., Sudom, K., et al. (2014). Postmilitary adjustment to civilian life: Potential risks and protective factors. *Physical Therapy, 94*(8), 1186–1195.

Maguen, S., Madden, E., Cohen, B. E., Bertenthal, D., & Seal, K. H. (2012). Time to treatment among veterans of conflicts in Iraq and Afghanistan with psychiatric diagnoses. *Psychiatric Services, 63*(12), 1206–1212.

Manser, L. (2015). *The needs of medically releasing Canadian Armed Forces personnel and their families – A literature review*. Ottawa, Ontario, Canada: Military Family Services.

Martikainen, P., Bartley, M., & Lahelma, E. (2002). Psychosocial determinants of health in social epidemiology. *International Journal of Epidemiology, 31*(6), 1091–1093.

Mellotte, H., Murphy, D., Rafferty, L., & Greenberg, N. (2017). Pathways into mental health care for UK veterans: A qualitative study. *European Journal of Psychotraumatology, 8*, 1.

Messinger, S. D. (2010). Getting past the accident. *Medical Anthropology Quarterly, 24*(3), 281–303.

Ministry of Defence. (2017a). *Annual medical discharges in the UK regular armed forces*. Available at https://assets.publishing.service.gov.uk/government/uploads/system/uploads/attachment_data/file/627223/20170713-MedicalDisBulletinFinal-O.pdf.

Ministry of Defence. (2017b). *UK Armed Forces recovery capability: Wounded, injured, and sick in the recovery pathway, 1 October 2010 to 1 April 2017*. Retrieved from https://assets.publishing.service.gov.uk/government/uploads/system/uploads/attachment_data/file/633445/20170727_-_WIS_Official_Statistic-April_2017_-O.pdf.

Ministry of Defence. (2018). *Annual medical discharges in the UK regular armed forces*. https://assets.publishing.service.gov.uk/government/uploads/system/uploads/attachment_data/file/723715/20180712-MedicalDisBulletinFinal-O.pdf.

Mojtabai, R., Rosenheck, R. A., Wyatt, R. J., & Susser, E. S. (2003). Use of VA aftercare following military discharge among patients with serious mental disorders. *Psychiatric Services, 54*(3), 383–388.

Morin, R. (2011). *The difficult transition from military to civilian life*. Washington, DC: Pew Research Center.

Murphy, D., Palmer, E., Wessely, E., Oddy, M. J., da Silva Ramos, S., Fortescue, D., et al. (2015). Prevalence and associations between traumatic brain injury and mental health difficulties within UK veterans accessing support for mental health difficulties. *Psychology Research, 5*(11), 613–623.

National Defence and the Canadian Armed Forces. (2018a). *About the Canadian Armed Forces Transition Group*. https://www.canada.ca/en/department-national-defence/

corporate/reports-publications/transition-guide/about-the-caf-transition-group.html.

National Defence and the Canadian Armed Forces. (2018b). *DAOD 5023-1, Minimum operational standards related to universality of service*. http://www.forces.gc.ca/en/about-policies-standards-defence-admin-orders-directives-5000/5023-1.page.

National Defence and the Canadian Armed Forces. (2018c). *The guide to benefits, programs, and services for CAF members and their families*. Ottawa, Ontario, Canada: c, Department of National Defence.

O'Connell, M. J., Kasprow, W., & Rosenheck, R. A. (2008). Rates and risk factors for homelessness after successful housing in a sample of formerly homeless veterans. *Psychiatric Services, 59*(3), 268–275.

Office of the Auditor General of Canada. (2012). *fall report of the Auditor General of Canada* (p. 2012). Ottawa, Ontario, Canada: Author. http://www.oag-bvg.gc.ca/internet/English/parl_oag_201210_04_e_37348.html#hd3a.

Ouimette, P., Vogt, D., Wade, M., Tirone, V., Greenbaum, M. A., Kimerling, R., et al. (2011). Perceived barriers to care among veterans health administration patients with posttraumatic disorder. *Psychological Services, 8*(3), 212–223.

Pease, J. L., Billera, M., & Gerard, G. (2015). Military culture and the transition to civilian life: Suicide risk and other considerations. *Social Work, 61*(1), 83–86.

Quartana, P. J., Wilk, J. E., Thomas, J. L., Bray, R. M., Rae Olmsted, K. L., Brown, J. M., et al. (2014). Trends in mental health services utilization and stigma in US soldiers from 2002 to 2011. *American Journal of Public Health, 104*(9), 1671–1679.

Schlossberg, N. K., Lynch, A. Q., & Chickering, A. W. (1989). *Improving higher education environments for adults*. San Francisco: Jossey-Bass.

Schnurr, P. P., Hayes, A. F., Lunney, C. A., McFall, M., & Uddo, M. (2006). Longitudinal analysis of the relationship between symptoms and quality of life in veterans treated for posttraumatic stress disorder. *Journal of Consulting and Clinical Psychology, 74*(4), 707.

Schuy, K., Brants, L. M., Dors, S., Strohle, A., Zimmermann, P. L., Willmund, G. D., et al. (2018). *Mental health stigma: An influencing factor in healthcare utilization by veterans of the German Armed Forces*. Gesundheitswesen.

Sharp, M.-L., Fear, N. T., Rona, R. J., Wessely, S., Greenberg, N., Jones, N., et al. (2015). Stigma as a barrier to seeking health care among military personnel with mental health problems. *Epidemiologic Reviews, 37*, 144–162.

Shields, N., White, M., & Egan, M. (2009). Battlefield Blues: Ambivalence about treatment among military veterans with depression. *Canadian Family Physician/Medecin de famille canadien, 55*(8), 799–802.

Siegel, S., Rau, H., Dors, S., Brants, L., Borner, M., Manhke, M., et al. (2017). Barriers to treatment-seeking among German veterans: Expert interviews. *The Journal of Evidence and Quality in Health Care, 125*, 30–37.

Silins, S., Coulthard, J., & Lee, J. E. C. (2017). *Operational stress injury social support (OSISS) peer support study: Participant access and outreach* (DRDC-RDDC-2017-L288). Ottawa, Ontario, Canada: Defence Research and Development Canada – Director General Military Personnel Research and Analysis.

Statistics Canada. (March 14, 2018). *Canadian Armed Forces transition and well-being survey, 2016*. The Daily. Ottawa, Ontario, Canada: Statistics Canada.

St Cyr, K., McIntyre-Smith, A., Contractor, A. A., Elhai, J. D., & Richardson, J. D. (2014). Somatic symptoms and health-related quality of life among treatment-seeking Canadian forces personnel with PTSD. *Psychiatry Research, 218*(1), 148–152.

Taft, C. T., Weatherill, R. P., Woodward, H. E., Pinto, L. A., Watkins, L. E., Miller, M. W., & Dekel, R. (2009). Intimate partner and general aggression perpetration among combat veterans presenting to a posttraumatic stress disorder clinic. *American Journal of Orthopsychiatry, 79*(4), 461–468.

Tanielian, T., Haycox, L. H., Schell, T. L., Marshall, G. N., Burnam, M. A., Eibner, C., et al. (2008). *Invisible wounds of war. Summary and recommendations for addressing psychological and cognitive injuries*. Santa Monica, CA: RAND Corp.

Thompson, J., Hopman, W., Sweet, J., VanTil, L., MacLean, M. B., VanDenKerkhof, E., et al. (2013). Health-related quality of life of Canadian forces veterans after transition to civilian life. *Canadian Journal of Public Health, 104*(1), 15–21.

Thompson, J. M., & Lockhart, W. (14 May 2015). *Backgrounder for the road to civilian life (R2CL) program of research into the mental health and well-being of Canadian Armed Forces members/veterans during military-civilian transition* (Vol. 52, pp. 51–58). Charlottetown, PE: Veterans Affairs Canada. VAC Research Directorate Technical Report.

Thompson, J. M., Lockhart, W., Roach, M. B., Atuel, H., Bélanger, S., Black, T., et al. (2017). *Veterans' identities and well-being in transition to civilian life—A resource for policy analysts, program designers, service providers and researchers (Technical Report 01).* Charlottetown, Prince Edward Island, Canada: Veterans Affairs Canada Research Directorate.

Thompson, J. M., Pranger, T., Sweet, J., VanTil, L., McColl, M. A., Besemann, M., & Pedlar, D. (2015). Disability correlates in Canadian Armed Forces Regular Force veterans. *Disability and Rehabilitation, 37*(10), 884–891.

Thompson, J. M., MacLean, M. B., Van Til, L., Sudom, K., Sweet, J., Poirier, A., et al. (2011). *Survey on transition to civilian life: Report on regular force veterans*. Charlottetown, Prince Edward Island, Canada.: Veterans Affairs Canada Research Directorate.

Van Hooff, M., Forbes, D., Lawrence-Wood, E., Hodson, S., Sadler, N., Benassi, H., et al. (2018). *Mental health prevalence and pathways to care: Summary report*. Canberra, Australia: Department of Veterans' Affairs.

Van Til, L., Fikretoglu, D., Pranger, T., Patten, S., Wang, J., Wong, M., et al. (2013). Work reintegration for veterans with mental disorders: A systematic review to inform research. *Physical Therapy, 93*(9), 1163–1174.

Veterans Ombudsman. (2017). *Transitioning successfully: A qualitative study.* Ottawa, Ontario, Canada: Office of the Veterans Ombudsman.

Warner, C. H., Appenzeller, G. N., Grieger, T., Belenkiy, S., Breitbach, J., Parker, J., et al. (2011). Importance of anonymity to encourage honest reporting in mental health screening after combat deployment. *Archives of General Psychiatry, 68*(10), 1065–1071.

CHAPTER

8

Disability and compensation principles in military-to-civilian transition support

Mary Beth MacLean[1], *Ryan Murray*[1], *Raun Lazier*[2]

[1] Veterans Affairs Canada, Charlottetown, PE, Canada; [2] United States Department of Veterans Affairs, Washington, DC, USA

OUTLINE

Military Veteran Reintegration
https://doi.org/10.1016/B978-0-12-815312-3.00008-5

© 2019 Crown Copyright and Elsevier Inc.
All rights reserved.

Introduction

Historically, there have been at least two parallel tracks for providing disability benefits,[1] one for former military members and another for the civilian population (Gerber, 2016). Veteran disability benefits were seen as entitlements for serving their nation and putting their lives at risk and therefore distinct from the civilian welfare system. This distinction often implied a higher standard of welfare for disabled veterans who were seen as deserving given their sacrifices (Gerber, 2016). Today, working-age disability policy has been described as one of the biggest social and labor-market challenges for policy makers. This may be an even greater challenge for policy related to veteran disability compensation as reforms to compensation have been challenging for some nations. Another unique circumstance of military service is that members must be able to perform their duties or be released from service on medical grounds, with no duty to accommodate for permanent impairments. Conversely, civilian employers often do have a duty to accommodate.

Before the end of World War I, many nations implemented entitlements such as disability pensions, health care, and vocational rehabilitation. Disability compensation was used for recruitment, retention, and ultimately to reintegrate disabled veterans into civilian life (Gerber, 2016). As nations set about developing the finer points of disability compensation, many questions were raised. How to authenticate disability claims to ensure that injuries and illnesses were actually incurred in the line of duty? Should there be distinctions between officers and enlisted men in pension rates? Should pensions be geared to compensation for injury or the loss of earnings potential? Would compensation serve as a disincentive to work? Should disability or illness incurred at home be dealt with as generously as cases in which they were incurred at the front? Was the purpose of restoration efforts to return a man to the exact same position he was before the war or to enable him to improve on that

[1] Disability benefits, in this chapter, refers to income and related medical care and/or rehabilitation benefits that are received to compensate for reduced earning capacity, including public programs for the general population as well as workers' compensation.

position (Gerber, 2016). The answers to these preceding questions would have been based on a concept of disability and a set of principles at the time, which shaped the veteran disability compensation systems of today.

Veteran disability compensation schemes were generally developed during World War I and II; however, the concept of disability has evolved over time. These schemes involved compensation for earnings loss and quality of life losses, with disability characterized by impairment. However, the social model of disability emerged in the 1960s as a reaction to the dominant medical model of disability. The medical model is a functional analysis of the body as a machine to be fixed to conform to normative values. On the other hand, the social model of disability recognizes that disabilities are the result of the interaction between a person's functional limitations and an unsupportive environment (Gade, 2013; Hasler, 1993). The World Health Organization defines disability as an umbrella term, covering impairments, activity limitations, and participation restrictions. An impairment is a problem in body function or structure; an activity limitation is a difficulty encountered by an individual in executing a task or action; while a participation restriction is a problem experienced by an individual in involvement in life situations (WHO, 1998). For example, hearing loss is an impairment; however, with a hearing aid many people do not experience activity limitations or participation restrictions. Disability is thus not just a health problem or impairment. It is a complex phenomenon, reflecting the interaction between injuries or diseases which affect a person's body and the features of the society in which they live (WHO, 1998). A modern concept of disability recognizes that an impairment does not necessarily lead to loss in quality of life or earnings and that instead these losses can be mitigated through interventions to remove environmental and social barriers. This is an influential concept for the design and reform of modern disability compensation schemes.

This chapter describes the modern principles in designing and reforming veteran disability compensation and provides recommendations for each principle based on compensation schemes in 11 nations: 9 NATO nations (Canada, Croatia, Estonia, Latvia, the Netherlands, Norway, Slovenia, the United Kingdom, and the United States) and 2 non-NATO nations (Australia and New Zealand). We also examined how disability is assessed, how compensation is structured and identified gaps in knowledge relating to the principles of disability compensation. This was initially explored through a survey and then interviews with subject matter experts in NATO and selected non-NATO nations as well as through a literature review. The aim of this chapter is to provide useful recommendations that can help guide nations without compensation schemes in their development and to guide reforms among nations with existing schemes by highlighting strategies and methods used in existing disability compensation schemes.

Description of disability compensation

The context of national coverage for disability and health care differs greatly between nations and has likely shaped veteran disability compensation schemes. It has been noted that comparisons of schemes are difficult owing to the widely varying social, welfare, and health care arrangements across nations (UK Ministry of Defence, 2017). For example, nations such as Norway have comprehensive national coverage for disability and health care, while nations such as the United States have limited national coverage for both, except for the elderly where coverage is universal. Canada has national piecemeal coverage for disability involving eight different private and public programs. While there is comprehensive national coverage for physician services and acute care hospitals, public coverage for prescription drugs and other health care providers is limited.

In several nations, the rehabilitation and reintegration of veterans in civilian life is mainly the role of government. For example, veterans' administrations in Australia, Canada, New Zealand, and the United States have rehabilitation programs with case managers who coordinate treatment and vocational rehabilitation. However, in the United Kingdom, there is an expectation that the care of veterans and their families is a societal obligation and not just the role of government. This is set out in the Armed Forces Covenant, which outlines a moral obligation of British society to veterans and their families.

Most nations examined have disability compensation programs operated by the department of defense and/or the veterans' administration, while others such as Estonia, Latvia, Norway, and Slovenia rely mainly on programs administered nationally with special provisions for veterans. The United States and Canada have separate schemes administered by defense and the veterans' administration and both nations have multiple disability compensation programs administered by the veterans' administration. The defense programs cover those releasing on medical grounds regardless of whether or not the condition is service related, and the veterans' administration programs cover service-related conditions of those both medically and nonmedically released.

The extent to which rehabilitation (medical and vocational programs) is integrated with compensation differs between nations. Australia, Canada, Estonia, the Netherlands, and New Zealand all have a post-release recovery/rehabilitation programs. Australia, Canada, Estonia, and New Zealand all require participation in these programs to receive earnings loss compensation, while no such requirement exists in the United States. Nations such as Croatia, Slovenia, and the United Kingdom do not have veteran-specific rehabilitation programs.

Most nations have comprehensive coverage for earnings loss and quality of life loss. Australia, Canada, Latvia, the Netherlands, Slovenia, the United Kingdom, and the United States cover regular or active force and reserve force veterans, deployed and not deployed. The Republic of Croatia and Norway do not have reserve forces but disability compensation covers regular forces and conscripts both deployed and nondeployed. In Australia, Canada, and the United Kingdom, still serving members are eligible to apply for and receive disability lump sum payments. Families are also covered by compensation under varying circumstances in Canada, Croatia, New Zealand, Norway, the United Kingdom, and the United States. In Norway, special provisions for veterans were added to disability compensation provided by the state and employers over the last 10–20 years. Before this, veterans received the same compensation as the general population. The provisions made for veterans are more beneficial than that of civilian employees. For example, veterans on international operations are covered 24/7 for every type of injury, service-related or not, and veterans are covered for mental health conditions which are not covered for civilians.

Disability compensation for veterans in some nations such as Croatia, Estonia, and Latvia relies on the civilian system to administer benefits but provide for greater benefits to more recent veterans than that provided to civilians and other veterans. Estonia and Latvia both gained independence from Russia in 1991 and additional earnings loss and quality of life benefits are for those who served after 1991. The Republic of Croatia provides additional earnings loss benefits to veterans of the Homeland Wars of 1991–95. Other veterans receive the same benefits as civilians.

Australia, Canada, New Zealand, and the United States all use the American Medical Association (AMA) Guides to the Evaluation of Permanent Impairment, which was updated and enhanced in 2009, as a basis of the assessment of impairment level. The impairment levels are used for quality of life compensation in

Australia, Canada, and New Zealand and for earnings loss compensation in the United States. The Netherlands assesses level of invalidity percentage based on the War Pension Committee scale which is a NATO booklet dating from 1949. This scale does not cover mental health conditions and to compensate they developed their own protocol for mental disorders which was completed in 2007/08. The protocol consistently results in double the percentage assessment for mental health conditions compared with the AMA edition 6.

Several nations have restructured compensation to a dual award approach involving lump sum payments for loss of quality of life and monthly or biweekly earnings loss benefits. These reforms often involve a greater focus on rehabilitation and reintegration to civilian life. New Zealand was the first to move to this approach in 1974, followed by Australia in 1988 (revised in 2004), the United Kingdom in 2005, and Canada in 2006. In Australia and New Zealand, this coincided with modernization of workers compensation schemes. In Canada, these reforms were driven by several studies and reviews including a report by the Veterans Affairs Canada Canadian Forces Advisory Council (VAC-CFAC) called "Opportunity with Security" (VAC-CFAC, 2004). In nations with a dual award approach, earnings loss payments are either provided until age 65, in the case of Australia and Canada, or for life, as in the United Kingdom. Both the United Kingdom and Canada allow for claims for service-related lump sum benefits to be made while still serving. However, the United Kingdom aims to make these payments full and final with a time limit on application post-release of 10 years. Canada allows for reassessments and does not have any time limit.

Modernization reforms in several countries have recently been reviewed. The disability compensation scheme in New Zealand is currently under review, and the new scheme in the United Kingdom was recently reviewed and found to provide realistic levels of compensation for service-related conditions. Australia's 2004 scheme was reviewed in 2011. This review resulted in many recommendations but none involved major changes to the fundamental aspects of the scheme. While, for the most part, fundamental changes are not being recommended, there have been some challenges to disability compensation reform. In Canada, a recent review of the 2006 New Veterans Charter (NVC) (MacLean & Lockhart, 2016, p. 35) found that key aspects of the design were still relevant today. This review found that none of the previous evaluations/reviews recommended fundamental changes. Despite this, due to pressures from veteran advocacy groups, a return to the option for a pension for life is being implemented by government (Veterans Affairs Canada, n.d.).

While disability compensation in the United States has not undergone any major restructuring, there have been several recommendations for reforms. These include integrating vocational services into disability compensation, providing separate quality of life payments, systematically factoring the effects of assistive technology to improve functioning and medical interventions into rating decisions (Government Accountability Office, 2012), and simplifying the delivery of medical care and disability programs (Dole-Shalala Commission, 2007).

Several nations including Canada, Norway, the United Kingdom, and the United States have expanded financial compensation over the last 10 years. Canada expanded eligibility, raised payment levels, and added programs several times over the past decade. Norway recently expanded coverage for veterans to include mental health conditions. In 2008, lump sum payments in the United Kingdom were doubled, from £285,000 to £570,000, for the most serious disability.

Key principles of disability compensation

Five main principles for developing adequate, equitable, and sustainable compensation were identified through the literature and interviews with subject matter experts. Principles to guide the development of effective disability compensation systems include adequacy of compensation for losses; program affordability; integration of rehabilitation; simplicity; and comprehensiveness.

Adequacy of compensation for losses

Veteran disability compensation programs involve compensation for earnings losses, quality of life losses, or both. In regard to earnings losses, the literature suggests that income adequacy is typically measured by what is known as the earnings replacement rate (MacLean & Campbell, 2014, p. 35). However, there is no accepted benchmark for the adequacy of earnings replacement, nor is there a consistent methodology. More recent studies compared the earnings of injured workers or veterans to uninjured control groups, thereby more accurately reflecting actual earnings losses over time. Social adequacy, defined as income above poverty or a low-income threshold, was also measured in some studies. A few of these studies that considered the adequacy of workers' compensation benefits found average earnings replacement rates of at least 90%, and even greater than 100% in cases with the highest impairment ratings.

Equity concerns in the adequacy of earnings loss compensation have also been highlighted. In the United States, concerns have been raised that the 1945 model involving a medical concept of disability does not reflect actual earnings losses leaving some former members overcompensated and others undercompensated (GAO, 2012; VA Office of Inspector General, 2005). In the United States, a large-scale study conducted in the late 1960s found that while overall ratings generally overcompensated loss, for almost half of conditions losses were overestimated and for another 10% losses were underestimated (GAO, 1997). Some of those conditions underestimated included mental health conditions. A more recent study found that, on average, earnings losses were more than offset by disability compensation (Buddin & Han, 2012). However, some groups were found to suffer earnings losses not offset by compensation including officers, veterans who had a disability separation, and those with low impairment ratings (Buddin & Han, 2012).

In the United States, the overcompensation of disability benefits has been partially attributed to the lack of regular updates to disability rating schedules, despite significant advances in science, medicine, technology, and the labor market (GAO, 2012). As a result, the United States has been pressured to consider individual factors that may impact future earning potential, such as differences in veterans' education, training, occupation, earnings trajectory, or motivation to work (CBO, 2014).

In the United Kingdom, earnings loss benefits are adjusted to provide more for younger veterans in recognition of their steeper earnings trajectory. In Canada, the importance of accounting for age was highlighted in a recent study (MacLean, Van Til, & Poirier, 2016). This study found that younger veterans in receipt of disability benefits experienced earnings losses, while those who were older at release (aged 55 or older) had virtually no earnings losses. Veterans without disability benefits and under age 40 replaced 122% of their prerelease earnings, while those aged 55 or older replaced 22% of their prerelease earnings. Earnings loss compensation, however, is based on 90% of prerelease earnings regardless of age. Also in the United Kingdom, females were found to have a lower rate of award; although the reasons are unknown, gender differences in musculoskeletal injury, risk type, and treatment course have been highlighted as a possible sources of inequity in compensation (UK Ministry of Defense, 2017).

In terms of equitable compensation for quality of life, Australia adjusts lump sum quality of life compensation to reflect the longer life expectancy of younger injured veterans and females. In both Australia and Canada, compensation is based on impairment levels with self-reported quality of life to improve the adequacy of compensation. Recently, in the United Kingdom, there were concerns expressed about the adequacy of compensation for quality of life losses for some conditions such as back pain. In the United Kingdom, where compensation is for earnings losses only, there are calls for disability compensation to also account for loss of quality of life (GAO, 2012).

Social adequacy or income above poverty or some low-income threshold is also a concern of some disability compensation schemes. Canada and the United States both have specific disability compensation benefits aimed at preventing poverty. Canada's program, Canadian Forces Income Support (CFIS), is for veterans who have completed the rehabilitation program, are seeking employment, and are experiencing low income. CFIS benefits depend on veteran's income and increases if the veteran has a dependent spouse or children (Aiken & Buitenhuis, 2011). In the United States, compensation has been shown to reduce poverty and homelessness in veterans (Murdoch et al., 2011).

While concerns have been raised as to whether benefits adequately compensate for lost earnings (Buddin & Han, 2012; GAO, 1997; Tompa, Scott-Marshall, Fang, & Mustard, 2010), the generosity of benefits can be a financial disincentive undermining employment goals and ultimately impacting program costs. The rise in disability compensation costs among former military members has raised questions as to the impact of compensation on participation in work and ultimately successful transition to civilian life (CBO, 2014). These questions have led to various studies which have found compensation to have a negative impact on participation in rehabilitation and work (Autor & Duggan, 2007; Autor, Duggan, & Lyle, 2011; Drew et al., 2001; Duggan, 2014; Frueh et al., 2003; Organization for Economic Co-operation and Development, 2003; Organization for Economic Co-operation and Development, 2009; Organization for Economic Co-operation and Development, 2010; Tsai & Rosenheck, 2013). For example, Drew et al. (2001) found that veterans receiving disability benefits worked fewer hours in compensated work therapy each week, earned less income, had a higher dropout rate, and were less likely to be competitively employed at discharge. While more generous benefits and higher disability levels can negatively affect employment integration, there is no clear threshold at which this effect comes into play. However, thresholds of $800 per month payments (Greenberg & Rosenheck, 2007) and 50% or higher disability ratings (Tsai & Rosenheck, 2013) have been observed in US veterans. In the general population, more generous disability policies were also found to be associated with higher numbers of beneficiaries, whereas more comprehensive employment and rehabilitation programs were associated with lower recipiency rates (Organization for Economic Co-operation and Development, 2009).

While the literature suggests that the adequacy of compensation involves the extent to which benefits compensate for losses and the equitable distribution of compensation, the adequacy of benefits has been interpreted as benefits that are the same as those available to previous generations of veterans or greater than those provided to civilians. The unique nature of military service has been used as an argument that compensation for veterans should be more generous than that provided to civilians. Canada, for instance, has been pressured to return to pensions for life, which the current government committed to.

Program affordability

Today, disability in the general population in many nations is much more prevalent than unemployment. In addition, spending on disability benefits is typically twice as high as spending on unemployment benefits; incapacity benefits account for 2.1% of Gross National Product in OECD nations compared with 0.9% for unemployment benefits (Organization for Economic Co-operation and Development, 2016). Over the last decade, many nations faced with growing disability benefit beneficiaries, and costs, have tightened access to these benefits while improving employment integration to ensure program affordability and sustainability (Organization for Economic Co-operation and Development, 2009).

Disability compensation costs for veterans have also been growing. In the United States, total expenditures in 2013 were $54 billion, almost five times more than expenditures 16 years earlier in 1995 (Congressional Budget Office, 2014; GAO, 1997). The United States has seen a growth in the number of veterans receiving disability compensation and the average annual disability payment. The proportion of US veterans receiving compensation increased from 9% in 2000 to 16% in 2013, a 55% increase, and the average payment has increased from $8100 to $12,900 per year, a 60% increase (CBO, 2014). This growth has been attributed to changes in policy such as the Veterans Claims Assistance Act of 2000 and the Veterans' Benefits Improvement Act of 2008. These changes required the VA to help veterans apply for disability benefits, help with substantiating claims, and allowed applications to be submitted online, making it easier for veterans to claim benefits. Growth has also been attributed to the recent conflicts in Iraq and Afghanistan and difficult labor market conditions (CBO, 2014). Recommendations to reduce costs have included eliminating concurrent receipt of military and VA compensation, restricting the time limit for applications, and taxing benefits.

There are signs that costs will continue to rise with the growing numbers of Afghanistan veterans transitioning to civilian life (MacLean et al., 2015, p. 20; Zamorski & Boulos, 2014) and the higher prevalence of mental health problems observed among more recent veterans (Thompson, Zamorski et al., 2014). In Canada, participation in disability benefits, at 13%, among the more than 40,000 who served in Afghanistan already exceeds the peaks for Second World War and Korean War veterans (MacLean et al., 2015, p. 20). Australia, the Netherlands, and the United States have also seen rising costs related to participation in Afghanistan missions and, in particular, for mental health conditions. In Australia, compensation costs under the 2004 scheme have been rising quickly and were forecast in 2009 to treble over the next decade (Australia DVA, 2011). In the United States, the wars in Iraq and Afghanistan have produced historically unprecedented rates of disability compensation claims. Possible explanations include high rates of PTSD, delayed onset PTSD, and financial need (McNally & Frueh, 2013).

The Republic of Croatia has been faced with pressures to increase disability compensation despite mounting foreign debt levels and rising disability pension costs (Badun, 2017). Veterans have been unsatisfied and have protested over rights including previously reduced pensions. In 2016, Croatia's new government announced that pension amounts would be reinstated in accordance with the economic and financial recovery in the nation.[2] Similarly, before the 2006 introduction of the NVC in Canada, participation rates and expenditures were also rising. In the year before the NVC coming into effect, disability pension expenditures among Canadian Armed Forces veterans rose by almost 20% and the number of clients rose by 11%. The size of the eligible population, however, did not change. There were concerns not only about rising costs but also about poor outcomes among disability compensation recipients (MacLean & Lockhart, 2016, p. 35).

[2] https://inavukic.com/2016/01/20/setting-right-croatian-war-veterans-rights/.

Disability compensation schemes that provide monthly annuities, similar to the ones offered in the Republic of Croatia and the United States, can potentially increase administrative costs due the routine costs associated with monthly payments (Schaefer & Christensen, 2006). Some recommendations were proposed to combat the potential economic burden of monthly annuities in the Republic of Croatia, including improvement in the medical screening procedure, stricter assessment of disability, and more frequent assessment of current health status (Badun, 2017).

Lump sum programs have shown promise, as they can potentially benefit both veterans with disabilities and reduce program costs. Veterans with minimal disabilities may find it more useful to receive concentrated support at the point of transition to civilian life, and program savings could be realized if the lump sum payment is less than the present value of the veteran's lifetime monthly payment and if reassessments are restricted (Veterans' Disability Benefits Commission, 2007). One of the concerns related to lump sum payments is that veterans will not use the money responsibly. Australia, Canada, and New Zealand provide funding for financial advice to mitigate this concern. Many nations have coupled monthly annuities with lump sum benefits to address the short-term and long-term needs of veterans with disabilities.

However, lump sum payments may not reduce costs. In Canada, the NVC introduced a dual award approach to compensation as well as a post-release rehabilitation programs. Monthly disability pensions based on impairment levels, in place since WWI, were replaced by earnings loss payments based on prerelease earnings and lump sum payments for quality of life losses. While the NVC was designed to be cost neutral, in the 5 years before 2014–15, costs for financial benefits programs compensating for earnings losses more than tripled (Veterans Affairs Canada, 2016). This has been related to the expansion of benefits, rising participation in the program, and high rates of veterans continuing to receive compensation until age 65 due to having been deemed to have diminished earnings capacity (MacLean & Lockhart, 2016, p. 35; MacLean & Pound, 2014, p. 24; Veterans Affairs Canada, 2016).

Some nations have also been more restrictive with claims. For example, the United Kingdom adopted a time limit on claims for lump sum quality of life payments. In addition, Latvia has time limits in place for soldiers who were not injured during an international operation. In the United States, time limits on applications for ongoing monthly disability compensation have also been suggested as a cost saving measure (CBO, 2014).

Integration of rehabilitation

Important to a modern concept of disability is that best practices involve interventions to remove barriers to participation in society. One such intervention, used in civilian workers compensation and by military and veteran rehabilitation programs, is early comprehensive management of disability which (1) begins soon after the onset of a physical or mental impairment; (2) seeks to optimize treatment of physical and mental impairments so as to prevent or minimize long-term impairment; (3) removes or minimizes physical and social environmental barriers to full participation in life; (4) employs a case manager to coordinate care; and (5) improves the individual's ability to manage their disability and improve function in activities of daily living, family and social roles, work and leisure, and community participation (Thompson & MacLean, 2009, p. 51).

Veterans seek disability benefits not only because of financial need but also for access to health care and vocational rehabilitation, to identify and clarify their health problems and for recognition of injury related to service (Sayer et al., 2011). While income and access to other benefits provided by compensation are important for financial security and health, having a purpose provides a sense of identity and social integration essential for successful transition to civilian life. Research suggests that people experiencing disability should be encouraged and supported to remain in or to (re)-enter work as soon as possible because it is therapeutic; helps to promote recovery and rehabilitation; leads to better health outcomes; minimizes the harmful physical, mental, and social effects of long-term sickness absence; reduces the risk of long-term incapacity; promotes full participation in society; promotes independence and human rights; reduces poverty; and improves quality of life and well-being (Waddell & Burton, 2006).

Findings related to the role of employment in transition to civilian life suggest that the prevention of work disability is important for improving transition outcomes for veterans. The Life After Service Studies in Canada found that among veterans working, the prevalence of activity limitations at work was three times greater than among Canadians (Thompson, Pranger et al., 2014). Veterans who reported that their main activity was disabled or being on disability were also more likely to report difficulty in transitioning to civilian life and had lower rates of satisfaction with their main activity, life, and finances (Keough et al., 2015).

Work reintegration, an important part of participation in society, is often complex involving multiple stakeholders across multiple systems. Interactions between stakeholders and systems can have a positive or negative impact on work disability. Developing effective interventions therefore requires identifying each of the stakeholders and associated barriers. A model originally developed to describe the factors related to return-to-work of persons with musculoskeletal disorders organizes these factors into four broad categories, namely personal (ex. coping), health care, workplace, and compensation systems (Loisel et al., 2005).

There is a requirement to participate in rehabilitation to receive earnings loss compensation in several nations. In Australia, Canada, and New Zealand, individual barriers to reintegration into civilian life are assessed and those experiencing barriers are offered traditional medical, psychological, and/or social rehabilitation and related earnings loss benefits. In addition to traditional rehabilitation programs, one promising intervention that integrates the personal, health care, workplace, and compensation systems is "Individual Placement and Support" or supported employment. This effective program recognizes that work disability is the result of complex interactions between health and work, and returning to work can improve health and mental health (Van Til et al., 2013). The effectiveness of United States Department of Veterans Administration supported employment programs for veterans has been demonstrated in several studies (Davis et al., 2012; Ottomanelli et al., 2012; Ottomanelli et al., 2014; Rosenheck & Mares, 2007). Other interventions such as benefits counseling (Rosen et al. 2014), work experience programs (Drebing et al., 2005; Kerrigan et al., 2000; Penk et al., 2010), strength-based case management (Siegal et al., 1996), and interventions to improve mental health (Burnett-Zeigler et al., 2011; Humensky, Jordan, Stroupe, & Hynes, 2013; Schnurr & Lunney, 2012; Smith, Schnurr & Rosenheck, 2005; Zivin et al., 2012) have also been found to be effective for improving labor-market outcomes for veterans.

The importance of integrating rehabilitation into compensation has been highlighted in the United States. An evaluation of veteran disability compensation in the United States (GAO, 2012) suggested that "the VA focuses too singularly on compensation without adequate focus on rehabilitation to maximize a veteran's recovery and reintegration," an issue which had been raised in two past commissions (Bradley Commission, 1956; Dole-Shalala Commission, 2007). A previous evaluation also reported that only a small proportion of veterans participate in the VA's vocational services (GAO, 2007). The 2012 report suggested that the goal of the VA's disability program should be to build a veteran's capacity to work rather than only providing income support or cash benefits. They concluded that participation in work leads to better integration into civilian life and other more intangible benefits like greater satisfaction and self-esteem (GAO, 2012). They also suggested that, if vocational assistance increases a veteran's earning capacity, the VA should consider that when determining losses in earnings. That is, veterans should be rated after they reach maximum medical improvement. In 2004, the VA Vocational Rehabilitation and Employment Task Force (2004) reached a similar conclusion, stating that VA had reduced its focus on the ultimate mission of returning veterans with service-connected disabilities to the workforce and stressed the preeminent role of vocational rehabilitation in achieving that goal.

Evaluations and reviews of compensation in Australia and Canada have also highlighted the importance of integrating rehabilitation into the compensation system. Australia is currently conducting a 5-year study on the effectiveness of rehabilitation within both the Australian Defence Forces and the Department of Veterans Affairs, as recommended by a review conducted in 2011 (Australia DVA, 2011). The review set out modern approaches to rehabilitation and compensation as one of several guiding principles in recommending improvements.[3]

Although rehabilitation programs have been found to be effective in helping veterans transition into civilian life, some nations identified potential challenges with program implementation and sustainability. In the United States, GAO identified the program cost and program capacity limitations are potential challenges with integrated vocational services (GAO, 2012). Additionally, veteran groups in the United States have expressed concerns that participation in early vocational services may result in reduced disability payments, and believe that payments should remain the same regardless of increased work potential (GAO, 2012). In Canada, a recent evaluation found that financial benefits for earnings losses are having a negative impact on rehabilitation program completion rates (Veterans Affairs Canada, 2014). They recommended that this relationship be examined and that adjustments be made to support veteran outcomes. The evaluation also found that veterans may choose to stay in the program longer than necessary (Veterans Affairs Canada, 2014).

[3] Other principles included reducing complexity, flexible compensation to meet needs of claimants, recognition of the special nature of military service, that military members and former members of the ADF are supported and cared for, and responsible economic management.

Simplicity

As disability benefit programs in many nations have evolved, often dating back to WWI, policies have become more complex. Many nations have a patchwork of programs, rules, and regulations related to disability compensation. Some nations, such as Canada and the United States, have separate disability compensation programs in defense and the veterans' administration as well as multiple programs in each department. In these nations, the consequences of this complex system have been described as adding to the stress of injured members and their families related to difficulties navigating the system, getting timely access to services, and understanding a rating process that differs between departments and that takes months to complete (Dole-Shalala Commission, 2007; Auditor General of Canada, 2012; Auditor General of Canada, 2014).

There have been recommendations related to reducing complexity in Australia, Canada, and the United States. In Australia, a review of compensation in 2011 included reducing complexity among the principles for developing recommendations (Australia DVA, 2011) and in 2017, Australia announced Veteran Centric Reform aimed at simplifying the process for disability compensation (Australia DVA, 2017). In Canada, the Auditor General has recommended that Veterans Affairs Canada should analyze the disability benefits application process to determine reasons for delays and help those veterans who may require additional assistance with the application process. To reduce delays they recommended that the Department of National Defence and the Canadian Armed Forces should accelerate the transfer of service and medical records to Veterans Affairs Canada. Veterans Affairs Canada committed to exploring the potential for new decision models, working with partners/stakeholders to simplify the process and reduce delays, focusing on processing the oldest disability claims first, and end-to-end electronic enablement of disability programs (Auditor General of Canada, 2014).

In the United States, a complete restructuring of disability compensation and creation of comprehensive recovery plans have been recommended to simplify the system (Dole-Shalala Commission, 2007). To effectively modify and strengthen the current disability compensation scheme, it was recommended that the VAs assume all responsibility for establishing disability ratings and for all disability compensation and benefits programs and initiating work and education-related benefits early in the rehabilitation period. Secondly, to provide a smooth transition into civilian life, the VA should create a patient-centered "Recovery Plan" and provide veterans with "Recovery Coordinators," so that veterans have a single point of contact for all their needs, including disability benefits, and to ensure that potential delays in treatment and services are eliminated (Dole-Shalala Commission, 2007).

Comprehensiveness

Comprehensiveness involves the populations eligible for benefits, the service relationship, and the types of conditions covered. Many nations have quite comprehensive coverage which includes regular and reserve forces, those deployed and not deployed, and often additional compensation provided for families. However, there are some nations that are more restrictive. For example, Veterans Affairs compensation in New Zealand is restricted to injuries and illnesses arising from deployment.

Coverage also tends to be more comprehensive for veterans compared with that offered to civilians. In Norway, veterans deployed to international operations are covered 24/7 regardless of whether or not the injury or condition is related to service; this is not the case for civilians. In Canada, those deployed are also covered 24/7 whether on duty or not. Compensation in Australia was designed to be more beneficial for veterans in recognition that their primary role is to defend Australia (Australia DVA, 2011).

Many nations have seen an increase in mental health claims over the years and have expanded their disability compensation programs to be more inclusive of these conditions. For instance, Norway recently added a provision to national coverage to include mental health conditions, which are not covered for civilian workers. In the United Kingdom, a compensation for mental health conditions was increased from a maximum tariff level of 8 to 6 (a tariff level of 1 reflects the most severe rating, following a review of the compensation scheme (UK Ministry of Defence, 2010) (Table 8.1).

Knowledge gaps

While many nations provide greater compensation to veterans than to civilians, there does not appear to be an accepted benchmark to quantify an excess level of compensation. There is, however, an accepted method for measuring for the adequacy of earnings loss compensation, but it is less clear how to measure the adequacy of quality of life compensation. In addition, it is often difficult to identify the purpose and the basis of assessment methods of various compensation programs. Several nations use AMA guidelines to

TABLE 8.1 Principles for guiding disability compensation.

Principle	Concepts	Examples
1. Adequacy in compensation for losses	• Refers to the effectiveness of compensation in replacing earnings and quality of life losses. For earnings losses, this is often a comparison of the earnings of injured workers with uninjured control groups, thereby more accurately reflecting actual earnings losses over time. • Social adequacy—i.e., income above poverty or some low-income threshold is often a concern of disability compensation. • Equity in compensation, i.e., overcompensation or undercompensation is also a concern. • There is no clear threshold for adequate earnings replacement and support that is too generous can lead to financial disincentives for work.	• Some groups have been found to be undercompensated for earnings losses including younger veterans and those with mental health conditions. • The United Kingdom adjusts earnings loss compensation benefits to provide greater amounts for younger veterans who have greater lifetime earnings losses. • Canada and Australia adjust impairment levels for self-reported quality of life to more adequately reflect loss of quality of life. • Canada and the United States both have disability compensation benefits aimed at preventing poverty. • Australia and Canada provide more generous benefits than those available to civilian employees.
2. Program affordability	• Costs have been rising in many nations due to more generous coverage as well as growth in demand. • Approaches to addressing program affordability include restricting program eligibility, rates of compensation, time limits on coverage, restructuring compensation to include lump sums for quality of life losses, and putting greater emphasis on rehabilitation.	• Cost increases appears to be of most concern in Canada and the United States. • Despite adding a rehabilitation program, costs continue to rise in Canada under the restructured scheme of 2006. • The United Kingdom restricted time limits for application and reassessments for lump sum quality of life awards put in place in 2005 keeping costs down.

3. Integration of rehabilitation	• The more modern concept of disability recognizes that disabilities are the result of the interaction between a person's functional limitations and an unsupportive environment. • Given this concept, the goal of disability compensation should be the rehabilitation and reintegration of veterans into civilian life to the maximum extent possible. • This often involves integration of rehabilitation programs into the compensation system.	• Compensation systems in Australia, Canada, and New Zealand assess individual barriers to reintegration into civilian life. Those assessed as experiencing barriers are offered medical, psychological, and/or social rehabilitation and related earnings loss benefits. • Some nations require rehabilitation participation to receive earnings loss compensation. • Evidence-based supported employment programs implemented by the United States Department of Veterans Administration have proven to be effective but have faced challenges.
4. Simplicity in administration of benefits	• Compensation schemes have become complex involving multiple programs with complex rules and various players. • This has led to delays in compensation and treatment and added stress in transitioning to civilian life.	• Canada and the United States have separate disability compensation programs in defense and the veterans' administration as well as multiple programs in each department. • Reviews in Australia, Canada, and the United States recommended reforms to simplify the process.
5. Comprehensiveness	• Comprehensiveness involves the populations eligible for benefits, the service relationship, and the types of conditions covered. • Most nations have quite comprehensive coverage which includes regular and reserve forces, as well as those deployed and not deployed and often additional compensation is provided for families.	• In Australia, Canada, the United Kingdom, and the United States coverage extends to injuries sustained in deployment and in other service contexts. • Norway recently added a provision to national coverage to include mental health conditions which are not covered for civilian workers. • Canada and Norway provide 24/7 coverage on deployments regardless of service relationship.

assess impairment, and therefore compensation levels. However, these guidelines specifically state that they are not to be used to assess disability. The usefulness of these guidelines is therefore limited in both assessing earnings and quality of life losses. Further research is needed on the various methods used to assess disability in veteran compensation in comparison with best practices.

Nations that have moved to dual award approaches to compensation often include a greater focus on rehabilitation and reintegration to civilian life aimed at improving the outcomes for veterans. In addition, the growth in the prevalence of mental health conditions has created challenges for providing adequate compensation and ensuring program affordability. While evidence-based supported employment programs in the United States have shown promising outcomes for veterans with mental as well as physical conditions, more research is needed on how best to integrate rehabilitation into the compensation system to improve veteran outcomes. An important component of this research may be to examine how best to integrate the systems that influence work disability. This research could include how best to structure compensation to encourage work among veterans.

Conclusions

Compensation schemes in 11 nations were examined, and while there are some similarities, substantial differences were found in the components of the schemes and the context in which they operate. This makes best practices difficult to identify and limits the application of certain aspects of program design to other nations. Instead, this chapter presents five key interrelated guiding principles in designing effective compensation systems: adequacy of compensation for losses; program affordability; integration of rehabilitation; simplicity; and comprehensiveness, as well as a description of modern concepts of disability.

In general, adequacy of compensation involves the effectiveness of compensation in replacing earnings and quality of life losses. Equity in compensation has been a concern as younger veterans, those with mental health conditions, and others have been found to be undercompensated for earnings losses. While quality of life losses are difficult to measure, some nations adjust impairment ratings to reflect veteran reports of quality of life losses. The adequacy of loss compensation can also be interpreted as compensation that is more generous than that provided to civilians, ensures income above poverty, and is as generous as that provided to previous generations of veterans. In this regard, public opinion, often driven by the media, likely plays a greater role than evidence in the development of veteran compensation policy.

One of the biggest challenges for policy makers is balancing the adequacy of compensation and program affordability. The challenge of balancing these two principles is particularly evident in the area of mental health which has implications for both the adequacy and affordability of compensation. While programs can be made more affordable by restricting coverage, greater integration of rehabilitation into compensation systems can lead to improved labor-market engagement as well as improved program affordability. Integration of rehabilitation involves recognizing that a modern concept of disability is not simply an impairment of the person but involves interventions to remove barriers to participation in society in which there is an important role for the compensation system to play. In terms of removing barriers, evidence-based supported employment programs have proven to be effective but have faced challenges.

Several nations have modernized their compensation systems; others have remained essentially the same as they were post WWII. These reforms have been guided mainly by concerns related to the adequacy of compensation, affordability, and integration of rehabilitation principles. However, the unique role that veteran compensation plays in recognizing the sacrifices of soldiers has led to challenges in modernizing veteran disability compensation. Nations, such as Australia and New Zealand that modernized compensation in conjunction with that for civilians in the 1970 and 1980s, or have a different view of the role of government, such as the United Kingdom, appear to have not been faced with pressures to return to previous schemes. However, Canada modernized its compensation scheme at a time when the death toll and numbers of deployments were rising in the Afghanistan conflict and has been faced with pressures to expand financial compensation and to return to the previous scheme.

Perhaps, given the sometimes daunting challenges related to operationalizing the principles of adequacy, affordability, and integration of rehabilitation in disability compensation, more recent efforts guiding disability compensation policy have focused on comprehensiveness and simplicity. Compensation schemes have become complex, involving multiple programs with complex rules and various players. This has led to delays in compensation and treatment in addition to the added stress in transitioning to civilian life. At the same time, most nations have quite comprehensive coverage which includes regular and reserve forces, as well as those deployed and not deployed, and often additional compensation provided for families. On the other hand, some nations are more restrictive.

As disability compensation has been viewed as an entitlement and assessed mainly using the medical model of disability, both the purpose and the outcomes appear unclear. A modern concept of disability, however, would contend that preventing disability is a shared responsibility with society and the veteran. Under this concept, the compensation system would be viewed as having positive and negative impacts on reintegration to civilian life. While a set of guiding principles is useful in developing or reforming compensation, an evaluation framework that includes integration with the labor-market and health care systems as well as full participation of the veteran is needed to improve veteran outcomes while at the same time ensuring the sustainability of programs for veterans.

Recommendations

1. Take a principle-based approach, based on modern concepts of disability, to program design instead of adopting program elements of other nations which likely have a different context in which their systems operate.
2. Compensate for both earnings loss and quality of life losses related to disability. Separate compensation allows for measurement of the adequacy of such compensation as well as the ability to tie participation in rehabilitation to earnings loss compensation. A systematic methodology and benchmarks for evaluating and compensating for earnings and quality of life losses should be developed that include equity concerns.
3. Integrate the disability compensation system with health care, personal and labor-market systems all with the aim of work reintegration, continued supported employment, and improved health and well-being. In doing so, NATO nations should consider (1) implementing policies and processes that make preventing work disability a shared responsibility between veterans, employers, and compensation providers, (2) adopting a modern concept of disability and evidence-based approaches to work reintegration, and (3) evaluating the disability compensation system on the adequacy of disability compensation, program affordability, and its ability to improve the health and well-being of the veterans.
4. Establish user-friendly processes to increase accessibility of benefits and regularly evaluate disability compensation

schemes to determine client experience and to identify opportunities for process improvements.
5. Provide as comprehensive coverage as possible given budgets. However, with a greater focus on work reintegration programs, coverage should become more affordable.

Acknowledgments

Alexandra Ralling and Jason Buss of the Policy and Research Division of Veterans Affairs Canada for research into the structure of disability compensation schemes in the nations covered in this chapter and reviewing.

Subject Matter Experts

Veterans Affairs Canada

Mary Rogers, National Rehabilitation Consultant, Rehabilitation.

Wendy Lockhart, Senior Project Officer, Research Directorate.

Jovette Bouchard-Doucet, Disability Benefits Program Specialist, Disability Programmes and Income Support.

Susan Howarth and Teresa Pound, Senior Policy Analysts, Policy Development.

Corey Miller, Service Delivery Advisor, Rehabilitation.

United Kingdom

Beryl Preston, Assistant Head Armed Forces Compensation and Insurance, Ministry of Defense.

Netherlands

Han Lankhorst, Insurance Doctor, Special Medical Reviews, Department of Defense.

Norway

Line Merete Lileng, Legal advisor, Veterans Affairs Division, Ministry of Defense.

Australia

Mark Tonkin, Assistant Director, Benefits and Payments Policy, Department of Veterans' Affairs.

References

Aiken, A., & Buitenhuis, A. (2011). *Supporting Canadian veterans with disabilities: A comparison of financial benefits*. The Claxton Papers, 1491-137X; 13. Kingston, ON: Queens University Defence Management and Studies Program, School of Policy Studies. Retrieved from http://www.queensu.ca/dms/publications/claxton/Claxton13.pdf.

Auditor General of Canada. (2012). *Fall report of the auditor general of Canada: Chapter 4-transition of ill and injured military personnel to civilian life*.

Auditor General of Canada. (2014). *Fall report of the auditor general of Canada* (Chapter 3)—Mental Health Services for Veterans. Retrieved from http://www.oag-bvg.gc.ca/internet/English/att__e_39979.html.

Australia Department of Veterans Affairs. (2017). *Veteran centric reform: Budget 2017-18*.

Autor, D., & Duggan, M. (2007). Distinguishing income from substitution effects in disability insurance. *AEA Papers and Proceedings, 96*(2), 119–124.

Autor, D. H., Duggan, M. G., & Lyle, D. S. (2011). Battle scars?: The puzzling decline in employment and rise in disability receipt among Vietnam era veterans. *Papers and Proceedings, 101*(2).

Badun, M. (2017). Determinants of disability pensions in Croatia: The role of institutions. *Public Sector Economics, 41*(1), 109–128.

Bradley Commission. (April 1956). *Veterans' benefits in the United States. Washington, D.C.: A report to the president by the president's commission on veterans' pensions.*

Buddin, R., & Han, B. (2012). *Is military disability compensation adequate to offset civilian earnings losses from service-connected disabilities*. RAND National Defense Research Institute.

Burnett-Zeigler, I., Valenstein, M., Ilgen, M., Blow, A. J., Gorman, L. A., & Zivin, K. (2011). Civilian employment among recently returning Afghanistan and Iraq National Guard, veterans. *Military Medicine, 176*(6), 639–646.

Congressional Budget Office. (2014). *Veterans' disability compensation: Trends and policy options*.

Davis, L. L., Leon, A. C., Toscano, R., Drebing, C. E., Ward, L. C., Parker, P. E., … Drake, R. E. (2012). A randomized controlled trial of supported employment among veterans with posttraumatic stress disorder. *Psychiatric Services (Washington, D.C.), 63*(5), 464–470. https://doi.org/10.1176/appi.ps.201100340.

Dole-Shalala Commission. (July 2007). *Service, support, simplify*. Washington, D.C.: US report of the President's Commission on Care for America's Returning Wounded Warriors.

Drebing, C. E., Van Ormer, E. A., Krebs, C., Rosenheck, R., Rounsaville, B., Herz, L., et al. (2005). The impact of enhanced incentives on vocational rehabilitation outcomes for dually diagnosed veterans. *Journal of Applied Behavior Analysis, 38*(3), 359–372.

Drew, D., Drebing, C. E., Van Ormer, A., Losardo, M., Krebs, C., Penk, W., et al. (2001). Effects of disability compensation on participation in and outcomes of vocational rehabilitation. *Psychiatric Services (Washington, D.C.), 52*(11), 1479–1484. https://doi.org/10.1176/appi.ps.52.11.1479.

Duggan, M. G. (2014). *The labor market effects of the VA disability compensation system, policy brief*. Retrieved from http://siepr.stanford.edu/sites/default/files/publications/Policy-Brief-Nov14-Duggan_0.pdf.

Frueh, B. C., Elhai, J. D., Gold, P. B., Monnier, J., Magruder, K. M., Keane, T. M., et al. (2003). Disability compensation seeking among veterans evaluated for posttraumatic stress disorder. *Psychiatric Services, 54*(1), 84–91.

Gade, D. M. (2013). *A better way to help veterans*. National Affairs, 16(Summer) (pp. 53–69). Retrieved from https://www.nationalaffairs.com/publications/detail/a-better-way-to-help-veterans.

Gerber, D. A. (2016). *Disabled veterans in history*. Ann Arbor, MI: University of Michigan Press. https://doi.org/10.3998/mpub.3874458.

Government Accountability Office. (1997). *VA disability compensation: Disability ratings may not reflect veterans' economic losses*.

Government Accountability Office. (2007). *Disabled veterans' employment: Additional planning, monitoring, and data collection efforts would improve assistance*. Washington, D.C.: United States Government Accountability Office Report to Congressional Committees. GAO-07-1020. Retrieved from https://www.gao.gov/assets/270/266681.pdf.

Government Accountability Office. (2012). *VA disability compensation: Actions needed to address hurdles facing program modernization*. Washington, D.C: United States Government Accountability Office Report to Congressional Committees. GAO-12-846.

Greenberg, G. A., & Rosenheck, R. A. (2007). Compensation of veterans with psychiatric or substance abuse disorders and employment and earnings. *Military Medicine, 172*(2), 162–168.

Hasler, F. (1993). Developments in the disabled people's movement. In J. Swain, et al. (Eds.), *Disabling barriers-enabling environments*. London: Sage.

Humensky, J. L., Jordan, N., Stroupe, K. T., & Hynes, D. (2013). Employment status of veterans receiving substance abuse treatment from the U.S. department of veterans affairs. *Psychiatric Services, 64*(2), 177–180.

Keough, J., MacLean, M. B., VanTil, L., Campbell, L., McKinnon, K., Poirier, et al. (2015). *Regular force veterans not in the labour force*. Charlottetown, PE: Veterans Affairs Canada, Research Directorate Data Report.

Kerrigan, A. J., Kaough, J. E., Wilson, B. L., Wilson, J. V., Boeringa, J. A., & Monga, T. N. (2000). Vocational rehabilitation outcomes of veterans with substance use disorders in a partial hospitalization program. *Psychiatric Services, 51*(12), 1570–1572.

Loisel, P., Buchbinder, R., Hazard, R., Keller, R., Scheel, I., van Tulder, M., et al. (2005). Prevention of work disability due to musculoskeletal disorders: The challenge of implementing evidence. *Journal of Occupational Rehabilitation, 15*(4), 507–524. https://doi.org/10.1007/s10926-005-8031-2.

MacLean, M. B., & Campbell, L. (2014). *Income adequacy and employment outcomes of the new veterans charter*. Charlottetown, PE: Veterans Affairs Canada, Research Directorate.

MacLean, M. B., Campbell, L., O'Connor, T., Van Til, L., Poirier, A., Sudom, K., et al. (2015). *Profile of personnel deployed to Afghanistan*. Charlottetown, PE: Veterans Affairs Canada, Research Directorate Technical Report.

MacLean, M., & Lockhart, W. (2016). *Rapid review of the literature since the 2006 new veterans charter*. Charlottetown, PE: Veterans Affairs Canada Research Directorate.

MacLean, M. B., & Pound, T. (2014). *Compensating for permanent losses: Totally and permanently incapacitated*. Charlottetown, PE: Veterans Affairs Canada, Research Directorate.

MacLean, M. B., Van Til, L., & Poirier, A. (2016). *Economic loss: Is it related to age or disability rating? Life after service studies secondary analysis* (p. 18). Charlottetown, PE: Veterans Affairs Canada, Research Directorate Data Report.

McNally, R. J., & Frueh, B. C. (2013). Why are Iraq and Afghanistan war veterans seeking PTSD disability compensation at unprecedented rates? *Journal of Anxiety Disorders, 27*(5), 520–526. https://doi.org/10.1016/j.janxdis.2013.07.002.

Murdoch, M., Sayer, N. A., Spoont, M. R., Rosenheck, R., Noorbaloochi, S., Griffin, J. M., … Hagel, E. M. (2011). Long-term outcomes of disability benefits in US veterans with posttraumatic stress disorder. *Archives of General Psychiatry, 68*(10), 1072–1080. https://doi.org/10.1001/archgenpsychiatry.2011.105.

Organization for Economic Co-operation and Development. (2010). *Sickness, disability and work: Breaking the barriers; A synthesis of findings across OECD nations*. Paris: OECD. Retrieved from http://www.oecd.org/publications/sickness-disability-and-work-breaking-the-barriers-9789264088856-en.htm.

Organization for Economic Co-operation and Development. (2016). *Society at a glance: OECD social indicators*. Paris: OECD.

Organization for Economic Co-operation and Development OECD Employment Outlook. (2009). *Chapter 4: Pathways onto (and off) disability benefits: Assessing the role of policy and individual circumstances*.

Organization for Economic Co-operation and Development OECD Policy Brief. (2003). *Disability programmes in need of reform, march 2003*.

Ottomanelli, L., Barnett, S. D., & Goetz, L. L. (2014). Effectiveness of supported employment for veterans with spinal cord injury: 2-year results. *Archives of Physical Medicine and Rehabilitation, 95*(4), 784–790. https://doi.org/10.1016/j.apmr.2013.11.012.

Ottomanelli, L., Goetz, L. L., Suris, A , McGeough, C., Sinnott, P. L., Toscano, R., et al. (2012). Effectiveness of supported employment for veterans with spinal cord injuries: Results from a randomized multisite study. *Archives of Physical Medicine and Rehabilitation, 93*(5), 740–747. https://doi.org/10.1016/j.apmr.2012.01.002.

Penk, W., Drebing, C. E., Rosenheck, R. A., Krebs, C., Van Ormer, A., & Mueller, L. (2010). Veterans health administration transitional work experience vs. job placement in veterans with co-morbid substance use and non-psychotic psychiatric disorders. *Psychiatric Rehabilitation Journal, 33*(4), 297–307. https://doi.org/10.2975/33.4.2010.297.307.

Rosen, M. I., Ablondi, K., Black, A. C., Mueller, L., Serowik, K. L., Martino, S., ... Rosenheck, R. A. (2014). *Work outcomes after benefits counseling among veterans applying for service connection for a psychiatric condition*. Washington, D.C.: Psychiatric Services. https://doi.org/10.1176/appi.ps.201300478.

Rosenheck, R. A., & Mares, A. S. (2007). Implementation of supported employment for homeless veterans with psychiatric or addiction disorders: Two-year outcomes. *Psychiatric Services (Washington, D.C.), 58*(3), 325–333.

Sayer, N. A., Spoont, M., Murdoch, M., Parker, L. E., Hintz, S., & Rosenheck, R. (2011). A qualitative study of U.S. veterans' reasons for seeking department of veterans affairs disability benefits for posttraumatic stress disorder. *Journal of Traumatic Stress, 24*(6), 699–707. https://doi.org/10.1002/jts.20693.

Schaefer, E., & Christensen, E. W. (2006). *Lump sum alternatives to current veterans' disability compensation*. Alexandria, VA: The CNA Corporation.

Schnurr, P. P., & Lunney, C. A. (2012). Work-related outcomes among female veterans and service members after treatment of posttraumatic stress disorder. *Psychiatric Services, 63*(11), 1072–1079. Retrieved from https://ps.psychiatryonline.org/doi/pdf/10.1176/appi.ps.201100415.

Siegal, H. A., Fisher, J. H., Rapp, R. C., Kelliher, C. W., Wagner, J. H., O'Brien, W. F., et al. (1996). Enhancing substance abuse treatment with case management. Its impact on employment. *Journal of Substance Abuse Treatment, 13*(2), 93–98.

Smith, M. W., Schnurr, P. P., & Rosenheck, R. A. (2005). Employment outcomes and PTSD symptom severity. *Mental Health Services Research, 7*(2), 89–101.

Thompson, J. M., & MacLean, M. B. (2009). *Evidence for best practices in the management of disabilities*. Charlottetown, PE: Veterans Affairs Canada, Research Directorate Technical Report.

Thompson, J. M., Pranger, T., Sweet, J., VanTil, L. D., McColl, M. A., Besemann, M., et al. (2014). Disability correlates in Canadian Armed Forces regular force veterans. *Disability and Rehabilitation, 37*(10), 884–891.

Thompson, J. M., Zamorski, M., Fikretoglu, D., VanTil, L., Sareen, J., MacLean, M. B., et al. (2014). Out of the shadows: Mental health of Canadian Armed Forces veterans. *International Psychiatry, 11*(4).

Tompa, E., Scott-Marshall, H., Fang, M., & Mustard, C. (2010). *Comparative benefits adequacy and equity of three Canadian workers' compensation programmes for long-term disability*. Working Paper # 350. Toronto, ON: Institute for Work & Health.

Tsai, J., & Rosenheck, R. A. (2013). Examination of veterans affairs disability compensation as a disincentive for employment in a population-based sample of veterans under age 65. *Journal of Occupational Rehabilitation, 23*(4), 504–512. https://doi.org/10.1007/s10926-013-9419-z.

UK Ministry of Defence. (February 2010). *The review of the Armed Forces compensation scheme,*.

UK Ministry of Defence. (2017). *The Armed Forces compensation scheme quinquennial review*.

VA Office of the Inspector General. (2005). *Review of state variances in VA disability compensation payments* (Washington, DC).

VA Vocational Rehabilitation, & Employment Task Force. (2004). *Report to the secretary of veterans affairs: The vocational rehabilitation and employment program for the 21st century veteran* (Washington, D.C).

Van Til, L., Fikretoglu, D., Pranger, T., Patten, S., Wang, J., Wong, M., et al. (2013). Work reintegration for veterans with mental disorders: A systematic literature review to inform research. *Physical Therapy, 93*(9), 1163–1174. https://doi.org/10.2522/ptj.20120156.

Veterans Affairs Canada. (September 2014). *Rehabilitation services evaluation*. Audit and Evaluation Division.

Veterans Affairs Canada. (September 2016). *Evaluation of the financial benefits program*. Audit and Evaluation Division.

Veterans Affairs Canada. (n.d.). *Introducing pension for life*. Retrieved from http://www.veterans.gc.ca/GCWeb/pdf/Factsheets/Introduction.pdf.

Veterans Affairs Canada – Canadian Forces Advisory Council's Report. (2004). *Honouring Canada's commitment: "Opportunity with security" for Canadian forces veterans and their families in the 21st century, 2004*.

Veterans' Disability Benefits Commission. (2007). *Honoring the call to duty: Veterans' disability benefits in the 21st century* (Washington, D.C).

Waddell, G. B., & Burton, A. K. (2006). *Is work good for your health and well-being?* London, UK: The Stationary Office (TSO).

World Health Organization. (1998). *Health promotion glossary*. Geneva: WHO/HPR/HEP/98.1, 36 pp.

Zamorski, M. A., & Boulos, D. (2014). The impact of the military mission in Afghanistan on mental health in the Canadian Armed Forces: A summary of research findings. *European Journal of Psychotraumatology, 5*(0), 423–435.

Zivin, K., Campbell, D. G., Lanto, A. B., Chaney, E. F., Bolkan, C., Bonner, L. M., et al. (2012). Relationships between mood and employment over time among depressed VA primary care patients. *General Hospital Psychiatry, 34*(5), 468–477. https://doi.org/10.1016/j.genhosppsych.2012.05.008.

CHAPTER

9

The transition of military veterans from active service to civilian life: impact of transition on families and the role of the family, support, and recognition

Matt Fossey[1], *Linda Cooper*[1], *Kadri Raid*[2]

[1] Veterans and Families Institute for Military Social Research, Anglia Ruskin University, Chelmsford, United Kingdom; [2] Faculty of Social Sciences and Education, University of Tartu, Estonia

OUTLINE

Military Veteran Reintegration
https://doi.org/10.1016/B978-0-12-815312-3.00009-7

© 2019 Elsevier Inc. All rights reserved.

Introduction

Models of military service, societal and political expectations of the military, and the definition of what constitutes a military veteran vary significantly between countries (Dandeker, Wessely, Iversen, & Ross, 2006). As a result, when military service ends, the process of the transition to civilian life is managed differently across nations. However, for the families of former service personnel, many transition issues remain the same, and it is these matters on which we focus in this chapter. The challenges facing veterans in transition are briefly discussed, but the focus of this chapter is on the challenges of transition for the civilian, family unit. We will consider the wider findings of the pan-NATO survey on families (described elsewhere in this book) and will draw heavily on what we know of the support systems and experiences of families in Estonia, Canada, Norway, the United States, and the United Kingdom.

The definition of veteran is varied and is covered in greater detail in Chapter 2. In the United Kingdom, Dandeker et al. (2006) have considered the challenges faced by policy makers in defining who a military veteran is, and the authors identified that there is considerable variation across nation states. Unsurprisingly, these definitions have a providence that is driven by different historical, political, and social contexts.

When considering military families in transition, we will explore the journey of the military family and in general the challenges that they may face, although ultimately some of the support available to families will be associated with the serving spouse's status (for example, are they a veteran, how long have they served, have they been medically discharged, or was their discharge honorable?). There are also a broad range of practical and emotional challenges that will be inextricably linked to the families' experience of military service and military living.

Definition of a family within the military context

In this section, we aim to consider the forms and definitions of family that are used by the military (Gribble, Mahar, Godfrey, &

Muir, 2018). We will explore why these particular definitions are used and then propose a definition that could be adopted by NATO.

In Western cultures, the notions, identification, and definition of the family are driven by pervasive social values and norms, and these notions are subject to change, with a diversity of family forms that are recognized within these cultures. These definitions are also bounded by legislation and shaped by religious views and tolerances. Even within different countries, the definitions of families are shaped by different social and cultural expectations. The concept of family is therefore neither fixed nor bounded and a number of different models can operate in parallel. It is not our intention to enter into detail about the social construction of the family, but an overview may be helpful.

Traditionally "family" has been defined as a group of people related to one another by marriage, kinship, or adoption, stereotypically consisting of husband, wife, and their children, or other close relatives lived with them. Family bonds used to be quite clearly fixed through bonds of blood, sexual mating, or legal ties. Everybody in the family had their certain roles and role-related duties as husband, wife, parent, etc. Family acted as a primary socialization for children as the environment where the child learns basic values and norms. Therefore, the traditional family was seen as community of need, held together by the obligation of solidarity (Beck & Beck-Gernsheim, 2002). The bond of marriage between a man and woman was a cornerstone of family. Over recurring decades, the proportion of family based on marriage has declined and a multiplicity of choices has defined family life. According to the UK Office for National Statistics (ONS, 2018), in England and Wales, being married continues to be the most common marital status for those aged 16 and over in 2016. This is despite the proportion of the population who are married decreasing by 3.9% since 2002 and the proportion of the population who are single increasing. The proportion of same-sex marriages has more than doubled since 2015 (Office for National Statistics, 2018). It is also helpful to consider statistics from Estonia as these are similar to other Nordic countries. Marriage continues to be the most common form of partnership in Estonia; however, cohabitation is becoming increasingly more popular. The last Estonian population and housing census, taken in 2011, shows that 69% of couples were married and 31% cohabiting (Statistics Estonia, 2019). Since 2004, more children have been born to cohabiting couples than to married ones, and according to the OECD (2016) Estonia has surpassed Sweden in the proportion of children living with cohabiting parents.

As the statistics from the UK ONS and the Estonian census suggest, it is now more socially acceptable in Western cultures not to marry to start a family; couples may also choose to cohabit and have children in cohabiting relationships and marry later or stay in cohabitation. Similarly, societal attitudes and legislation have changed to enable same-sex couples to marry. Therefore, the number of families based on cohabitation and also single parent families has increased (Office for National Statistics, 2018).

With respect to the military, studies have found that US service members are significantly more likely to be married than a matched sample of civilians (Karney, Loughran, & Pollard, 2012; Hogan and Seifert, 2010), with the odds of being married about three times greater for those in the military. In the United States, the probability of divorce was found to be significantly greater for those who have served two or more years on active duty and Hogan and Seifert (2010) conclude that " *It is likely that government policies affecting taxes, welfare benefits, medical insurance, immigration, and other areas that vary by marital status may have behavioral effects on marriage rates and marriage timing*" (p.436). Similar results have also been identified in the United Kingdom (Keeling, Wessely, & Fear, 2017); however, in this analysis, women in the military and younger military personnel (<30 years old) were more likely to report divorce than a matched civilian cohort.

This multiplicity of choices has also turned our understanding of family into a more diverse definition. It is no longer the traditional rules of ascription (descent and marriage) which determine the family bond. In this situation, the family still acts in its function as primary socialization for children, but families are more diverse than ever before.

Defining military families

Gribble et al. (2018) undertook a rapid synthesis of online resources from government departments from the participating countries (United Kingdom, United States, Australia, and Canada) and in turn they reviewed the policy definitions of military families. They were able to conclude that "*only the US Department of Defense provides a definition of both a 'military' and a 'veteran' family. The remaining countries define or allude to a definition of military or veteran families* via *policy related to access to benefits or services for those within the military community*" (p.18). The table below provides a guide to the countries that have reached consensus on military family definitions and eligibility (Table 9.1).

TABLE 9.1 Overview of similarities and differences in government definitions of military/veteran families.

Overarching government definition

	United Kingdom	United States	Australia	Canada
Definition of military family	X		X	X
Definition of veteran family	X		X	X
Eligibility for benefits and services				
Spouse/partner				
Married (including same sex)				
Common law/de facto	X	X		
Children/adolescents				
Children (biological, adopted, step)				
Other family members				
Parents (if dependent)				
Other relatives (if dependent)		X	X	
Siblings	X	X	X	X

*Includes recognition of same-sex civil partnerships/unions in the United Kingdom and Australia.

Produced with kind permission of Gribble, R., Mahar, A., Godfrey, K., and Muir, S. (2018) What does the term "military family" mean? A preliminary comparison across four countries. Military Families Working Group, Canadian Institute for Military and Veteran Health Research.

As Gribble et al. (2018) have shown, the definition of military families in the United States is very much driven by access to services, and in turn the overall cost of provision. As such, the definitions tend to be tight and conservative. There is little flexibility for nontraditional family structures and even within the United States definitions that reach beyond the service person only extends to spouses and do not encompass siblings unless they are dependent on the service person. The pervasive conservative constructs of family are being challenged, especially the right to same-sex marriage (*Obergefell v.* Hodges, 2015; see Isaacson, 2015 for a full discussion of the case), and it is inevitable that the effect of this judgment will be tested, at some point, in full in the military context. Gribble et al. (2018) found that unmarried partners are mostly not recognized within the definition of the military family and blended families (e.g., when children from previous relationships are brought into a new relationship) when recognized by the military are limited to stepchildren and parents/stepparents that are dependent on the military family member.

Gribble et al. (2018) explain that *"The United States governmental agencies define 'military families' by who is eligible for enrollment in the Defense Enrollment and Eligibility Reporting System (DEERS) and the definitions set forth in Title 38 of US Code that outlines veteran benefits within the US. Benefits such as installation access, Department of Defense school access, health care through the Military Health System, benefit enhancements during deployment and housing contain more explicit and restrictive definitions regarding the dependents who are eligible for access to their services"*. pp. *11).*

What though, of the role of the broader constituents of the family? There is a nexus of other members of a wider family network. Individuals transitioning out of the military may rely on members of an extended family unit, and this may especially be the case where personnel are medically discharged from the military, due to the greater demands of care. Parents, grandparents, brothers, and sisters may all be affected by the transition process, and in some cases may take on intimate caring responsibilities. Recent research has shown the paucity in addressing the care needs of families of injured personnel (Fossey & Hacker Hughes, 2014) and the disparity between the expectations of coping between injured veterans and their families (Engward, Fleuty, & Fossey, 2018). In the United Kingdom, these gaps have led, in part, to the emergence of peer-led, not-for-profit support networks such as The Ripple Pond (TRP). In the absence of any assistance from the Ministry of Defence, TRP has evolved to specifically support the parents of wounded personnel who have transitioned out of the military.

As military families have broadly been defined in international policy as a function of entitlement to services, the definitions are both reductionist and easy to qualify. However, these definitions do not represent the broad diversity of relationship types and changing views and attitudes toward the perception of family that are increasingly commonplace in wider society. We propose that a broader, holistic, and less restrictive definition be adopted, and this should be guided by a set of principles. These principles also need to be considered within the context of a series of questions that should be legitimately posed to policy makers.

Firstly, when do military families begin and end? This is an important concept as the values, culture, and sense of identity associated with the military are influenced by both geopolitical and subjective circumstances and do not simply stop at the point of transition (Cooper, Caddick, Godier, Fossey, & Cooper, 2019). This is discussed in more detail later in this chapter, but from a policy perspective is it legitimate to determine wheather a military family ceases to exist on transition to civilian life? The question also needs to be applied to the structural composition of the family. As mentioned earlier, the impact of poor transition may be experienced by family members who fall outside of the currently adopted, reductionist policy definition of a nuclear family. Should policy makers be prepared to extend their definitions to include wider family members?

Secondly, some areas of the military are known to have higher divorce rates than matched civilian counterparts (Keeling et al., 2017; Hogan and Seifert, 2010). Who then are the military families? Are they the ones that are currently "married" to the service person or are all of the families associated with the service member, military families? Situations arise where a spouse or partner has supported the service person through successive tours of operation, raised children, and been immersed in the military culture, only to become divorced. Should it be the responsibility of policy makers to consider the commitment and sacrifices (by proxy or otherwise) made by these families?

Thirdly, it is, of course, very common for people to get married or have long-term relationships after they have completed their service career. In some cases, spouses may be experiencing secondary psychological effects from a military relationship. Although far more clear-cut from a policy perspective, the consequences of pre-relationship military experiences may have challenging or even traumatic consequences, with the associated economic and societal burden, both to the individual and the wider society following the family member's discharge. Should postservice families be offered support if distress or relationship problems can be attributed to service experiences?

Fourthly, how does this apply to the military reservist community? Should reservist families be considered as military families with any associated benefits or access to services? This is probably one of the most challenging points for policy makers to consider as the reservist experience is even more heterogeneous than that of their full-time counterparts (Table 9.2).

Relationship between the military, family, and society

Irrespective of the definitions set within the context of policy that Gribble et al. (2018) identify as being driven, in the main, by entitlement to statutory services, military families need to be considered with respect to their relationships with the military per se, and general society in particular. This relationship dynamic is important as it is postulated that this will shape and potentially define the experience of the family through the transition period (Gribble et al., 2018).

In Fig. 9.1, we consider a number of different relationships that exist between the military, society, and the family. These relationships are shaped by the geopolitical situation and a range of intrinsic, extrinsic, internal, and external factors, and the model simplifies these across two continua, "internal stability" and "external threat." Internal stability relates to the stability of internal structures within society and how these relate to the functioning of both the family and society: these range from the impact on countriesat different states of conflict (civil war, internally to occupation

TABLE 9.2 Principles for defining a military family.

• The definition should be guided by the legislative framework of individual nations • There should be a recognition that the family may be fluid and change over time and mechanisms should be adopted to enable flexibility for the service person • Families also include other close relatives, such as parents, grandparents, and siblings, and this needs to be considered when developing policy • It is inappropriate to place prejudicial restrictions on the subjective definition, thus allowing for nontraditional and/or blended family structures to have equal status. Definitions should be inclusive enough to recognize the key individuals, etc. • Family structures should not be bounded by criteria that are deliberately imposed to restrict access to services.

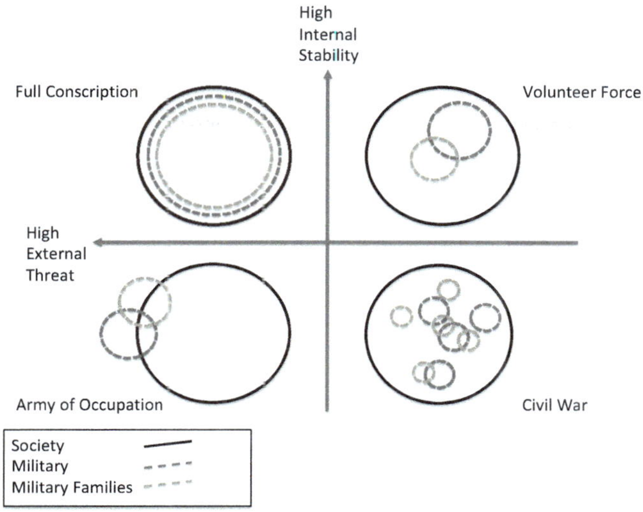

FIGURE 9.1 Military family systems model.

by a foreign power, externally). The other axis illustrates external threat and describes countires that are either at a high state of existential threat or countries who are not currently engaged in significant conflict.

Across the two continua, four illustrative relationship models are suggested and these are affected by relative internal/external challenges. This Military Family Systems Model (MFSM) described in this chapter shares some broad similarities to Bronfenbrenner's (1995) Ecological Model, where the concentric relationships and interactions between family, external, and societal environments effect, impact, and influence each other over time. Bronfenbrenner (1995) considers a number of concentric sets to describe the relationship between the individual (at the center) and other more and more distant actors in the individual's life. The MFSM is analogous with Bronfenbrenner's Ecological Model in that the military family equates to the Bronfenbrenner's "microsystem," the military to the "exosystem" and society to Bronfenbrenner's cultural "macrosystem." Importantly, Bronfenbrenner's work describes an ecological model for human development, whereas our model suggests a changing relationship between existing, but dynamic societal structures such as the family and the military, within the context of a cultural macrosystem, and posits all of these within different geopolitical paradigms.

Most of the countries surveyed for this NATO work on transition occupy the upper portion of the model with stable societies, but with varying degrees of external threat. As the relationship model indicates, these economies tend to adopt either a volunteer or conscription military. Where there is full conscription, the military and, by default, the military family are closely bound with society and there is an intimate mutuality of experiences and expectations. In countries that have a model of conscription most young people (in the main, men) will be expected to contribute a small number of years to military service. Their relative young age and expectation of only a limited period of service means that the "military family" in this instance will be their birth or adoptive families. It is unlikely that many of these young people will be married. Consequently, the challenges posed earlier in this chapter about the size and the scope of the military family are even more important. If young conscripts are expected to contribute to combat action (as is the current case in Israel or historically in the United States during the Vietnam War or in the United Kingdom during the Korean War, Aden, Palestine, etc.), then the families that these individuals return to is not one of marriage with children (see *The Virgin Soldiers* trilogy by Leslie Thomas for a comic example of the British conscription experience).

Where there are smaller volunteer militaries (as illustrated on the top right of Fig. 9.1.), the bond between military family and the military is partial and is a much smaller subset of society. In this example, there are fewer shared experiences as the proportion of the society employed in military careers is relatively small and contact with the military, for most people, will be through the lens of the media. This lack of intimacy and the influence of media reporting and/or propaganda has a polarizing effect on public perceptions. In the United Kingdom, for instance, there is a misconception that military veterans are "mad, sad, or bad" (Ashcroft, 2014), whereas in the United States there is a pervasive public narrative that all veterans are heroes, although the media continues to present a narrative of the veteran as a health victim. Neither of these extremes is truly representative. Table 9.3 below provides an overview of the facets of familial characteristics used in the MFSM model.

Adopting a new model of transition for families

In Chapter 3, Pedlar et al. describe a number of emerging models that explore military-to-civilian transition. For the purposes of this chapter, we aim to explore how the ideas of *capital* explored by the French sociologist Pierre Bourdieu and expanded on to describe military-to-civilian transition (Cooper et al. 2017, Cooper, Caddick, Godier, Cooper, &, Fossey, 2018) can be applied to military families

TABLE 9.3 Characteristics of the different military family systems.

	Type	Characteristics	The military family
A	Full conscription	High levels of existential threat Boarder security threats Stable internal government—often demographic Generational experience of military service Intimate family involvement Most families are or have been military families Young military Large military as a ratio of population Extensive use of reserve forces	Most people in society belong to or have experience of a military family. The relationship between society, the military, and family is intimate.
B	Volunteer force	Low levels of external threat although internal threat from terrorism may be high Stable internal government—often democratic Small military as a ratio of population General population have little military experience—most families have no military links Military families are not fully immersed in military culture Professional military Lower use of reserve forces	Relatively small militaries mean that the experiences of military families are not common or shared. Military families are not fully immersed in military culture and the media drive preconceptions of the military.
C	Army of occupation	Very high levels of external threat Internal government imposed and potentially unstable Military drawn from external threat and sympathetic population Military families are	Military families are generally drawn from the occupier; however, there will be assimilation over time.

Continued

TABLE 9.3 Characteristics of the different military family systems.—cont'd

	Type	Characteristics	The military family
		mainly external but collaboration and internal sympathetic recruitment produces hybrid families High levels of geopolitical chaos	
D	Civil war	Threats are internal Different warring factions including different militia which may or may not be state sponsored Unstable government High numbers of military and pseudomilitary families Families divided by loyalties Heterogeneous experiences	Families may become "military families" unwittingly or by necessity. A very chaotic situation can be destructive to the fabric of society and family life.

during the transition phase. In this chapter, we will be focusing on the family/military/society relationships characterized as types A and B in Table 9.2 above (full conscription and volunteer force) as these are the overwhelming circumstances currently experienced across NATO.

Even using the definition set out above, military families are still heterogeneous in their relationships with both civil society and the military itself. Describing these relationships is consequently complex and using the illustrative models described in Fig. 9.1, these will be explored in more detail.

Within the majority of NATO nations, the circumstance illustrated by type B, volunteer force, is most commonplace. Of the 28 NATO countries, only a few maintain the conscription model—most recently: Austria, Cyprus, Estonia, Finland, Greece, Norway, and Turkey (DW.com, 2018). Within this model, a proportion of military families will be fully immersed in the culture and way of life of the military, as illustrated in Fig. 9.2. A further proportion will live within civilian society, while still retaining links to the military via the serving person family member. These proportions will differ between different NATO nations and will be affected by national and local policy as well as history/traditions, cultures, and circumstances. The approach explored later in this chapter, where we consider the theoretic approaches to transition proposed by the

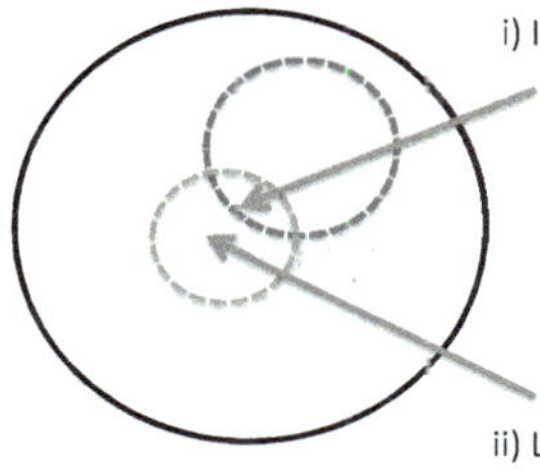

FIGURE 9.2 Volunteer force (Military Family Systems Model).

French sociologist Pierre Bourdieu, will take into consideration the challenges faced by those families that are more immersed in military culture and may have the most difficulty in adapting to civilian life. Using a Bourdieusian perspective, both the military and civilian spaces can be regarded as social spaces, or "fields," with military families immersed in both fields during the service person's military service, with the need to separate and shift into different lifestyles once the family members become a civilian unit. This may prove to be a particular challenge in nations where the military presents as a "total" (Goffman, 1961) or "greedy" (Coser, 1974) institution and operates in distinct separation from the rest of society. Although it is unusual for a military in Western democracies to be totally isolated from the rest of civil society, the inculcation of ideas, cultures, and expectations of practice experienced during basic training or "boot camps" are analogous with Goffman's definition. "*a place of residence and work where a large number of like-situated individuals cut off from the wider society for an appreciable period of time together lead an enclosed formally administered round of life*" (Coser, 1974, p. 11).

The complete absorption of the service person tends to occur during basic training where there is an immersion into military culture. Total institutions in their purest sense are incompatible with family life (Davies, 1989) and no military is completely divorced from the society in which it operates; there is always some degree of interaction. Military families span the gap between the military institution and a normative family life, which can also be very demanding and greedy (Segal, 1986). Both the family and military are "greedy" as they both make all-encompassing demands on the commitment and loyalty of individuals and tend to discourage involvement in other social spheres (Coser, 1974). When a person is involved in two greedy institutions, task and role conflicts may arise. This may pose challenges for military personnel who have an emotional attachment to the family and a legal obligation to the military (Segal, 1986).

In the second, most commonly found example of the military family relationship, type A full conscription (Fig. 9.3), the

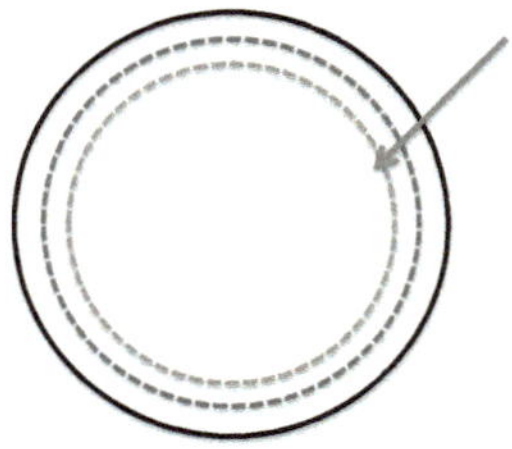

FIGURE 9.3 Full conscription (Military Family Systems Model).

relationship between society, military, and the family is very different. In this example, a smaller volunteer force is supplemented by a larger conscripted body with a proportion of reserve forces. As the military is an integral element of society, most families will be affected in some way, either through family members serving in the standing forces, through conscription, or as members of the military reserve. Consequently, the relationships between the military, society, and the family are very porous and the experiences of military service are commonplace. Where full conscription is the norm, the definition of military families will need to be expanded by policy makers to accommodate families whose constituents sit on a vertical as well as horizontal plane, i.e., parents/grandparents as well as partners. Where conscription is a generational experience, other family members will inevitably have served in the military and consequently have a shared frame of cultural reference, consequently there are far more "military families" in this example.

The following two examples of family/military relationships described in the MFSM, i.e., "Army of Occupation" (Fig. 9.4) and "Civil War" (Fig. 9.5) are not commonplace within NATO countries. However, within living memory, the World Wars and regional conflicts have resulted in these two phenomena and their consequent impact on family relationships.

In the example of Armies of Occupation, the assimilation between the invading force and local population will depend on a number of factors. Firstly, the degree of sympathy felt to the invading military by the indigenous population: are they freeing the population from tyranny or an aggressive invader? For instance, during WWII in Europe, the hostile actions of the Axis Powers were eventually displaced by the advance and victory of the Allies. During these periods of occupation and liberation, relationships were formed (and children sometimes ensued). The subsequent outcome of the conflict meant that (usually) women who fraternized with the Axis soldiers were accused of *collaboration horizontale:* stripped, beaten,

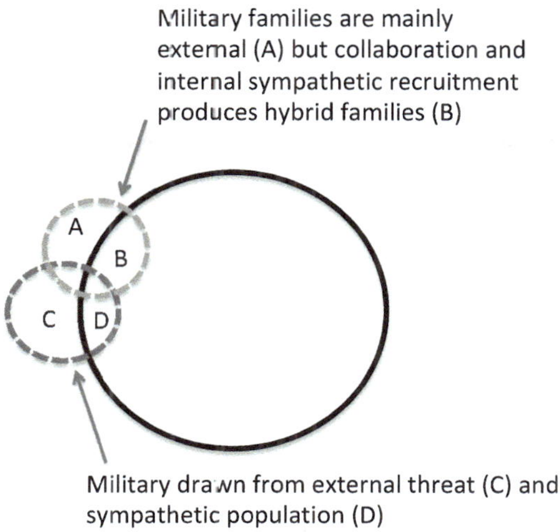

FIGURE 9.4 Army of Occupation.

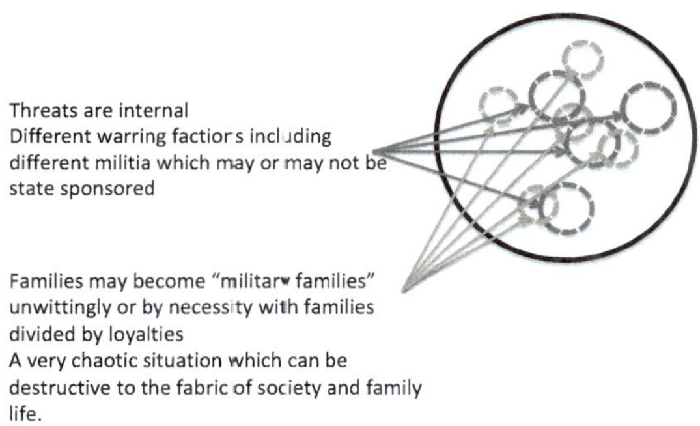

FIGURE 9.5 Civil war.

and shorn. Women having relationships with the liberators, on the other hand, may have been accused of loose morals but were not humiliated and vilified in the same way (Beevor, 2009). Secondly, the absolute outcome of "an invasion" also needs to be taken into consideration: the geopolitical map continues to fluctuate, and new boundaries are drawn and redrawn. Invading militaries who become established, in time, will become assimilated with the indigenous population. The relationships that arise out of occupation and conflict are illustrated in Fig. 9.4.

Military families emerging out of civil wars are complex. Across NATO, the after-effects of internal civil wars still resonate through the Balkan States and are a distant but still-present shadow in the

United States and England. Divided loyalties, brother against brother, father against son, all add to the complexity and bitter animosities that evolve from these crises.

Across the MFSM, the relationship between the military, society, and families is dynamic and changes depending on the geopolitical landscape. We therefore propose that this model presents a convenient framework for researchers and policy makers to consider the role, function, and position of military family, which, as we have described, is complex and convoluted.

Pierre Bourdieu and transition theory

Pierre Bourdieu is arguably one of the most influential of late 20th century sociologists. His theories relating to the dynamics of power and the individual's ability to transfer different forms of capital have influenced the development of policy and practice in many diverse disciplines, including religion (Rey, 2007), geography (Benson & Jackson, 2013), and medicine (Brosnan, 2014).

Although Bourdieu (1990) is synonymous with the theoretical construct and practical application of "transition," military-to-civilian transition is one of the few areas where the application of his theories has hitherto not been considered in any detail. Cooper et al. (2017, 2018) have explored how the transfer and application of capitals from the military sphere to civilian life can aid a more successful transition. The three most common forms of capital are social capital, the access to social and friendship networks; the ownership of economic capital with wealth and associated financial acumen; and cultural capital, i.e., to have knowledge, competencies, and understandings of how to fit in to certain situations (Bourdieu, 1986). The application of these capitals during the transition period, both for the veteran and their families, can be immensely valuable in supporting a smoother transition period. Cultural capital is particularly important in the transition phase, as the serving person and family may be tasked with finding new employment, housing, childcare, and schools at short notice.

The Model of Transition in Veterans (MoTiVe) (Cooper et al., 2017) has been devised to consider the changing, competing demands of moving between the two different fields of military and civilian life and the effects this has on the transition process. It demonstrates the opposing forces of different cultural contexts that have to be negotiated when moving between the two competing environments. While the model was originally devised to understand transition through the lens of the veterans, we propose to use the MoTiVe model to consider the issues facing families during transition. Fig. 9.6 below illustrates the model.

In the original papers (Cooper et al., 2017; 2018), the MoTiVe model was proposed as a way to consider the factors that a service person faces when they are immersed within their service role and away from their civilian responsibilities. By looking at the model from a new perspective, we can consider the issues faced by families and spouses of serving personnel.

Although this chapter relates to the challenges faced by families as serving personnel make the transition from a military role to becoming a civilian, it is very important to remember that frequent, often daily, microtransitions are an inevitable feature of military family life. Once they are off duty (or come back from training or an operational tour) and return to their family, serving personnel need to negotiate the subtle but complex change in relationship dynamics, and the many differences between the military and the home environment. The physical situation of the family (in military quarters or civilian housing) and the engagement of the family with military culture, etc., will all impact on this negotiation. This dynamic is described in some detail in the MFSM above, especially Fig. 9.2. It is, though, the application of the theories of Bourdieu that we believe help to describe the complexity of these transitions with more clarity.

For the service person, the separation of civilian and military roles is necessary to successfully negotiate the dichotomy between life in uniform and the responsibilities that may arise as a parent or

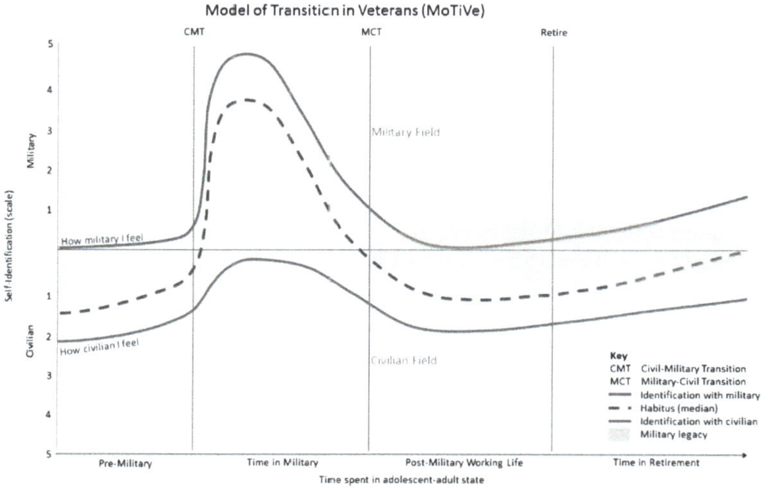

FIGURE 9.6 The Model of Transition in Veterans (MoTiVe).

partner. During service life, the movement between fields is as important for the family as for the service person, particularly when living within the military environment "behind the wire." To transition successfully, it requires the service person to return to the norms of day-to-day family life. Bourdieu (1990) referred to this way of living subconsciously as the "doxa." In a similar vein, a military spouse has to renegotiate the roles within the household and norms of a returning family member.

Fig. 9.6 illustrates the highs and lows of personal identification that can be experienced by the service person. Their commitment and engagement to their military responsibilities is countered by their material disengagement with their domestic obligations. We would suggest that as the service person is more immersed in their working life and by its nature, often without contact with the family, the onus is placed on the spouse to maintain the family unit. On returning home on leave, responsibility for certain roles within the family may need to be renegotiated, as the spouse will have continued to run day-to-day living, including childcare, their own employment, and running a household. Bourdieu (2005) describes social spaces, which include work and the home, as "fields." Fields maintain their own sets of power, for example, the hierarchal nature of the military brings inherent power to certain ranks, but would carry no weight in the civilian home. If the position of family members is considered the responsibility of the family, the maintenance of family life falls completely with the civilian spouse or responsible family members, potentially including young carers, parents, or others. Different sets of rules therefore exist within the military field and familial home. As discussed in the following section, these rules need to be negotiated on a permanent basis on transition, which affects not only the veteran but all members of the family and in particular the spouse who may have assumed a larger role in the absence of the partner.

A further area of family life that is not clearly understood is the role of parents of service personnel during transition. Families of service people are more likely to have involvement with the military in countries within the full conscription model (Fig. 9.3) as a characteristic of this model is that the military and family are often connected. Parental involvement in the transition process will be particularly pertinent to those who joined the armed forces at a young age, who were in the family home until conscription, and are returning to the family home following discharge. As noted earlier in this chapter, the full conscription model is more likely to have intergenerational service within the family, with shared experiences. Families with intergenerational service are likely to have a stronger sense of military legacy (Cooper et al., 2018). The military legacy is a "looking back" at peak experiences that provides an enduring attachment to the military across the life span. The legacy is likely to be more embedded in families who have had cultural ties to the military over successive generations. In terms of returning to the family home, it is likely that, rather than the veteran him/herself, the family will need a greater adaption of the habitus, as the person returning home not only brings a military legacy but it is also inevitable that he or she will have transitioned into adulthood since leaving the home to join the armed forces (another significant adjustment that is explored in some detail by Hogan and Astone,1986). The family will need to renegotiate the individual's maturation and needs during the transition process in a different way from an older service person or one returning to a partner or spouse. As with all transition processes, the military habitus needs to be adjusted for successful transition to occur (Cooper et al., 2018).

Military families and transition

On transitioning out of the military, the service person moves back into the civilian field, while the family has to negotiate their return, on both practical and emotionally levels. The family must also face their own adjustments to a new way of living at the same time as also supporting the veteran to successfully surmount any challenges they may face during the transition journey. Across NATO states, there are a range of differences in social and health care systems of provision, and the types of support that are generally available for veterans. In this section, we will explore the provision that is available for service families during and after the transition process.

Some of the NATO states who contributed to the development of this chapter have universal support for all citizens in the form of access to free health care and education (for example, Estonia, Norway, and the United Kingdom). In the United Kingdom, for instance, the Armed Forces Covenant states that no veteran or his family should be disadvantaged by service to their country (Ministry of Defence, 2011). This includes the right to equal access to health care and education services on return to civilian life, particularly for those who have been living within the armed forces community "behind the wire." Findings from an evaluation of a UK intervention model supporting veterans in the criminal justice system (Fossey, Cooper, Godier, & Cooper, 2017) highlighted the paucity of understanding as to how former service personnel and their families access the types of support that are readily available for civilians. Additionally, the study identified that hypermasculine traits among veterans that contributed to delayed and often unhealthy help-seeking behaviors (Cooper, 2019), findings not dissimilar to those identified in research within the United States (Hoge et al., 2004; Jakupak, Blais, Grossbard, Garcia, & Okiishi, 2014). Ironically, in some NATO states, the abundance of organizations with a specific remit to support veterans and families may have an overwhelming and confusing effect, which is compounded by a deficit in interagency collaboration and coordination (FiMT, 2013). Additionally, where the health and social needs of service families are met by the military system, a basic knowledge of the idiosyncrasies and vagaries of civilian health and social care may be lacking (Cooper, Andrews & Fossey, 2016, p. 68). This may include seemingly obvious commonplace occurrences from waiting lists to see a GP, to the necessity to pay utility bills or local area taxes.

When partners are away on duty, spouses have to compensate for the loss both practical and emotional support of their partner. For example, if a soldier is on exercise and not in contact with his family,the partner will be responsible for all issues relating to the family and home, including care and schooling of children, paying of bills, and general day-to-day living arrangements, potentially while holding down a job themselves. That is a burden to take emotionally and physically, at a time when the spouses are on their own and can only rely on themselves or their support network. Spouses establish their own rules to ensure that everyday life continues to run smoothly for the family, in the absence of the partner. In the absence of the service person, the family gets used to alternative living arrangements. The dynamic further changes when the service person returns and moves from the military field back into the civilian field and has to renegotiate family life. Having to intermittently adapt back into new rules and ways of living for both partners can inevitably cause conflict and lead to family disruption. Bourdieu and Passeron (1977) describe this mismatch and tension between two competing fields as hysteresis. Not only does the service person need to relearn how to live within the civilian field but also the adaption and restructuring of the family unit on a permanent basis. Therefore, the family life has to be renegotiated again.

Bergman, Burdett, and Greenberg (2014) argue that during transition, a "reverse culture shock" is experienced by some service personnel. This suggests that a time of adjustment into civilian life is necessary, both personally and to navigate the civilian environment. It is overlooked that the wider family also encounters these issues, particularly if the family has relocated on postings away from the wider family and friends support network. It will regularly require the spouse to organize work, schooling, and accommodation needs, also evoking a new or renewed engagement within new fields in civilian life. The spouse has to acquire cultural capital regarding information in the civilian field and social capital through new networks. Within the home, the rules of the habitus will change as the family dynamic adapts to the service person fully engaged in the family home on a permanent basis. The spouse and their family are often overlooked as key actors who also undergo fundamental changes in their lifestyle at this stage in the transition process.

What support is available for families in transition?

The NATO Research Panel (HFM-RTG 263) undertook a pan-NATO survey that is described in detail in its accompanying NATO technical report. One of the areas of focus of the survey was the assistance provided to military families during military-to-civilian transition. Table 9.4 is an overview of the responses to that survey.

Although there are a range of services available for families across NATO countries, very few, if any, were specifically established to help families cope with some of the more difficult challenges of transition, as described earlier in this chapter. Although a number of countries also indicated that there was evaluation of the services available, this tended to be developmental or specific research as opposed to routine monitoring or evaluation of the effectiveness and impact of the services provided.

In North America, for instance, there are currently programs of work to better understand the well-being of service personnel through the transition phase. The Life after Service Study (LASS) in Canada and the Veteran Metric Initiative (TVMI) in the United States including the development of a well-being inventory (Vogt et al., 2018), aim to understand well-being better and gather information on social relationships (TVMI) and subjective reports of family's experiences of transition (LASS). *"LASS 2016 included new content on families. When asked about the effect their release had on the family, most Veterans reported that the transition was easy for their partner (57%) and their children (60%). However, 28% of Veterans indicated their partners had difficulty with their release, and 17% reported their children had difficulty with their release"* (Veterans Affairs Canada, 2018). Neither of these initiatives currently directly asks family members about their experiences of transition and the VAC figures on ease of transition for families, as reported by the veteran, have not been validated with the families themselves. Understanding the well-being of Canadian

TABLE 9.4 Overview of findings of pan-NATO survey.

Type of family support	Country where this support is available	Is there any evaluation of these services?
Caregiver support	United States	√
	New Zealand	√
	Canada	
Case management/care coordination	United States	√
	New Zealand	
	Netherlands	
	Australia	
	Canada	
Counseling	United States	√
	New Zealand	√
	Netherlands	
	Australia	
	Slovenia	
	Estonia	
	Canada	
	Norway	
Disability compensation	United States	√
Education assistance	United States	√
	New Zealand	√
Employment assistance	United States	√
	Slovenia	
	United Kingdom	√
	Canada	
Information and referral	United States	√
	New Zealand	√
	Netherlands	
	Australia	√
	United Kingdom	√
	Canada	

TABLE 9.4 Overview of findings of pan-NATO survey.—cont'd

Type of family support	Country where this support is available	Is there any evaluation of these services?
Home care	United States	√
	New Zealand	
	Canada	√
Housing	United States	√
	New Zealand	√
	United Kingdom	√
Mental health and substance abuse	United States	√
	New Zealand	√
	Australia	√
	Slovenia	
	Estonia	
	Canada	
Psychoeducational group programs	Australia	√
Physical health	United States	√
	Netherlands	
Transportation support	United States	√
	Canada	
Family peer support	Canada	

personnel and veterans remains a priority for VAC and the Canadian DoD (Thompson et al., 2016) and this is reflected in Chapter 3 that considers different models and approaches to transition.

In the United Kingdom, the Well-Being Inventory (WBI), developed by Vogt and colleagues in the US Department for Veterans Affairs (Vogt et al., 2018), is currently being adapted for use in collecting important information about the impact of services for veterans and their families. This work is being designed to collect valuable well-being data directly from family members, as well as veterans, helping to reduce reporting bias. Although this work is not currently focused on transition, the framework for data collection that is in development could be modified for this purpose.

The Australian Department for Veterans Affairs are undertaking a comprehensive Transition and Wellbeing Research Programme

(Australian Government DVA, 2018) that incorporates a family well-being study (Australian Government AIFS, 2018). A total of 1448 surveys were completed, which will be complemented by a qualitative component. The study will investigate the impact of military service on the well-being of families of serving and ex-service personnel. The report is due imminently and it is hoped that this research will help to inform the following areas:

- The well-being of families after transition from the Australian Defence Force (ADF) to civilian life and how it compares with the well-being of families of current serving members;
- Some of the challenges experienced by families of transitioned ADF members and how these compare to families of current serving members;
- What military families do to get help during challenging times and what they actually find helpful; and
- The relationship between the well-being of families and ADF members, current and ex-service.

The findings of the Australian DVA research may help to shape the way future services for veterans and their families are structured, irrespective of whether the findings show positive outcomes, and these outcomes should be considered in the international context.

In a number of countries surveyed, psychological support was offered to families both in service and through the transition to civilian life. However, this support tended to be restricted to families who had experienced vicarious or secondary trauma as a result of the service person's military experience. As Table 9.3 indicates, a number of nations offer psychological interventions, but these were not signposted toward providing assistance with the management of the potential stresses involved in the transition process. As the VAC figures indicate, 28% of veterans who were surveyed in the 2016 Life After Service Survey reported that their partners had difficulty with transition back to civilian life.

The Australian DVA's 2014 Vietnam Veterans Family Study examined the physical, mental, and social health of Vietnam veterans and their families, covering a broad range of health outcomes for these people. Over 27,000 people participated in the studies, comprising veterans, partners, and their children.

The study found that the majority of sons and daughters born to Vietnam veterans are leading healthy and productive lives. However, analysis found that the families of Australia's Vietnam veterans are more likely to have significant emotional, physical, and social problems when compared with families of those who served in that era who did not go to Vietnam (Commonwealth of Australia, 2014; Cretchley,

Laffan, Ross, & Treloar, 2014; Forrest, Edwards, & Daraganova, 2014a, 2014b), although other evidence has concluded that there is no difference in risk taking between civilian and military children and the Australian Defence Force (Australian Government DVA, 2015). In a US study, parental distress and cumulative length of parental combat–related deployments during the child's lifetime independently predicted increased child depression and externalizing symptoms. Although behavioral adjustment and depression levels were comparable to community norms, anxiety was significantly elevated in these children (Lester et al., 2010). It is unclear as to the impact of military-to-civilian transition on these findings, but the military service itself appears to have a deleterious impact on families post-transition. The findings of this research highlight the need to better understand the longitudinal impact of military operations on families.

Research gaps

Very little is known about the experiences of military families during the transition process. While there has been international research investigating the impact of military service on families, notwithstanding the expected Australian DVA research, there has been very little on the impact of military-to-civilian transition and the types of services or inputs that may benefit military families during this period. There is emerging research in Canada, with the LASS and in the United States with the development of the Veterans Measurement Initiative (TVMI). Although very welcome, this work has, to date, relied on service personnel and veterans reporting on their perceptions of how families cope.

In short, very little is currently known about how military families cope during the transition period and what could be done to improve outcomes for this important but poorly understood cohort. Furthermore, the impact of the experiences of military families during service and through transition need to be better understood. We do not know if families struggle during the transition process and what effect military culture has on their abilities to function.

Conclusions and recommendations

In this chapter, we argue that military families that are fully immersed in military culture may find transition to civilian life more of a challenge. We propose a model of understanding the relationships between the military, society, and military families. Using the sociological ideas of Bourdieu, we have explored the complexity of transition and the effect a military legacy might have on military families after transition. We have used the MoTiVE model at Fig. 9.6 to investigate how a veteran may be pulled between the competing demands of the military and civilian fields during service and the need for a renegotiation of the habitus, both for the veteran and his family, as they adapt to the veteran permanently living back in the familial home.

The services that are available for military families are broad and differ between countries. These services though do not focus on transition, except where spouses are invited to engage in their service partners "transition interview."

Finally, and importantly, military families tend to be defined by entitlement to services, rather than as a reflection of family life in the 21st century. Militaries, by and large, appear to adopt a conservative definition of families which may prove discriminatory for those who chose not to adopt a traditional model of family life.

There are a number of recommendations that fall out of this chapter:

Recommendation 1: Not enough is known about the transition experiences of military families and NATO nations should consider funding research in this important area.
Recommendation 2: NATO nations should consider adopting the set of principles set out in this chapter when defining military families.
Recommendation 3: Following the outcomes of any research, military families in NATO nations should be consulted on and help to develop any programs or interventions.

References

Ashcroft, M. (2014). *The veterans' transition review.* Retrieved from http://www.veteranstransition.co.uk/.

Australian Government, Australian Institute of Family Studies. (2018). *Family wellbeing study.* Retrieved from https://aifs.gov.au/projects/family-wellbeing-study.

Australian Government, & Department for Veteran Affairs. (2015). *Summary report what is the prevalence of risk-taking behaviours in the children of former or current military personnel? Summary of the rapid evidence assessment august 2015.* Retrieved from www.evidencecompass.dva.gov.au.

Australian Government, & Department for Veteran Affairs. (2018). *Transition and wellbeing research programme.* Retrieved from https://www.dva.gov.au/health-and-wellbeing/research-and-development/social-research/transition-and-wellbeing-research.

Beevor, A. (2009). *An ugly carnival.* retrieved from: https://www.theguardian.com/lifeandstyle/2009/jun/05/women-victims-d-day-landings-second-world-war.

Beck, U, & Beck-Gernsheim, E (2002). *Institutionalized individualism and its social and political consequences*. Ann Arbor: University of Michigan Press.

Benson, M., & Jackson, E. (2013). Place-making and place maintenance: Practices of places and belonging among the middle classes. *Sociology, 47*(4), 793–804.

Bergman, B., Burdett, H., & Greenberg, N. (2014). Service life and beyond – institution or culture? *The RUSI Journal, 159*(5), 60–68.

Bourdieu, P. (1986). The forms of capital. In J. Richardson (Ed.), *The handbook of theory and Research for the sociology of education*. USA: Greenwood.

Bourdieu, P. (1990). *The logic of practice*. Cambridge: Polity Press.

Bourdieu, P. (2005). *The social structures of the economy*. Cambridge: Polity Press.

Bourdieu, P., & Passeron, J.-C. (1977) *Reproduction in education, society and culture*. London: Sage.

Bronfenbrenner, U. (1995). The bioecological model from a lifecourse perspective. In P. Moen, et al. (Eds.), *Examining lives in context*. USA: Washington: American Psychological Association.

Brosnan, C. (2014). Medical education and Pierre Bourdieu. In W. Cockerham, R. Dingwall, & S. Quah (Eds.), *The Wiley-Blackwell encyclopedia of health, illness, behavior and society*. USA: Wiley-Blackwell.

Commonwealth of Australia. (2014). Vietnam veterans health study. In *Introduction and summary of the studies of Vietnam veterans families* (Vol. 1). Canberra: Department of Veterans' Affairs.

Cooper, L., Andrew, S., & Fossey, M. (2016). Educating nurses to care for military veterans in civilian hospitals: An integrated literature review. *Special Issue: Nurse Education Today, 47*, p68–73.

Cooper, L., Caddick, N., Godier, L., Cooper, A., & Fossey, M. (2018). Transition from the military into civilian life: An exploration of cultural competence. *Armed Forces & Society, 44*(1), 156–177.

Cooper, L., Caddick, N., Godier, L., Cooper, A., Fossey, M., & Engward, H. (2017). A model of military to civilian transition: Bourdieu in action. *Journal of Military, Veteran and Family Health, 3*(2), 53–60. Available at: https://doi.org/10.3138/jmvfh.4301.

Cooper, L., Caddick, N., Godier, L., Fossey, M., & Cooper, A. (2019). *Shifting identities during military-to-civilian transition: A practical application of the model of transition in veterans (MoTiVe)*. In preparation (Military Psychology).

Cooper, L. (2019). *Difficulties following discharge: Supporting veterans in the UK criminal justice system*. in preparation.

Coser, L. A. (1974). *Greedy institutions; patterns of undivided commitment*. Free Press.

Cretchley, J., Laffan, W., Ross, A., & Treloar, S. (2014). Vietnam veterans health study. In *Part One, social factors that impact on sons and daughters of Vietnam veterans and Vietnam-era Servicemen* (Vol. 4). Brisbane: The University of Queensland.

Dandeker, C., Wessely, S., Iversen, A., & Ross, J. (2006). What's in a name? Defining and caring for 'veterans': The United Kingdom in international perspective. *Armed Forces & Society, 32*(2), 161–177.

Davies, C. (1989). Goffman's concept of the total institution: Criticisms and revisions. *Human Studies, 12*, 77–95.

DW.com. (2018). *EU nations continue to phase out military conscription*. Available at: http://www.dw.com/en/eu-nations-continue-to-phase-out-military-conscription/a-5749541.

Engward, H., Fleuty, K., & Fossey, M. (2018). *Caring and coping: The family perspective on living with limb loss*. London: Blesma. Availabe at: http://www.fim-trust.org/wp-content/uploads/2018/06/20180611-FINAL-Families-Project-Report.pdf.

Forces in Mind Trust. (2013). *The transition mapping study: Understanding the transition process for service personnel returning to civilian life*. Available at: http://www.fim-trust.org/wp-content/uploads/2015/01/20130810-TMS-Report.pdf.

Forrest, W., Edwards, B., & Daraganova, G. (2014a). Vietnam veterans health study. In *A study of health and social issues in Vietnam veteran sons and daughters* (Vol. 2). Melbourne: Australian Institute of Family Studies.

Forrest, W., Edwards, B., & Daraganova, G. (2014b). Vietnam veterans health study. In *Part Two, a study of Mortality patterns of Vietnam veteran families* (Vol. 3). Melbourne: Australian Institute of Family Studies.

Fossey, M, & HackerHughes, J. (2014). *"Traumatic limb loss and the needs of the family"*. London: Blesma. Available at: https://www.researchgate.net/profile/Matt_Fossey/publication/308617252_Traumatic_Limb_Loss_and_the_Needs_of_the_Family/links/57e8edcd08ae9e5e455946e3/Traumatic-Limb-Loss-and-the-Needs-of-the-Family.pdf.

Fossey, M., Cooper, L., Godier, L., & Cooper, A. (2017). *Project Nova: A pilot study to support veterans in the criminal justice system*. Available at: http://www.fim-trust.org/wp-content/uploads/2017/04/Project-Nova-Report.pdf.

Goffman, E. (1961). *Asylum* (New York, New York).

Gribble, R., Mahar, A., Godfrey, K., & Muir, S. (2018). *What does the term "military family" mean? A preliminary comparison across four countries*. Military Families Working Group, Canadian Institute for Military and Veteran Health Research. Available at: http://cimvhr.ca/documents/Military-families-definitions.pdf.

Hogan, D. P., & Astone, N. M. (1986). The transition to adulthood. *Annual Review of Sociology, 12*(1), 109–130.

Hogan, P. F., & Furst Seifert, R. (2010). Marriage and the military: Evidence that those who serve marry earlier and divorce earlier. *Armed Forces & Society, 36*(3), 420–438.

Hoge, C., Castro, C., Messer, S., McGurk, D., Cotting, D., & Koffman, R. (2004). Combat duty in Iraq and Afghanistan, mental health problems and barriers to care. *Journal of Medicine, 351*(1), 13–23.

Isaacson, S. E. (2015). Obergefell v Hodges: The US supreme court decides the marriage question. *Oxford Journal of Law and Religion, 4*(3), 530–535.

Jakupak, M., Blais, R., Grossbard, J., Garcia, H., & Okiishi, J. (2014). Toughness in association with mental health symptoms among Iraq and Afghanistan war veterans seeking veterans affairs health care. *Psychology of Men and Masculinity, 15*(1), 100–104.

Karney, B. R., Loughran, D. S., & Pollard, M. S. (2012). Comparing marital status and divorce status in civilian and military populations. *Journal of Family Issues, 33*(12), 1572–1594.

Keeling, M., Wessely, S., & Fear, N. T. (2017). Marital status distribution of the UK military: Does it differ from the general population? *Military Behavioral Health, 5*(1), 26–34.

Lester, P., Peterson, K., Reeves, J., Knauss, L., Glover, D., Mogil, C., et al. (2010). The long war and parental combat deployment: Effects on military children and at-home spouses. *Journal of the American Academy of Child & Adolescent Psychiatry, 49*, 310–320.

Ministry of Defence. (2011). *The armed forces covenant*. Available at: https://www.gov.uk/government/uploads/system/uploads/attachment_data/file/49469/the_armed_forces_covenant.pdf.

OCED: Family Database. (2016) Retrieved from http://www.oecd.org/social/family/database.htm.

Rey, T. (2007). *Bourdieu on religion*. Sheffield: Equinox.

Segal, M. W. (1986). The military and the family as greedy institutions. *Armed Forces & Society, 13*(1), 9–38.

Statistics Estonia (2019)[Online]. Estonian Population and Housing Census 2011. Available at: https://andmebaas.stat.ee/Index.aspx?lang=en (Accessed: 22.07.19)

The Money Advice Service. (2017). *Average childcare costs*. Available at: https://www.moneyadviceservice.org.uk/en/articles/childcare-costs#full-time-childcare-costs.

The Office for National Statistics. (2018). *Statistical bulletin: Population estimates by marital status and living arrangements, England and Wales: 2002 to 2016 population by legal marital status and cohabitation status by age and sex for England and Wales*. Available at: https://www.ons.gov.uk/peoplepopulationandcommunity/populationandmigration/populationestimates/bulletins/populationestimatesbymaritalstatusandlivingarrangements/2002to2016.

Thompson, J. M., MacLean, M. B., Roach, M. B., Banman, M., Mabior, J., & Pedlar, D. (2016). *A well-being construct for veterans' policy, programming and research*. Research Directorate Technical Report. Charlottetown: PEI: Research Directorate, Veterans Affairs Canada.

Veteran Affairs Canada. (2018). *Life after service survey 2016 executive summary*. Available at: http://www.veterans.gc.ca/eng/about-us/research-directorate/publications/reports/lass-2016.

Vogt, D., Perkins, D. F., Copeland, L. A., Finley, E. P., Jamieson, C. S., Booth, B., … Gilman, C. L. (2018). The Veterans Metrics Initiative study of US veterans' experiences during their transition from military service. *BMJ open, 8*(6), e020734.

CHAPTER

10

Public support for veterans leaving the Armed Forces

Jacco Duel[1], *Tiia-Triin Truusa*[2], *Martin Elands*[1]

[1] Netherlands Veterans Institute, Doorn, the Netherlands;
[2] Ühiskonnateaduste Instituut, Institute of Social Studies Tartu Ülikool, University of Tartu, Estonia

OUTLINE

Military Veteran Reintegration
https://doi.org/10.1016/B978-0-12-815312-3.00010-3

© 2019 Elsevier Inc. All rights reserved.

Old, unhappy, far-off things...

History has showed more than once that public appreciation and support for veterans are important for veterans to successfully transition into society. First and foremost, it is a necessary condition for developing and improving of a veteran's policy in general. Without strong public support, a veteran's policy is probably doomed to become marginalized in the long run. Furthermore, to varying degrees, a lot of veterans already feel alienated from society when they are returning home from a theater of war. They are convinced that ordinary citizens, journalists and politicians included, do not know what it means to have been deployed in a hostile and dangerous environment, do not understand loss and camaraderie, and cannot imagine what veterans are going through afterward because of these military experiences (Treseder, 2014). Critical reports and public comments, at the time of the war or years later, widen this emotional and psychological gap. Public appreciation and support can help bridge that gap.

The Second World War set the bar high. When the victorious allied veterans came home, they were cheered and—in most cases—supported in transitioning back into society, on a national level as well as on a local level (Taylor, 2007). Veterans from the war in Korea (1950–53) experienced quite a different welcome home in, for example, the United States, the United Kingdom, and the Netherlands. The war itself was not very popular, ended in an unsatisfactory cease fire, and, except for the first year, got little media attention. "The world hurried to forget Korea, those who returned, and those who never did" (Taylor, 2007, p. 113). The lack of support for veterans widened the gap between them and the society that had deployed them. This certainly was the case for American veterans who had been prisoners of war in Korea and had suffered the greatest hardships. These prisoners of war "were scorned, accused of collaboration, suspected of having turned communist, or were simply ignored" (Taylor, 2007, p. 118). All together it was no wonder that in all three countries it took more than 40 years, in the United Kingdom almost 60 years, before a public Korean War memorial was unveiled.

History reveals many recent conflicts that—at the time—were considered to be unimportant, unpopular, controversial, or unsuccessful. This is true in, for example, the United States (Vietnam 1957–75, Bosnia 1991–95), the Netherlands (Indonesia 1945–49, Bosnia 1991–95), the United Kingdom (Suez 1951–56, Northern Ireland 1969–2008, Bosnia 1991–95), and Estonia (Afghanistan 1979–89). Veterans of these conflicts, in general, lacked public sympathy and support. Sometimes they even came home to an outright hostile environment or at least an environment the veterans themselves experienced as being hostile to them (Klep, 2008; Taylor, 2007). Two of the most notorious examples are the homecoming experiences of the American Vietnam veterans, especially since 1968, and the Dutch soldiers that were not able to protect the Bosnian Muslim population of the safe area Srebrenica and prevent genocide by the Bosnian Serbs in 1995.

In the case of American Vietnam veterans and Dutch Srebrenica veterans, it became quite clear that the fierce public criticism on their military performance and conduct as soldiers was an obstacle for a successful transition. A lot of Vietnam veterans walked into a wall of silence or were even openly insulted or spat at. This, together with the massive protests against the war and the negative (and sometimes distorted) media coverage, made a lot of Vietnam veterans feel like the national scapegoats, depicted as drug addicts and baby killers. Who would hire a Vietnam veteran under these circumstances (Scott, 1993; Taylor, 2007)? Not surprisingly, 330,000 Vietnam veterans were unemployed at the end of 1971. Public antipathy apparently made it harder to transition, in particular in a struggling economy. Of course, thanks to the famous GI Bill, there was always the possibility of increasing one's chances through further education. But college campuses, where protests against the war were so fierce and attitudes to returning veterans often so hostile, were hardly the places to be for veterans, so a lot of them chose to leave this possibility unused (Taylor, 2007).

On a much smaller scale, Dutch veterans of the battalion that was deployed in the Bosnian safe area Srebrenica suffered the same inevitable fate. Because of their light armament, small numbers, the inadequate UN mandate, and lack of air support, they had been powerless against the Bosnian Serbian attack on the enclave and the following genocide of the Muslim population. In the Netherlands, the relief about the safe return of the battalion soon turned into strong criticism. In national and international media and other public comments, the Dutch veterans were accused of not having done enough to protect the local population, even of cooperating with ethnic cleansing and therefore complicity in the murder of 8000 Muslims. It took years before research commissioned by the government and a parliamentary inquiry both made it clear that the battalion was not to blame for the tragedy, but by then the harm was already done (Klep, 2008). Compared with other Dutch veterans of UN missions in the 90s, veterans of the Srebrenica battalion had a problematic transition into society and apparently are still not doing as well as others (RZO, 2016). Likewise, for a lot of American Vietnam veterans, the reception at home increased the damage caused by the experiences during deployment (Taylor, 2007).

Aim and outline of this chapter

So public support for veterans matters, especially when veterans transition out of the military into civilian society (see, e.g., Berndtsson, Dandeker, & Ydén, 2015). Therefore, in this chapter, we will describe and analyze how public support may either help or hamper veterans successfully transitioning into society. To do that, we will describe the situation of public support for veterans in four countries. For each country, we try to answer three broad questions. First, how does the public view veterans and does this view vary for different groups of veterans? Second, how does this public view materialize into support for veterans in general, and more specifically into support for veterans transitioning out of the military? In doing so, we will pay attention to both, support directly provided by the public, in the form of public opinion polls and media analysis, and also to government-provided support. We recognize that both types of support are far from the same thing, but we see the latter as a tangible manifestation of support endorsed by the public that is much easier to keep track of (see Kleykamp, Hipes, & MacLean, 2018). Third, what is the impact of public perception on the veteran in general, and more specifically how does that influence transitioning out of the military?

The countries we selected are quite different: the United States, the Netherlands, the United Kingdom, and Estonia. These countries differ regarding military experiences, military capacities, civil–military relations, and veteran definitions. In addition, the armed forces may be based on different principles (for example, all volunteer vs. conscript). These countries also have dissimilar social welfare systems and varying degrees of private sector organization involvement in veterans' issues. By analyzing these four rather different contexts, we can delineate important issues and challenges regarding public support that apply for most countries. These issues are worthwhile to be addressed by governments if they want to enhance or make use of public support that contributes to veterans successfully transitioning out of the military, or to give extra support and attention to compensate specific groups of veterans that lack public support so these veterans are not hampered in making a successful transition.

The outline of this chapter is as follows. First, we will answer the broad questions for the United States, followed by the Netherlands, the United Kingdom, and Estonia. Second, we will highlight issues that emerge when analyzing these four cases. For each issue, we will indicate what should be done to work on a solution. We close this chapter with some concluding remarks.

Public support in the United States

"Public support for increased spending on veterans at highest level in two decades," read the headline of Pew Research Center's announcement on their webpage, on April 24, 2017. The finding was based on an opinion poll among adult citizens of the United States in response to the question of what people would do if they could make up the federal government's budget that year. It must be noted that there was broad public support for either increasing spending or maintaining it at current levels for a broad range of other programs, such as education, rebuilding highways, and Medicare. However, public support for increasing spending on veteran's benefits was the largest (Pew Research Center, 2017). The finding was in line with Gallup's finding that 91% of the public supported the then presidential candidate Donald Trump's idea to allow American veterans to get health care at any health care provider that accepts Medicare, not just Veterans Administration medical facilities (Newport, 2016). In addition, a 2014 Gallup poll showed that 9 in 10 US adult citizens found it very or extremely important that the president and the Congress deal with improving the way in which health care services are provided to US veterans. It was Americans' top legislative priority for the government, according to the general public (Saad, 2014).

Good news for US veterans. Especially since the government already "pours more than $140 billion into veterans every year" (Meyer, 2013, p. 8). Where does this support originate from? That is a difficult question to answer. It will surely have helped that American citizens hold the military in high regard with about four in five US adults saying that "members of the armed services contribute 'a lot' to society's well-being." Although esteem for the military modestly decreased from 84% in 2009 to 78% in 2013, the military is still on top of the list of various professions that contribute to society, and overall, there was a modest decline for several professions (Pew

Research Center, 2013). Likewise, it will have helped that 9 in 10 American citizens are proud of the soldiers who have served in the military (Drake, 2013). It will also have helped that most American citizens still have close connections with people who serve or have served in the military (Livingston, 2016). It may also have helped that around 60% of the people in the United States think that post-traumatic stress disorder (PTSD) and suicide are more prevalent among current military personnel as compared with the general public (Maher et al., 2017) so veterans may be in need of help.

Thus, there appears to be ample public support for about 21 million veterans in the United States, although research shows that the public somewhat overstate their support (Kleykamp, Hipes, & MacLean, 2017).[1] Does this "mental support" also materializes into "real support," not only from the government but from the public as well? It appears it does. In 2015, 45,559 nonprofit organizations for veterans and their families were registered with the IRS (Guidestar, 2015).[2] Eighteen percent of the veterans organizations are charitable organizations, whereas the remaining are, for example, non-charitable, or organizations of past or present members of the US Armed Forces. According to Charity Navigator (n.d.), in the United States, people donate more than $2.5 billion annually to the American charities with military-related objectives.

Together, the veterans' organizations provide a wide array of services depending on the mission of the organization, such as helping wounded veterans heal physically and mentally and cope with challenges presented by long-term injuries, provide financial assistance to veterans' families and wounded veterans, and help veterans transition to civilian life (Guidestar, 2015). More specifically, the activities of these organizations are focused on: employment (e.g., training and certification; placement); education (e.g., academic support); physical health (e.g., amputations; burns; spinal injuries); mental health (e.g., increasing access to care; reducing stigma); family and community (e.g., community reintegration); and legal, financial, and housing issues (e.g., homelessness; Meyer, 2013). Moreover, Meyer (2013) points at a governmental publication that estimates a total of 400,000 service organizations that in one way or another touch veterans or men and women who are still serving.

[1] See https://www.va.gov/vetdata/veteran_population.asp (visited October 4, 2017).

[2] The IRS is the revenue service of the United States federal government.

In addition, commercial organizations may also support veterans, for example, in providing jobs for veterans.[3]

Although this picture may seem rosy, there are some concerns as well. According to Charity Watch (2015), "Even though the government, tens of thousands of nonprofit organizations, and millions of caring Americans try to provide support for veterans and military families, many are not receiving the help they need. Much of the blame for this lies with the US government, which provides the lion's share of services to past and present military personnel and their families. A smaller share of the blame lies with the growing number of poorly run and inefficient charities claiming to serve veterans and the military."

Another concern is the danger of diminishing support for veterans. Although most of the American public is connected to someone with military experience, the connections between the general public and the military are loosening (Drake, 2013; Pew Research Center, 2011). The last decades showed a dramatic decline in the share of the US population with military experience (Livingston, 2016). Perhaps that is why the connection to military personnel is especially fading among younger people. "[W]hile about eight-in-ten adults (79%) ages 50 to 64 reported having an immediate family member who served, just one-third of those ages 18 to 29 said the same."[4] Moreover, today's wars are fought far away from home. Perhaps that is why half of the US public said that the wars in Afghanistan and Iraq had little impact on their own lives.[5] In addition, a large majority of veterans and the general public said that Americans do not understand military life (Drake, 2013). This may be also seen as in indicator that the connection from society to the military—and vice versa—is loose.

So, what is the situation for the American veteran? It appears that despite the overwhelming support available, large groups of veterans do not receive care for their health needs or other needs, such has housing problems, financial problems, the need for education, or the need to find a job. For a part, they do not receive support because some veterans want to solve their problems on their own—and they think they can do so successfully—but also because they perceive barriers to care. More strikingly, however, is that—depending on the study—one

[3] See for example https://corporate.walmart.com/_news_/news-archive/2013/05/27/today-walmart-launches-veterans-commitment-plans-to-hire-100000-over-the-next-five-years.

[4] 61% of the Americans had an immediate family member who served (Pew Research Center, 2011, November 23; see also: Livingston, 2016, November 11).

[5] http://www.pewresearch.org/fact-tank/2013/05/24/on-memorial-day-public-pride-in-veterans-but-at-a-distance-2/.

of six to one of two veterans do not know where to get help or whom to see (Castro, Kintzle, & Hassan, 2014, 2015; Kintzle, Rasheed, & Castro, 2016). Also worrying is that a fair amount of veterans are critical about civilian employers. Again, depending on the study and the specific concern they raise, 3–6 in 10 veterans say employers do not understand or are insensitive to the needs of veterans, employers think veterans do not have adequate skills, employers think veterans are dangerous or physically broken, or they do not want to hire a veteran (Castro et al., 2014, 2015).

Finally, despite the overwhelming support, about half of the veterans felt disconnected from the world around them, even their peers or the people with whom they were close (Kintzle et al., 2016). Overall, there seems to be a problem in connecting veterans in need to the abundant support available and the wider society they belong to. Apparently, public appreciation and support is important and help veterans transition successfully, but by no means all veterans. The latter do not feel understood or connected to society and—as a result of the overwhelming support available—may not see the forest for the trees. A personal and outreaching approach and providing a simple and clear road map to find high-quality care and support certainly would help.

Public support in the Netherlands

Comparable to the United States, the Dutch public appreciates its veterans. According to the most recent survey, 75% of the public said veterans deserve outright public appreciation (Ministry of Defence, 2017d). This finding has been more or less stable in recent years, as has been the public image of veterans as being "courageous," "dutiful," "helpful," "proud," and "brave" (Duel, 2015; Duel, Dirksen, De Reuver, Elands, & Algra, 2017; Ministry of Defence, 2017d). That said, it must be noted that the survey also made clear that 43% of the public did not have a correct image of who may be regarded as a veteran (according to the Dutch definition, about 115,000 "service and ex-service members who served during a war or peace mission") so the question is who the public had in mind when they assigned all those positive labels. Veterans and military personnel were also rated fourth on a scale of appreciation for seven uniformed services (with first responders, firemen, and policemen being the numbers 1, 2, and 3, respectively). In addition, 90% of the public did nothing or very little to show veterans their appreciation. If they said they did something, it was more or less passive like following the news coverage on veterans, being interested in veterans' issues, or visiting veterans' days (Ministry of Defence, 2017d). Moreover, the public is quite critical about the Dutch participation in several military missions since the Second World War; this finding is also stable in recent years (Ministry of Defence, 2017d). Regarding most missions, for example, the missions in Bosnia and more recently Iraq, Afghanistan, and Mali, a minority of the public said Dutch military participation was justified.

In general, the media are predominantly neutral toward veterans (see, for example, Van Tilburg, 2014, 2016; Van Tilburg & Elands, 2013). "The veteran" is not a big topic in the print media, and when it is written about it is mostly in regional newspapers and in a 4-month period encompassing Remembrance Day (May 4), Liberation Day (May 5), and Veterans Day (last Saturday of June).

How far does this lukewarm attention for veterans among the public and in the media affect their tangible support for veterans? It appears that support for veterans is for the most part a governmental responsibility in the Netherlands. That responsibility is embedded in the Veterans Act (2012) and the Veterans Decree (2014). Both documents stress that the government should enhance appreciation and recognition for veterans among the public but they also assign the task to support and care for veterans to the government. The attribution of that task to the government apparently suits the general idea among the Dutch public that the government has a responsibility in caring for those in need and that the government should play an active role in employment issues (see e.g., Kloosterman, 2013; see also Dekker, De Blok, & De Hart, 2016; Den Ridder & Dekker, 2012; Olsthoorn, Pommer, Ras, van der Torre, & Wildeboer Schut, 2017).[6]

[6] It is beyond the scope of this chapter to delve into this topic too deep. However, for example, within British society, more people are inclined to think that people themselves are responsible for their well-being as compared with people within the Dutch and Estonian societies. In the latter two, more people are inclined to think the government has a responsibility for the well-being of people than in British society (Den Ridder & Dekker, 2012). Perhaps that is why Dutch society relies less on charities than British society. A crude index to indicate the tendency to rely on charities is to determine the total income of charities as a percentage of the gross domestic product for each country. For 2015, these percentages were 2.1% (United States), 1.6% (United Kingdom), 0.2% (Estonia), and 0.8% (Netherlands). Sources used to calculate the indices are https://tradingeconomics.com; https://philanthropy.iupui.edu; https://data.ncvo.org.uk; http://www.geveninnederland.nl; https://heakodanik.ee/uudised/eesti-heategevuses-oli-rekordaasta/; https://www.stat.ee/news-release-2016-141. See the World Giving Index 2017 by the Charities Aid Foundation (https://www.cafonline.org) for other ways to map charitable behavior and generosity across the globe.

Interestingly, more recently, there has been criticism regarding this division of responsibilities as well, especially regarding the idea of the Ministry of Defence predominantly being responsible for veterans in the Netherlands. Voices from within the Ministry of Defence, from—representatives of—veterans and from several politicians uttered that the Ministry of Defence is not a health care department and that care for veterans should also be a responsibility of other departments and society (Ministry of Defence, 2016b).

Notwithstanding that, the government clearly expresses its support for veterans in an annual veterans' policy letter to the House of Representatives and in parliament. Likewise, the King, members of the cabinet or members of parliament regularly express their support for veterans.[7] Besides these forms of intangible support, the government organizes veterans' days, facilitates reunions, grants decorations, and provides all kinds of services to veterans. Moreover, it initiated a comprehensive national health care system for veterans (see: Duel, Elands, & Van den Berg, 2017). Furthermore, it supports the establishment of veterans' homes (meeting points). To execute most of these tasks, the government established two nongovernmental organizations (the Veterans Institute and the National Veterans Day) that are subsidized by the government. In addition to the activities already mentioned, these organizations closely cooperate in several activities to promote a nuanced view about veterans among the public. Yearly, the government spends about €140 million to execute its veterans' policy with about three quarters of that budget being spent on disability pensions, pensions for the relatives of fallen soldiers, compensation for loss of income, and financial compensations for damages sustained by veterans (Ministry of Defence, 2016b).

Besides governmental activities, there are hardly, if any, public activities that aim to support veterans. Some national activities have a knock-on effect on local communities. For example, municipalities organize local veterans' days or a meeting centers or veterans' cafes. Sometimes these activities are partly funded by the local government or via private initiatives. Furthermore, there are some initiatives that grant veterans all kinds of benefits. And more recently, several initiatives started that aimed at helping veterans to get a job, such as The Unknown Heroes Foundation (Dutch: Stichting Onbekende Helden). Likewise, the Veterans Platform (Dutch: Veteranen

[7] In fact, the Veterans Act was an initiative of the House of Representatives. It was carried unanimously by both the House of Representatives and the Senate which can be seen as a sign of broad—public—support for veterans as expressed by all representatives.

Platform)—an umbrella organization made up of more than 40 veterans' organizations and trade unions that looks after veterans' interests—launched its initiative "The proud veteran" that emphasizes the added value of veterans for society. In addition, the National Fund for Peace, Freedom, and Veteran Care (Dutch: vfonds) financially supports—among other objectives—initiatives that enhance appreciation and recognition for veterans (and other uniformed services). The fund receives its revenues from various national lotteries. In 2016, vfonds granted in total over €5 million to 93 initiatives aimed at enhancing appreciation and recognition for veterans (vfonds, 2017).

Now what does all of this mean for veterans in the Netherlands? Although it is impossible to measure, public appreciation and actual public support undoubtedly contributed to the fact that three quarters of the veterans had a good transition out of the armed forces and about six in seven feel settled in society (Duel, 2017). In general, veterans do fine in the Netherlands and most are very satisfied with their life (Van Wijngaarden & Meije, 2015). Overall, 6 in 10 veterans are satisfied with the veterans' policy in the Netherlands and about half of the respondents are satisfied with the current care for veterans. In addition, about half of the veterans feel appreciated by the government and the Ministry of Defence or the people in their vicinity, but only one in three feel appreciated by society in general or the media. The remaining veterans are predominantly neutral toward these issues (Duel, Dirksen, et al., 2017). Dissatisfaction is quite rare.

About one in nine veterans have a need for care, mostly for physical or mental health problems or because of financial problems, that is partly related to having been deployed (Van Wijngaarden & Meije, 2015). The latter is a necessary condition for getting access to the National Health Care System for Veterans (Dutch: LZV) or veterans' care by the Pension Fund (Dutch: ABP).[8] About half of them receive professional care—whether from these organizations or not, for example, because they see their General Practitioner—and the remaining veterans are supported by the people in their

[8] See Duel, Elands (2017) for an overview of the care for veterans in the Netherlands.

vicinity or they do not receive any care.[9] Overall, veterans are satisfied with the care that is provided to them, whether it is specific care for veterans or not (Van Wijngaarden & Meije, 2015). The main reasons for veterans with deployment related needs not to seek professional care are roughly because they wish to solve their problem themselves, they are adopting a wait-and-see approach and not taking the initiative themselves, they anticipate negative consequences, or they have insufficient confidence in the support services provided (Veteraneninstituut, 2015). Despite this group of veterans that may experience barriers to care, those who want help can get access to the care they need via the Veterans Office—as part of the Netherlands Veterans Institute—which acts as a one-stop shop for all help available according to the veterans' policy.

Although the overall picture is rosy, a minority of Dutch veterans experienced a difficult transition out of the armed forces and they do not feel appreciated and understood by society. One of the emerging issues is the gap between high public appreciation and the limited extent to which veterans feel appreciated by society. Research can determine whether this is also the case in other countries and—if so—should stimulate governments to close that gap by stimulating the public, local communities, and private organizations to show their appreciation for veterans more overtly.

Public support in the United Kingdom

In general, the British public holds the military in high regard. Based on their review of the literature from 2000 until 2014, Hines, Gribble, Wessely, Dandeker, and Fear (2014) found that the majority of the British public holds a positive view of the UK Armed Forces. Moreover, the public has a great deal of respect and admiration for the Armed Forces. These opinions appeared to be relatively stable over time. In addition, there appears to be a great deal of goodwill among the British public to help members of the Armed Forces (Gribble et al., 2014). A sign of this goodwill may be the existence of at least 2000 registered charities and several 1000 unregistered charities that are active in the veterans' sector in the United Kingdom. Together these charities raise approximately £200 million

[9] It must be noted that every person who lives or works in the Netherlands is legally obliged to take out standard health insurance to cover the cost of, for example, consulting a general practitioner, hospital treatment, and prescription medication. People may also opt to take out additional insurance to cover costs not included in the standard package (source: https://www.government.nl/topics/health-insurance).

per year which places these organizations among the most successful fundraising organizations in the charitable sector in the United Kingdom (Gribble et al., 2014). Charities provide a wide array of services to veterans, such as support on finance, housing, health issues, work programs and rehabilitation, and family support (Murphy et al., 2017).

The question Gribble and colleagues raise, however, is whether this goodwill among the public stems from a perceived failure of the government to provide services for veterans with health problems. Indeed, the publicity for charities tends to reinforce the idea among the public that charities are filling the gap left by the government or the Armed Forces (Ashcroft, 2017). On the other hand, it must be noted that in the United Kingdom, the Armed Forces Covenant explicitly calls on the moral obligation of the whole nation to respect, support, and fairly treat those who serve the Armed Forces, those who have served in the past, and their families (Ministry of Defence, 2017b). As such, the Covenant, which is rooted in the Armed Forces Act 2011, is a partnership between the Armed Forces and the wider society to recognize and mitigate the disadvantages that the unique demands of service life may have caused (Ministry of Defence, 2017b). However, the research by Lord Ashcroft (2017) tentatively raises doubts about whether the public is aware of the Covenant and, if so, understands what it is for.

Despite the positive attitudes and images of veterans among the public that emerge from several studies, and the apparent goodwill among the public to help veterans, there are some concerns as well. First, in its latest annual report on the aforementioned Armed Forces Covenant, the Ministry of Defence (2017b, p.17) concluded that

> [t]he [national] perception of veterans as a burden rather than a benefit to society is an enduring problem and clearly puts them at a 'disadvantage' to use the key word in the Covenant. The latest report by Lord Ashcroft highlights the issue. He reports that there has been no drop-off in the proportion of the public who believe Service Leavers were likely to have been damaged by their time in the Forces – even though we are no longer seeing casualties from Afghanistan, the military are less prominent in the media, and the campaign profile of the Forces charities is a good deal lower. This suggests that efforts to address this misconception are not succeeding. Lord Ashcroft calls for co-ordinated action and we agree.

In this regard, The Royal British Legion (2014, p. iv), one of the major UK charities related to veterans, calls it a pervading myth that serving and ex-service personnel are "mad, bad, and sad," implying that most have health problems, that most end up in prison or sleeping rough on the streets, and many are suicidal (see also

Ashcroft, 2014, 2017).[10] The Legion stresses the possible harms of this myth in hampering veterans finding a job outside the military or diverting resources away from addressing real problems. Gribble et al. (2014) point at the problematic situation that may emerge when, although it is important to draw attention to the needs of veterans such as mental health issues, too much emphasis on these needs may result in increased stigmatization of veterans. According to Hines et al. (2014), an issue with the success of charitable campaigns is their reliance on characterizing service personnel, and veterans in particular, as victims (see also Ashcroft, 2017). This effect may be enhanced when charities must compete for donations from the public, especially in times of economic austerity.

Second, Gribble et al. (2014) and Ashcroft (2017) both comment on the positive attitudes toward service members and veterans among the general public and people's willingness to donate to service charities. The question is whether the absence of military operations and the reduction of forces will lead to service members and veterans fading from the public eye. If that happens, the public opinion of service members and veterans may become less positive or more indifferent which in turn might lead to a reduction of donations to service charities. In addition to that, Ashcroft (2017) points at the vulnerability of being dependent on service charities when the charity sector as a whole comes under fire due to instances of misconduct or mismanagement by a few charities. As a consequence, public trust and confidence in charities has fallen lower than it has been since measuring began in 2005 (Charity Commission, 2016), and this loss of trust and confidence has led to a steady loss of income for the charity sector which "is certainly being experienced by some Armed Forces charities" (Ashcroft, 2017, p. 14).

Third, Gribble et al. (2014) mentioned the concerns uttered by others that the increase in the number of veterans' charities may lead to problems of coordination and replication of services and that the quality of services provided by some charities have been questioned. Indeed, the Ministry of Defence together with a consortium of charities noticed that the sheer number of organizations providing support confused many veterans. Therefore, in June 2017, the Veterans' Gateway was launched as a single point of contact for veterans and their families across the United Kingdom. The Veterans' Gateway directs those who are unsure where to turn to the appropriate organization that may support their needs (Ministry of Defence, 2017b). Likewise, the Confederation of Service Charities

[10] See for an overview of the well-being of service members and former service members, for example, Samele (2013) and Ministry of Defence (2017a, 2017e).

(Cobseo) promotes coordination and cooperation among service charities.[11] The future will show whether or not this new initiative will be effective.

What is the veteran's perspective? The community consisted of around 2.5 million veterans (Ministry of Defence, 2017a). According to the (Ministry of Defence 2016a, 2016b), the working age ex-service members are as likely to be employed as nonveterans (78% and 79%, respectively), were more likely to work in the public administration and the defence industry, but were less likely to have a degree.[12] Interestingly, one of the most pressing concerns UK service members have when thinking about leaving the armed forces is finding a good job (Ashcroft, 2012). Despite most service members thinking they have military skills that are transferable to the civilian work environment or say they gained recognized civilian qualifications while in the military, most think it will not be easy to find a job, for example, because employers do not understand what service members do in the military so they will not give a veteran a chance (Ashcroft, 2012). Related to that and the earlier mentioned myth of the veteran as "mad, bad, and sad," Ashcroft (2017) stresses the importance of developing the right narrative that explains the nature of service members and veterans to the nation. That narrative should also explain to future employers what valuable skills and traits veterans can offer those employers, making the transition for veterans into a civilian job easier. Indeed, it seems important for any government to take coordinated action if a substantial portion of the population believes veterans are "mad, bad, and sad."

Public support in Estonia

Estonia is one of the countries where veteran issues rose to public awareness during the Iraq and Afghanistan campaigns. The definition of veteran came about in 2012, through the "Policy regarding veterans of the Defence Forces and the Defence League." The definition is fairly exclusive (see, e.g., Dandeker, Wessely, Iversen, & Ross, 2006), pertaining mostly to soldiers who have

[11] See https://www.cobseo.org.uk.

[12] According to the Ministry of Defence (2016a, 2017c), there were no notable differences in the employment status of working age veterans residing in Great Britain in 2014 and 2016 as compared with the nonveterans' population. According to Pike (2016, a study by the Royal British Legion), however, the employment gap between veterans and civilians can be found in the study by The Royal British Legion (2014) and the study by the Ministry of Defence (2016a).

deployed on missions abroad since 1995. This means that the bulk of Estonian veterans are, at present, made up of those who participated in the Iraq and Afghanistan deployments, making the veteran population fairly homogenous, relatively young, and with over half of them still serving in the Estonian Defence Forces.

Public support in terms of money spent on supporting veterans and veterans' issues is around €1.2 million a year, including once-only subsidies for injuries, family support, medicine and rehabilitation, and recognition measures (Siplane, 2018). Like in the Netherlands, the support of veterans is predominantly viewed as an issue that should be handled mainly by the state and the armed forces; there are very few private or nongovernmental organizations that are involved in veterans' issues.

The Veterans Policy carried with itself notable measures for enhancing recognition of veterans in society. There were two main reasons for that. First, the term veteran, for historic reasons, has not always had positive connotations in Estonia. For example, during the Soviet period, only those who had fought in the Second World War on the Soviet side were war veterans. They enjoyed higher status in society, through special benefits and services allotted to them. This, however, created tensions within society as the Soviet forces were also the occupational forces. The second reason for recognition enhancing measures was that Estonian society, after regaining its independence from the Soviet Union in 1991, underwent rapid, profound social changes and the topic of military service members leaving the service and their issues did not surface in public debate until the policy was instituted in 2012.

Although there is a formal definition of who may be regarded a veteran, the biannual public opinion polls conducted by the Ministry of Defence make it clear that most people have another image of "the veteran" in mind than the official definition.[13] In 2016, over 60% of the people considered veterans to be those who had fought in the Second World War or in the Estonian War of Independence 1918-1920 (Kivirähk, 2017) War of Independence (1918–20; Kivirähk, 2017). The same polls reveal that Estonian professional military service members have enjoyed a continuously high (over 70%) regard in society; similarly, the Estonian military has been regarded as one of the three most trusted institutions in society.

Although there seems to be a diversion between who the public thinks is a veteran and who is entitled to be a veteran according to the policy, media analysis research of the two larger daily

[13] The public opinion polls are held twice a year. Since 2011, the poll addresses the question who may be regarded a veteran.

newspapers in Estonia showed that the image of a veteran and the attribution of issues to veterans have changed over the course of just a few years (Truusa, 2015). This research included articles from two periods, 2007–10 and 2012–14, with the aim to determine what, if any, were the differences in how veterans were portrayed before and after the implementation of the Veterans Policy. The themes from 2007 to 2010 concentrated on the motives of soldiers who deploy, the lack of state support for the wounded and injured, the poor support and understanding of the needs of veterans, and expressed concerns over the mental health of soldiers returning from deployments. In the later period, 2012–14, the two large daily newspapers shifted toward the new recognition-affirming themes, with more emphasis on introducing the definition of a veteran, explaining who veterans are, what they have given to society, what their stories are, and how they have managed to overcome their hardships. The change in public support and opinion has been partly made possible through a clear and well-organized recognition campaign regarding veterans' issues in which the Defence Forces stressed the Estonian participation in different missions, the capabilities of the soldiers, and the need to preserve Estonian independence (Jõesaar, 2015). The recognition campaign started in 2013 and at the end of that year the organizers of the campaign received an award for the "Best Media Campaign in the Public Sector 2013." Although the public relations' section of the Estonian Defence Forces was the primary force behind the campaign, the independent media publications were quite well aligned with the purposes of the campaign. To boot, the international security environment was conducive to the recognition-affirming campaign as the events in Ukraine and Crimea raised the publicly perceived threat levels (Republic of Estonia Ministry of Defence, 2014). Notably, in both periods, the official statements of Estonian dignitaries and politicians published in the press have always been expressions of their gratitude and appreciation for the work Estonian soldiers did and the sacrifices these soldiers made because of being deployed abroad.

One of the recognition measures was instituting Veterans Day on the 23rd of April, which is also Saint George's Day, the patron saint of soldiers. In the spirit of the poppy flower as a symbol of support for veterans, Estonians chose the hepatica flower to be such a symbol. On Veteran's Day, there are several commemorative gatherings across the country and also a 10-kilometer run to show support for veterans' issues. In 2012, this so-called "Hepatica run" took place only in Tallinn, the capital of Estonia, but by 2016, the Hepatica run was taking place in three locations in Estonia and also in Brussels, in support of Estonian veterans. In 2014, the Parliament made the 23rd of April a flag day, a day when national flags are compulsory on all public buildings. In addition, all through the month of April, people can buy and wear a blue hepatica pin to show support and appreciation for veterans' issues. The money raised during this Hepatica flower campaign has gone to public hospitals for mobility aid devices and also for raising awareness for mental health issues among young people, especially young men. The campaign raised €68,000 in 2014 and over €75,000 in 2016. These sums of money are noteworthy because the Estonian society is not very prone to giving money to charities (Charities Aid Foundation, 2017). The Veterans Day and Hepatica flower campaigns are organized jointly by the Estonian Ministry of Defence, Women's Voluntary Defence Organization, the Defence League, and the Veterans of the Estonian Defence Forces, a nongovernmental organization.

All these activities have generated a wider awareness of veterans' issues and have created favorable conditions for veterans' support. For example, in October 2017, the Estonian Ministry of Defence announced that the mental health issues of Estonian veterans will be studied more in depth to have a clearer understanding of what these issues in Estonia are and how to best address suicide prevention within the veteran population. This a step forward, because before 2010 the stance of the Estonian Ministry of Defence and the Estonian Defence Force was that suicide and PTSD were not of importance in Estonia, due to the selection process before entering the armed forces and the voluntary nature of military deployments (Truusa, 2015). In other words, while raising public awareness of veterans' issues, awareness within the Ministry of Defence and the Estonian Defence Force has also risen, leading to less stigmatizing attitudes regarding mental health problems among veterans.

Another example is that the Estonian Ministry of Defence had a monument built in 2017. The monument commemorates the Estonian soldiers and officers who took part in the Soviet–Afghan war (1979–89). This represents a conciliation of sorts, as the Soviet–Afghan war participants are not officially considered veterans in Estonia; it stands to reason that the more positive understanding of veterans has allowed more politically ambiguous groups of veterans to have some measure of recognition as well. However, the commemoration of veterans of the Second World War still remains somewhat controversial as Estonia had soldiers on both sides of the war.

The positive effects of the activities mentioned earlier and the increased general awareness of veterans' issues affect veterans themselves as well. Over time, more veterans feel recognized by society; in 2011, 33% of the veterans thought they were well regarded in society; in 2016, this had increased to about 80% of veterans (Raid, Truusa, & Kasearu, 2016). However, it is important to bear in mind that up to the year 2014, which is the end of the Estonian involvement in Afghanistan, a mission where Estonian troops suffered losses and many were severely injured, the percentage of veterans who felt recognized did not rise above 55% (Truusa & Kasearu, 2016). According to a survey carried out among Estonian veterans in 2016, veterans who felt that deployments had improved their recognition had a higher life satisfaction than those who felt that their recognition had been impaired by the deployment (Thompson et al., 2017). Even those who reported that deployments had no impact on their recognition still reported a higher satisfaction with life than those who reported that deployments had decreased their recognition. Moreover, those who considered that deployments had improved their recognition found their status in society to be higher than those who deemed that deployments had impaired their recognition. Those who considered that deployments had no impact on their recognition deemed their position in society to be roughly two times higher than those who felt that deployments had impaired their recognition. Thus, the more intangible public support that comes in the form of social recognition appears to be important in addition to other types of tangible support, such as subsidies.

Therefore, in conclusion, in Estonia, a well-organized recognition-enhancing campaign and clear communication from the Estonian Defence Force helped to turn public perception of veterans for the better in a fairly short period of time. This positive turn was supported by the continuous official consensus on Estonia's participation in international missions, as part of the county's security policy. The changed security situation in the region also contributed to raising public awareness and support for veterans. Social recognition is important as it provides a higher life satisfaction among veterans and veterans perceive their position in society as having a higher status.

Emerging issues

Let us start with a caveat. In our view, there is no blueprint for effective support for veterans that can be applied to all countries. Each country has its specific history of supporting the welfare of its citizens and providing health care. Likewise, each country has its own history of supporting and caring for veterans. Moreover, the way a society supports its veterans depends on the wider system of care—in the broadest sense—for citizens within that society.

Therefore, for example, in the United States and United Kingdom, charities play a more prominent role in supporting veterans than they do in the Netherlands or Estonia. In the latter two countries, the care for veterans according to the veterans' policy is executed by organizations that serve citizens as well. However, in the Netherlands, some of those public organizations also provide care specifically aimed at veterans and those organizations cooperate in proving that care supported by a governmental organization coordinates the veteran-related activities. There is no "better" or "worse" system of care for veterans, as long as there is an effective system of care that is aligned with the wider system of care in that country. Nevertheless, we think, several topics on how to sustain effective public support for veterans in transition emerge from the four case studies above. We will address these topics below.

Keep veterans on the radar of the general public and stimulate appreciation, especially for veterans of missions with a negative image

A real challenge for each country is to keep the general public and the veteran community connected, and governments should be aware of a widening gap between society and the military that may erode support for veterans. The reasons for that widening gap may be various, such as a diminishing veteran population as the older generations of veterans (deployed during or shortly after the Second World War)—that in some countries still form a substantial part of the veteran population— pass away. Other reasons may be the diminishing footprint of the military in society due to reductions in force size or because the military turns or turned from a conscription army to an all-volunteer army. In addition, most deployments are "far away from home" and most societies do not directly or evidently experience the effects of the mission. Besides that, other pressing issues, such as education, employment, health, the environment, and crime, to name a few, may absorb the public mind. Thus, indifference toward veterans and their needs is always looming, and this requires an ongoing effort of the government to keep veterans and the recognition of their sacrifices for society on the radar of the general public so support for veterans is maintained or even strengthened.

To add to that, as we implicitly pointed out earlier, the public image of a veteran may change over time, but the images that society has held as valid previously can also persist for quite a long time. This phenomenon is explained through the concept of social representations, where new concepts and understandings are attached to concepts already familiar in society. Therefore, a continuous, lively discourse within society is necessary to reach a well-structured representation of veterans (see, e.g., Wagner, 2012). Nowadays, this public debate inevitably involves the media, and increasingly social media plays a significant role in this process. However, with regard to the public discourse, it is important that the government—as an active core—keeps the discourse alive. Diversifying the image of veteran, dissolving a homogenous understanding of veterans, as for example "mad, bad, and sad," needs to be a continuous process, and veterans' issues need to be kept in public discourse.

Related to that, it is important to realize that recent research revealed that support for missions and support for veterans may be two different things (Gribble et al., 2012, 2014; Ministry of Defence, 2017d). Thus, although the public may no longer support a specific mission, it may well support the veterans that participated in that mission. The question, however, is whether veterans themselves can make that distinction. Can you really feel supported by the public when you know that the public is highly criticial of the mission you participated in? It can be expected that some groups of veterans have difficulty with that. For them, criticizing the mission itself feels like criticizing them. For example, as mentioned in the introduction, Dutch veterans who were deployed in Srebrenica when the genocide took place, in general, feel abandoned by the society that decided to send them on a mission which turned out to be a mission impossible. And every time this highly emotional and tragic issue is discussed in the Netherlands, and journalists suggest that the Dutch battalion should have done more to save the Muslim population, some of the veterans of Srebrenica feel offended despite the fact that public appreciation for veterans that participated in that mission is among the highest as compared with other groups of veterans (see: Ministry of Defence, 2017d). Likewise, groups of veterans that took part in the decolonization war in the former Netherlands Indies (1945–49) become upset when news coverage of war crimes committed by Dutch soldiers appears in the media, as if they were war criminals as well. Although this group of veterans is also appreciated highly by the public as well, public appreciation is seldom expressed and occasional criticism is still prominent in the media. Therefore, besides the generic encouragement toward governments to keep veterans on the radar of the public and to stimulate public appreciation for them, we think governments should do their utmost to stimulate public support for veterans of missions with a negative image or missions that are debated among the public.

This applies perhaps even more to those groups of veterans that were left on their own when they returned from a contested mission into a society hostile or indifferent toward veterans, such as the Vietnam veterans in the United States, the Dutch veterans of the aforementioned decolonization war, or Estonian soldiers from the Second World War or the Soviet–Afghan war in the 1980s. In addition, it is important to realize that criticism of certain missions may also affect veterans of other missions giving them the idea that society does not understand veterans. Thus, in government communication, it is important to remember that political messages need to be thought through also from the aspect of how to mitigate the averse outcomes for not only returning veterans but also for transitioning veterans.

State a compelling and clear reason why people should support veterans; make distinctions between groups of veterans when necessary

How should governments keep the veteran on the radar of the general public? What is the story to tell? We think there is not one specific story to be told. Different groups of veterans have different needs and for each there is a story to tell. We also think it is important to prevent the general public having an overly simplistic view of veterans, such as the veteran being a victim, a hero, or a perpetrator. Such simplistic views do no justice to the diversity of needs among the veteran population and the negative frames may stigmatize the group of veterans as whole. Thus, one size does not fit all. The question, for which we do not have an immediate answer, however, is how to strike the right balance between telling the different stories that address the diverse needs of groups of veterans and that genuinely gives veterans the idea that they count, their voices are heard, and that they are understood.

One fruitful avenue to harness public support may be in trying to seek solidarity between veterans and groups of people, instead of solely emphasizing the uniqueness of veterans' experiences for which they deserve respect and recognition and in doing that unintentionally set veterans apart from society. In trying to connect veterans to society by stressing solidarity, it is important that the veteran's situation—the military experiences and its consequences—is recognized as specifically theirs, but that the situation is shared in a different sense with others (see, e.g., Honneth, 1996). For example, soldiers with limb loss due to an improvised explosive device cannot really compare their experience to that of someone who lost a limb in a car accident. However, the experience of limb loss in daily life is shared to a certain extent. Likewise, veterans may experience mental health problems because of their deployment but the experience of having, or having had mental health problems, is shared by 4 in 10 Dutch adults (De Graaf, Ten Have, & Van Dorsselaer, 2010). On that line of reasoning, it is important not only to recognize veterans as a group but also to understand that veterans are a part of society sharing experiences that are common for many. In that regard, it helps to stimulate initiatives that bring veterans into interactions with the public where the feeling of solidarity is created through the exchange of experiences that are somewhat similar (see, e.g., Warming, 2015). Finally, solidarity toward a group is enhanced if that group is seen as a valuable group within society (see, e.g., Frost, 2016).

Make sure veterans can see the forest for the trees ... and perhaps there should be some thinning of the forest as well

Especially in the United States and United Kingdom, many thousands of organizations aim to help veterans in addition to the governmental organizations Despite the abundant sources of help, it appears difficult to connect groups of veterans to the support they need. Also in the Netherlands, where the situation is more transparent because there are few supporting organizations related to veterans' care, there are groups of veterans who do not know where to turn to when in need. Even the existence of a one-stop shop in the Netherlands, which in one form or the other has been in place for many years now, where veterans can turn to for deployment related care, does not guarantee that every Dutch veteran knows about its existence, or, more importantly, will find the support they need. Establishing such a one-stop shop in the United Kingdom, like the Veterans Gateway, may surely help connect veterans to the support they need. But in addition to that, it is important to find out how veterans can be helped to navigate their way to the support they need, especially when the sheer amount of support is daunting.

Related to that, sometimes there are doubts whether services provided to veterans are effective, if not harmful. This raises several questions. For example, who assesses the quality of public support? Is there a hallmark for effective and efficient organizations provided by an authoritative organization so veterans know where they can turn? If so, what organization is that authoritative organization? Is there a governmental responsibility for help provided to veterans by nongovernmental organizations? Again, we do not have all the answers, and they depend on the specific contexts in each country. However, we think that despite all good intentions of organizations that aim to support veterans,

veterans—especially when in need and vulnerable—must be safeguarded against ineffective organizations or organizations that provide services that may be harmful. Not every support is appropriate or desirable. It must be clear for veterans who they can trust and turn to when in need.

Three final comments

Finally, we would like to make three comments regarding public support. First, does the abundant availability of specific veteran-related services—and sometimes the need for veterans to use these services—hamper or facilitate the integration of veterans into society? Stated otherwise, is it really always an advantage to help veterans in care or support systems that are specifically developed for them? The answer could be yes, for example, because veterans would not be able to afford regular care or, for example, because services can be focused on the specific needs of veterans. Weaving a dense net of specific veteran support around the veteran may look comfortable at first sight. But in the end that situation may become stifling, contributing to veterans being disconnected from society rather than integrated.

Second, by comparison, there appears to be few public supports specifically aimed at supporting veterans making the transition out of the military. In general, public support for veterans aims to address the needs of veterans some time after they transition out of the armed forces. Moreover, it appears that organizations in which veterans are active are often the ones helping veterans transition out of the military. Thus, the general public can be more involved in supporting veterans in transition, especially because applying resources to prevent problems occurring are more effective than using those resources to try to address the problems once they have become chronic.

Third, notwithstanding all we mentioned above, veterans themselves have a responsibility in making a smooth transition out of the military into society as well. They have to make their own effort to connect to society again by telling civilians about their deployment experiences. Too often veterans regard the public as ignorant of what they have been through. They keep the public at a distance and thereby miss the opportunity to address misconceptions and make clear how they, with their skills and attributes, can contribute to society. If veterans do not trust the public, how can they expect the public to trust them and welcome them back?

Conclusion

Society in general can play an important role in supporting veterans leaving the military. Or as Ashcroft (2014, p. 7) puts it: "On joining, young volunteers adopt an ethos of selfless service, a lifestyle far removed from that of the civilian, ready to go wherever they are ordered, totally committed to the task at hand, and ultimately prepared to give their lives for their team and mission. As a result, ... society has a duty to ensure that on leaving the military they are integrated successfully back into civilian society and suffer no disadvantage as a result of having served." In our opinion, Ashcroft's argument, referring to the British situation, pertains to soldiers in other countries as well. Based on the four case studies we presented in this chapter, we highlighted topics that governments should address when trying to enhance or make use of public support that contributes to veterans successfully transitioning out of the military or to compensate specific groups of veterans that lack public support so these veterans are not hampered in making a successful transition.

In general, there is an overly positive image of veterans in the four countries. Veterans are held in high regard and the public holds a supportive attitude toward veterans. Especially in the United States and the United Kingdom as compared with the Netherlands and Estonia, there are many, many charities, nongovernmental organizations, and individuals who exert themselves daily in serving those who served. But there are issues regarding the public support for veterans that transcend the four nations and that may apply to other countries as well. These issues revolve around turning the overall goodwill toward veterans into tangible support for veterans' needs in an early stage to prevent chronic problems, to maintain that high level of overall goodwill in the future as veterans—for whatever reason—may escape the attention of the public in their respective societies, and to connect veterans to the support available and to the wider society in general. These issues are difficult to solve and they require an unwavering commitment by the government, the public, and of course veterans themselves to find the best possible solution. In describing the situations in the four countries, it appeared difficult to directly link public support to veterans in transition and mostly we described public support for veterans in general. We are nevertheless convinced that the goal for governments and society should be to relentlessly improve public support for veterans, especially the support at that critical moment when veterans leave the armed forces and return to the societies they once served.

References

Ashcroft, M. A. (2012). *The Armed Forces & Society. The military in Britain – through the eyes of service personnel, employers and the public.* Lord Ashcroft, KCMG. http://lordashcroftpolls.com/wp-content/uploads/2012/05/THE-ARMED-FORCES-SOCIETY.pdf.

Ashcroft, M. A. (2014). *The veterans' transition review.* Lord Ashcroft, KCMG PC. http://www.veteranstransition.co.uk/vtrreport.pdf.

Ashcroft, M. A. (October 2017). *The veterans' transition review.* Third follow-up report. Lord Ashcroft, KCMG PC http://www.veteranstransition.co.uk/vtr3_followup_2017.pdf.

Berndtsson, J., Dandeker, C., & Ydén, K. (2015). Swedish and British public opinion of the armed forces after a decade of war. *Armed Forces & Society, 41*(2), 307–328. https://doi.org/10.1177/0095327X13516616.

Castro, C. A., Kintzle, S., & Hassan, A. (2014). *The state of the American veteran: The Los Angeles county veterans study.* Los Angeles, CA: USC School of Social Work.

Castro, C. A., Kintzle, S., & Hassan, A. (2015). *The state of the American veteran: The Orange county veterans study.* Los Angeles, CA: USC School of Social Work.

Charites Aid Foundation. (2017). *CAF World Giving Index 2017. A global view of giving trends*. London, UK. See https://www.cafonline.org/docs/default-source/about-us-publications/cafworldgivingindex2017_2167a_web_210917.pdf?sfvrsn=ed1dac40_10.

Charity Commission. (2016). *Public trust and confidence in charities 2016*. London, United Kingdom: Charity Commission. https://www.gov.uk/government/uploads/system/uploads/attachment_data/file/532104/Public_trust_and_confidence_in_charities_2016.pdf.

Charity Navigator. (n.d.). *Support veterans and active duty service members*. Retrieved from Charity Navigator website on 31 January 2018 https://www.charitynavigator.org/index.cfm?bay=content.view&cpid=531.

Charity Watch. (January 26, 2015). *A donor's guide to serving the needs of veterans and the military.* Retrieved from Charity Watch website https://www.charitywatch.org/charitywatch-articles/a-donor-39-s-guide-to-serving-the-needs-of-veterans-and-the-military/150.

Dandeker, C., Wessely, S., Iversen, A., & Ross, J. (2006). What's in a name? Defining and caring for "veterans". The United Kingdom in international perspective. *Armed Forces & Society, 32*(2), 161–177. https://doi.org/10.1177/0095327X05279177.

De Graaf, R., Ten Have, M., & Van Dorsselaer, S. (2010). *De psychische gezondheid van de Nederlandse bevolking. NEMESIS-2: Opzet en eerste resultaten* [The mental health of the Dutch population]. Utrecht, Netherlands: Trimbos-instituut https://www.volksgezondheidenzorg.info/sites/default/files/nemesis_2_-_opzet_en_eerste_resultaten.pdf.

Dekker, P., De Blok, L., & De Hart, J. (2016). *Burgerperspectieven 2016|3* [Public opinion]. The Hague, Netherlands: The Netherlands Institute for Social Research.

Den Ridder, J., & Dekker, P. (2012). De publieke opinie over eigen verantwoordelijkheden [Public opinion on personal responsibilities] [An appeal to public. Less welfare state and more personal responsibilities?]. In V. Veldheer, J.-J. Jonker, L. van Noije, & C. Vrooman (Eds.), *Een beroep op de burger. Minder verzorgingsstaat, meer eigen verantwoordelijkheid? Sociaal en Cultureel Rapport 2012* (pp. 277–302). The Hague, Netherlands: The Netherlands Institute for Social Research.

Drake, B. (May 24, 2013). *On memorial day, public pride in veterans, but at a distance.* Retrieved from Pew Research Center website http://www.pewresearch.org/

fact-tank/2013/05/24/on-memorial-day-public-pride-in-veterans-but-at-a-distance-2/.

Duel, J. (2015). Hoe zien Nederlanders "de veteraan"? Plichtsgetrouw, behulpzaam en moedig [how does the general public views veterans]. *Checkpoint, 1*, 20–21.

Duel, J. (June 2017). Mind the gap! Military to civilian transition and the quality of life of Dutch veterans. In *Paper presented at the conference of the European research group on military and society (ERGOMAS), Athens, Greece.*

Duel, J., Dirksen, M., De Reuver, Y. M., Elands, M., & Algra, G. (2017, November). Thank you for serving! What affects the degree Dutch veterans feel appreciated for their service?. In *Paper presented at the biennial international conference of the inter-university seminar on Armed Forces and society, Reston, VA.*

Duel, J., Elands, M., & Van den Berg, C. E. (2017). Veteran psychological health and social care: A Dutch perspective. In J. Hacker Hughes (Ed.), *Military veteran psychological health and social care: Contemporary issues* (pp. 175–192). Abingdon, UK: Routledge.

Frost, L. (2016). Exploring the concepts of recognition and shame for social work. *Journal of Social Work Practice, 30*(4), 431–446. https://doi.org/10.1080/02650533.2015.1132689.

Gribble, R., Wessely, S., Klein, S., Alexander, D. A., Dandeker, C., & Fear, N. T. (2012). British social attitudes. Armed forces. In A. Park, E. Clery, J. Curtice, M. Phillips, & D. Utting (Eds.), *Britisch social attitudes: The 29th report* (pp. 138–154). London, UK: NatCen Social Research.

Gribble, R., Wessely, S., Klein, S., Alexander, D. A., Dandeker, C., & Fear, N. T. (2014). Public awareness of UK veterans' charities. *The RUSI Journal, 159*(1), 50–57. https://doi.org/10.1080/03071847.2014.895258.

Guidestar. (2015). *U.S. Veterans organizations by the numbers*. Retrieved from https://www.guidestar.org/downloadable-files/us-veterans-organizations.pdf.

Hines, L. A., Gribble, R., Wessely, S., Dandeker, C., & Fear, N. T. (2014). Are the Armed Forces understood and supported by the public? A view from the United Kingdom. *Armed Forces & Society, 41*(4), 688–713. https://doi.org/10.1177/0095327X14559975.

Honneth, A. (1996). *The struggle for recognition: The moral grammar of social conflicts*. Cambridge, MA: MIT Press.

Jõesaar, I. (July 11, 2015). *Kindralleitnant Riho Terras intervjuus Sõdurile: Vaim vajab samuti treenimist nagu füüsiski* [Lieutenant General Riho Terras in his interview to "Soldier": The spirit needs training just as the body does.]. Forte. Retrieved from http://forte.delfi.ee/news/militaaria/kindralleitnant-riho-terras-intervjuus-sodurile-vaim-vajab-samuti-treenimist-nagu-fuusiski?id=72868877.

Kintzle, S., Rasheed, J. M., & Castro, C. A. (2016). *The state of the American veteran: The Chicagoland veterans study*. Los Angeles, CA: USC School of Social Work.

Kivirähk, J. (2017). *Avalik arvamus ja riigikaitse* [Public opinion and defence.]. Tallinn, Estonia: Republic of Estonia Ministry of Defence.

Klep, C. (2008). *Somalië, Rwanda, Srebrenica. De nasleep van drie ontspoorde vredesmissies* [Somalia, Rwanda, Srebrenica. The aftermath of three failed peace missions]. Amsterdam, Netherlands: Boom.

Kleykamp, M., Hipes, C., & MacLean, A. (2017). Who supports U.S. veterans and who exaggerates their support? *Armed Forces & Society.* https://doi.org/10.1177/0095327X16682786. Advance online publication.

Kleykamp, M., Hipes, C., & MacLean, A. (2018). Who supports U.S. veterans and who exaggerates their support? *Armed Forces & Society, 44*(1), 92–115. https://doi.org/10.1177/0095327X16682786.

Kloosterman, R. (2013). *Meningen over het takenpakket van de overheid. Sociaaleconomische trends* [Public opinion on governmental tasks]. The Hague, Netherlands: Statistics Netherlands.

Livingston, G. (November 11, 2016). *Profile U.S. veterans is changing dramatically as their ranks decline*. Retrieved from Pew Research Center website http://www.pewresearch.org/fact-tank/2016/11/11/profile-of-u-s-veterans-is-changing-dramatically-as-their-ranks-decline/.

Mahar, A. L., Gribble, R., Aiken, A. B., Dandeker, C., Duffy, B., Gottfried, G., et al. (2017). Public opinion of the armed forces in Canada, U.K. and the U.S. *Journal of Military, Veteran, and Family Health*, 3(2), 1–2. https://doi.org/10.3138/jmvfh.3.2.002.

Meyer, T. (2013). *Serving those who served. A wise giver's guide to assisting veterans and military families*. Washington, DC: The Philanthropy Roundtable. Retrieved from http://www.philanthropyroundtable.org/file_uploads/Serving_Those_Who_Served.pdf.

Ministry of Defence. (2016a). *Annual population survey: UK armed forces veterans residing in Great Britain 2014*. London, United Kingdom: Ministry of Defence. https://www.gov.uk/government/statistics/annual-population-survey-uk-armed-forces-veterans-residing-in-great-britain-2014.

Ministry of Defence. (2016b). *Evaluatie veteranenbeleid 2011-2016* [Evaluation of the veterans' policy 2011-2016]. The Hague, Netherlands: Ministry of Defence.

Ministry of Defence. (2017a). *Annual population survey: UK armed forces veterans residing in Great Britain, 2016*. London, United Kingdom: Ministry of Defence. https://www.gov.uk/government/uploads/system/uploads/attachment_data/file/654734/20171023_-_APS_2016_Bulletin.pdf.

Ministry of Defence. (2017b). *Armed Forces covenant annual report 2017*. London, United Kingdom: Ministry of Defence. https://www.gov.uk/government/publications/armed-forces-covenant-annual-report-2017.

Ministry of Defence. (2017c). *Career transition partnership annual statistics: UK regular service personnel employment*. London, United Kingdom: Ministry of Defence. https://www.gov.uk/government/uploads/system/uploads/attachment_data/file/586072/20170126_CTPNewBulletinFormat_1516_-_O.pdf.

Ministry of Defence. (2017d). Nederlanders aan het woord. Veteranen en de Nederlandse Veteranendag 2017 [Public opinion on veterans and the Netherlands veterans day]. In *Utrecht, The Netherlands: Trends, Onderzoek en Statistiek*. The Hague, Netherlands: Ministry of Defence.

Ministry of Defence. (2017e). *UK armed forces mental health: Annual summary & trends over time 2007/8 – 2016/7*. London, United Kingdom: Ministry of Defence. https://www.gov.uk/government/uploads/system/uploads/attachment_data/file/619133/20170615_Mental_Health_Annual_Report_16-17_O_R.pdf.

Murphy, C., Brooke-Holland, L., Thurley, D., Wilson, W., Kennedy, S., & Bellis, A. (2017). *Support for UK veterans*. Briefing paper, number 7693. London, United Kingdom: House of Commons http://researchbriefings.parliament.uk/ResearchBriefing/Summary/CBP-7693.

Newport, F. (March 21, 2016). *Americans say "Yes" to spending more on VA, infrastructure*. Retrieved from Gallup News website http://news.gallup.com/poll/190136/americans-say-yes-spending-infrastructure.aspx.

Olsthoorn, M., Pommer, E., Ras, M., Van der Torre, A., & Wildeboer Scut, J. M. (2017). *Voorzieningen verdeeld. Profijt van de overheid* [Provisions distributed. Profit from the government]. The Hague, Netherlands: The Netherlands Institute for Social Research.

Pew Research Center. (November 23, 2011). *The military-civilian gap: Fewer family connections*. Retrieved from Pew Research Center website http://www.pewsocialtrends.org/2011/11/23/the-military-civilian-gap-fewer-family-connections/.

Pew Research Center. (July 11, 2013). *Public esteem for military still high*. Retrieved from Pew Research website http://www.pewforum.org/2013/07/11/public-esteem-for-military-still-high/.

Pew Research Center. (April 24, 2017). *Public support for increased spending on veterans at highest level in two decades*. Retrieved from http://www.people-press.org/2017/04/24/with-budget-debate-looming-growing-share-of-public-prefers-bigger-government/attachment/42/.

Pike, A. (2016). *Deployment to employment. Exploring the veteran employment gap in the UK*. London, United Kingdom: The Royal British Legion.

Raid, K., Truusa, T.-T., & Kasearu, K. (2016). *ÜRO rahuvalvemissioon UNFIL Liibanon ESTPLA-20. Aruanne 2016* [UN Peacekeeping mission Lebanon, ESTPLA-20. Report 2016]. Tallinn, Estonia: Republic of Estonia Ministry of Defence.

Republic of Estonia Ministry of Defence (2014). Avalik arvamus ja riigikaitse [Public opinion and defence.]. Tallinn, Estonia.

RZO. (2016). *Opzet en uitvoering van een onderzoek naar de zorgbehoeften van Dutchbat III (Advies nr. 21)* [Advice to the Ministry of Defence concerning a study into the needs for care among Dutchbatt III-veterans by the Civil-Military Care and Research Council]. Retrieved from http://rzoveteranen.nl/wp-content/uploads/2016/12/RZO-Advies-nr.-21-Onderzoek-Dutchbat-III-1.pdf.

Saad, L. (June 13, 2014). *Most in U.S. want to prioritize improving veterans' health*. Retrieved from Gallup News website http://news.gallup.com/poll/171596/prioritize-improving-veterans-health.aspx.

Samele, C. (2013). *The mental health of serving and ex-service personnel. A review of the evidence and perspectives of key stakeholders*. London, United Kingdom: Forces in Mind Trust. http://www.fim-trust.org/wp-content/uploads/2015/01/20130729-FiMT-MHF-Final.pdf.

Scott, W. J. (1993). *The politics of readjustment. Vietnam veterans since the war*. Hawthorne, NY: Walter de Gruyter, Inc.

Siplane, A. (2018). *Veteran support*. Tallinn, Estonia: Republic of Estonia Ministry of Defence.

Taylor, R. H. (2007). *Homeward bound. American veterans return from war*. Annapolis, MD: Naval Institute Press.

The Royal British Legion. (2014). *The UK ex-service community: A household survey*. London, United Kingdom: The Royal British Legion. https://media.britishlegion.org.uk/Media/2275/2014householdsurveyreport.pdf?_ga=2.98236447.1611296855.1516099496-521527159.1516099496.

Thompson, J., Lockhart, W., Roach, M. B., Atuel, H., Belanger, S., Black, T., et al. (2017). *Veterans' identities and well-being in transition to civilian life — a resource for policy analysts, program designers, service providers and researchers*. Report of the Veterans' Identities Research Theme Working Group, Canadian Institute for Military and Veteran Health Research Forum 2016. Charlottetown, Canada: Research Directorate, Veterans Affairs Canada.

Treseder, W. (April 14, 2014). *The gap is real: 7 out of 10 vets feel misunderstood by others*. Retrieved from website Military1 https://www.military1.com/army/article/461087-the-gap-is-real-7-out-of-10-vets-feel-misunderstood-by-others/.

Truusa, T.-T. (June 2015). Supporting the troops: The effects of Estonia's veterans policy. In *Paper presented at the 13th Biennial conference of ERGOMAS, Ra'anana, Israel*.

Truusa, T.-T., & Kasearu, K. (September 2016). The Estonian veteran and recognition. In *Paper presented at the NORDEFCO veteran conference, Lidingö, Sweden*.

Van Tilburg, A. (2014). *Dagbladmonitor Veteranen 2013* [Study into media coverage on veterans in Dutch newspapers –2013]. Doorn, Netherlands: Veterans Institute.

Van Tilburg, A. (2016). *Dagbladmonitor Veteranen 2015-2016. Onderzoek naar berichtgeving over veteranen in Nederlandse dagbladen (1 augustus 2015 – 31 juli 2016)* [Study into media coverage on veterans in Dutch newspapers – from 1 August 2015 until 31 July 2016]. Doorn, Netherlands: Veterans Institute. Retrieved from https://www.veteraneninstituut.nl/wp-content/uploads/2016/12/Dagbladmonitor-Veteranen-2015-2016-in-huisstijl.pdf.

Van Tilburg, A., & Elands, M. (2013). *Veteranen Dagbladmonitor 2012* [Study into media coverage on veterans in Dutch newspapers –2012]. Doorn, Netherlands: Veterans Institute.

Van Wijngaarden, B., & Meije, D. (2015). *Veteraan, hoe gaat het met u? Een onderzoek naar het welbevinden van de Nederlandse veteranen. Samenvatting* [Veteran, how are you? A survey of the well-being of the Dutch veteran. Summary]. Utrecht, Netherlands: Trimbos-instituut.

Veteraneninstituut. (2015). *Veteraan, hoe gaat het met u? Een onderzoek naar het welbevinden van de Nederlandse veteranen. Publiekssamenvatting* [Veteran, how are you? A survey of the well-being of the Dutch veteran. Lay person summary]. Doorn, Netherlands: Veterans Institute.

Veterans Act. (2012). *Staatsblad, Jaargang 2012, Nr. 133, Wet van 11 februari 2012 tot vaststelling van regels omtrent de bijzondere zorgplicht voor veteranen* (Veteranenwet). Retrieved from https://zoek.officielebekendmakingen.nl/stb-2012-133.html.

Veterans Decree. (2014). *Staatsblad, Jaargang 2014, Nr. 221, Besluit van 19 juni 2014, houdende nadere regels omtrent de bijzondere zorgplicht voor veteranen* (Veteranenbesluit). Retrieved from https://zoek.officielebekendmakingen.nl/stb-2014-221.html.

Veterans Institute. (2017). *Jaarverslag 2016* [Annual report 2016]. Doorn, Netherlands: Veterans Institute.

vfonds. (2017). *Jaarverslag 2016 [annual report 2016]*. 's-Hertogenbosch, Netherlands: Vfonds. Retrieved from: https://www.vfonds.nl/assets/Uploads/vfondsJaarverslag2016-2.pdf.

Wagner, W. (2012). Social representation theory. In D. J. Christie (Ed.), *The encyclopedia of peace psychology* (1st ed.). Oxford, United Kingdom: Blackwell Publishing Ltd.

Warming, H. (2015). The life of children in care in Denmark: A struggle over recognition. *Childhood, 22*(2), 248–262. https://doi.org/10.1177/0907568214522838.

CHAPTER

11

Essential components for a successful military-to-civilian transition

Carl Andrew Castro[1], *Sanela Dursun*[2], *Mary Beth MacLean*[3], *Raun Lazier*[4], *Matt Fossey*[5], *David Pedlar*[6]

[1] Suzanne Dworak-Peck School of Social Work, University of Southern California, Los Angeles, CA, USA; [2] National Defence Canada, Ottawa, ON, Canada; [3] Veterans Affairs Canada, Charlottetown, PE, Canada; [4] United States Department of Veterans Affairs, Washington, DC, USA; [5] Veterans and Families Institute for Military Social Research, Anglia Ruskin University, Chelmsford, United Kingdom; [6] Canadian Institute of Military and Veteran Health Research and Professor, School of Rehabilitation Queens University, Kingston, ON, Canada

OUTLINE

Military Veteran Reintegration
https://doi.org/10.1016/B978-0-12-815312-3.00011-5

© 2019 Elsevier Inc. All rights reserved.

Service members and their families need several essential components for a successful transition to civilian life. Before discussing these components, we consider some contextual factors that will shape how each nation develops veteran support initiatives. It should go without saying, first, that factors unique to each nation will influence the types of issues its veteran experience and, thus, the kind of support it offers to address them. Second, every nation should leverage what already exists. Creating veteran-specific agencies and programs is unnecessary if existing civilian organizations can be leveraged for the veteran population. Third, establish only affordable and sustainable veteran initiatives and programs because eliminating an unaffordable program once it is up and running may be more detrimental than not setting the program up in the first place. Fourth, stick to evidence-based approaches. As a rule, this means borrowing or adapting proven approaches to address veteran and family issues instead of developing new and speculative ones. If evidence does not exist for a particular program, the nation should evaluate it to assess whether the program meets the needs of veterans and their families. Finally, veteran services and support should prioritize meeting the demonstrated needs of veterans and their families over length of service or entitlement.

A transition framework that captures the key phases of transition

Military-to-civilian transition (MCT) occurs within a complex and dynamic ecosystem where service members, veterans, and their families will experience their own individual transition journey. Transitioning out of the military generally involves a series of adjustments, such as geographic location, career, relationships, family roles, support systems, social networks, and community. Thus, one of the foundational elements countries need to support successful transitions is an overarching MCT framework that positions governments to (1) define and organize the various aspects of MCT in a holistic way; (2) identify MCT-related objectives, activities, resources, and expected outcomes; and (3) design, monitor, and evaluate MCT processes, policies, and programs. The MCT framework will also align partnerships, research, and investment activities with one another and toward common outcomes. In the absence of such a framework, governments risk developing programs that do not achieve their intended purposes, use resources in an ineffective and inefficient manner, and fail to leverage the community of support for service members, veterans, and their families.

A definition of veteran

Every nation should develop a definition of a veteran that has wide consensus not only among veterans and their families but also among the civilian society. Establishing a formal definition of who is a veteran is important for determining eligibility, as well for determining who is not eligible for veteran benefits and entitlements. Who qualifies as a family member of a veteran should also be established. Factors to consider in defining a veteran include length of service, type of discharge, and operational deployment experience. Many nations reserve the designation *veteran* to a service member who has been on an operational deployment, often involving combat, while others consider anyone who has worn the uniform a veteran. Regardless of the definition of veteran, nations should ensure that the service-related health and well-being issues of all those who have served are addressed.

Focus on work disability prevention

Income and access to benefits and compensation are important for the health and financial security of veterans and their families. Having a purpose in work and life, however, provides a sense of identity and social integration that is essential for a successful transition to civilian life. Research suggests that people experiencing disability should be encouraged and supported to remain in or to re-enter the workforce as soon as possible. Furthermore, findings related to the role of employment in the transition to civilian life suggest that the prevention of work disability is important for improving transition outcomes for veterans. The Life After Service

Studies in Canada suggest that the prevention of work disability is important for generally improving post-service outcomes. Nonetheless, work reintegration is often complex, involving multiple stakeholders across multiple systems. Interactions between stakeholders and systems can have a positive or negative impact on work disability. Developing effective interventions therefore requires identifying the stakeholders and associated barriers. The main systems include personal (e.g., coping), health care, workplace, and compensation systems. It is important to integrate the disability compensation system with these systems with the aim of work reintegration, continued support in employment, and improved health and well-being.

Measuring outcomes: successes and failures

Most nations have developed programs to assist veterans and their families in the transition to civilian life that include employment preparation, health and disability assessments, housing support, and civilian educational opportunities. Yet these programs are rarely evaluated to determine whether they actually succeed (or fail) in their intent. Each nation must therefore establish clear, measurable outcomes that indicate whether a particular program has met its intended goals. Oftentimes, this will involve committing resources to conduct performance evaluations. But the additional resources are generally minimal when compared with the actual costs of a program, particularly a program that is failing in its intended purpose. It is also important to build in the outcome analyses by identifying the measurable outcomes upfront, before the program is implemented. Determining the success or failure of a program after implementation is more complicated, more expensive, and more time-consuming.

Timely and appropriate engagement

Engaging early on with service personnel planning to leave the military is important to the success of their transitions. Research suggests that personnel who have prepared themselves the least are more likely to experience challenges during transition. The need to encourage and incentivize the early engagement of service members and their family in resettlement is also important. In the United Kingdom, for example, members are able to access resettlement training up to 2 years before discharge, with graduated support dependent on how long the individual has served. In the United

States, transition is officially said to begin at the outset of a service member's military career. But service members leaving the US military often report that they had to "plead" with their superiors to attend resettlement or transition activities. Military leaders must actively support service members' early and continuous engagement in MCT programs to maximize the likelihood of a successful return to civilian life.

Address unique health and social care needs

The transition to civilian life can be highly challenging. Members being released from the military may experience cumulative stress from loss of employment, loss of military identity, and loss of military community, all while navigating a complex release system to access benefits, services, and programs. In addition to these challenges, medically released members must often live with the added burden of their health condition. Studies have shown that illness and injury is one of the main factors associated with difficulties experienced in the transition to civilian life, with medically released members often reporting every aspect of transition as more challenging than their non-medically released counterparts. Anticipating medical release can also exacerbate feelings of distress and anxiety as members prepare to begin a new identity as a civilian and a new career in the civilian workforce, and as they prepare to face upcoming challenges associated with such a transition.

These findings underscore that those undergoing medical release have greater requirements for assistance and support. Evidence suggests that personal resources, such as mastery and coping skills, and interpersonal resources, such as social support and organizational support, may assist these members in maintaining a better overall well-being and in overcoming the considerable challenges that can accompany illness or injury.

Culture, recognition, and military-to-civilian transition

The culture and recognition domain of civilian transition is concerned with the norms, values, and services of the society in which the member lives and how these change for members when they return to civilian life. Within the military culture, military members receive support in many aspects of well-being, such as health care, employment, income support, and housing. Recruit training is designed to develop their social identity as soldiers, sailors, or air personnel. When they leave the military, however, they leave the military culture and have to adapt to living in the civilian culture. They have to find civilian health care providers, civilian jobs, perhaps new homes, and learn to manage without military supports. They also have to develop new social identities, finding meaning through memberships in social groups whose norms and values they adopt. Of course, the social transition has two sides: transitioning members have to engage in new social groups and these social groups have to accept them. As with anyone else, social membership recognition provides veterans with meaningful roles through which they develop a sense of purpose. Transition programs and processes should include a strong recognition of the contributions and sacrifice veterans have made through their military service and recognize the importance of acceptance in civilian social groups and the sense of belonging such memberships provide in life after service.

Involvement of families in transition

Release from military service and transition into civilian life is also a stressful time for the families of service members. Although they are largely not included in the formal transition process, families transition at the same time as members, and all families experience some challenges during the transition period. Most families are able to cope well with these challenges using available administrative, family, and community supports. But some families experience greater stress levels and additional challenges, making them at risk for stress-related health problems. These families may require additional support, and many nations have established different programs and services to assist families during this stressful period.

Nevertheless, studies have found that the transition challenges commonly reported by families relate to their understanding of available benefits and services. Organizations must therefore ensure adequate communication with families so they are aware of the services and programs available to them. This is particularly important in the case of families of ill or injured service members because the entire family is affected by the injury or illness, with spouses often bearing the burden of supporting and caring for their military partners and families. Studies have highlighted the importance of a system perspective and recommend that therapeutic and educational programs include family members who serve as primary caregivers. Understanding the key stressors and unique risk factors is necessary to assist families transitioning to civilian life. In addition, it is essential to identify areas for improving existing services and for developing new services.

Provide employment assistance

Employment is important to health and well-being. While the majority of Canadian veterans work after release, veterans who are not working report more difficulty adjusting to civilian life than those who are working. Outcomes also vary by subgroup of the veteran population. Those looking for work (i.e., unemployed) are more likely to be younger, and those not in the labor force are more likely to be older, female, and released for medical reasons. Satisfaction with civilian employment also varies considerably by military rank, with officers being the most satisfied and privates being the least satisfied. These differences in outcomes suggest the need to account for demographic and service characteristics to improve employment-related outcomes among veterans. Many nations recognize the importance of employment assistance and most have programs available to both transitioning and former members of the armed forces. A few, such as the United Kingdom, have formally evaluated their programs, though research suggests more could be done in this important area of veteran well-being.

Conclusion

These nine essential components are intended to provide an MCT framework for nations developing or enhancing the services and support they provide to service members returning to civilian life. If each component is addressed, we believe that every service member and their family will have the best chance for success in their transition. After all, serving one's nation by performing military service is one of the highest acts of service an individual can perform. Those who have done so deserve all that their nation can do to ensure the success of their and their families' reintegration into civilian life.

Index

'*Note:* Page numbers followed by "f" indicate figures and "t" indicates tables.'

FSC
www.fsc.org
MIX
Papier | Fördert gute Waldnutzung
FSC® C083411

Kolibri 360 GmbH
Ferdinand-Jühlke-Straße 7
99095 Erfurt, Deutschland
produktsicherheit@kolibri360.de